An Economic History of
Modern Scotland
1660–1976

'In memoriam matris suae'

An Economic History of
Modern Scotland
1660–1976

BRUCE LENMAN

Lecturer in Scottish History,
University of St Andrews

B. T. Batsford Ltd *London*

First published 1977
© Bruce Lenman, 1977
ISBN 0 7134 0884 7 (cased)
ISBN 0 7134 0885 5 (limp)

Filmset by Elliott Bros. & Yeoman Ltd, Liverpool
and printed in Great Britain by Billing & Sons Limited
London, Guildford & Worcester
for the publishers
B. T. Batsford Ltd,
4 Fitzhardinge Street, London W1H 0AH

Contents

Maps

Introduction

Any study of a topic as complex as the economic history of Scotland from the Restoration of 1660 to North Sea Oil is bound to be fiercely selective, expecially in the modern period when source material is so abundant. I have chosen to discuss what I see as the two basic transitions in this era. One is the transition from pre-industrial to industrial society. The other is the transition from the peaks of Victorian industrial supremacy to the effectively de-industrialising Scotland of the 1970s. I am aware of the underlying problem of all modern Scottish History. It is whether the subject really exists. After 1603 Scotland was politically heavily involved with the English Crown. This trend accelerated after the failure of the Scottish Revolution of the 1630s and 1640s. Nevertheless, a distinct Scottish economy, linked to other economies but still distinctive, certainly existed down to 1707. Thereafter it is a fact that the industrial and agricultural development which shaped modern Scotland was very much part of a process of integration with a larger economy, world-wide in its scope even if not universal. Victorian Scotland is a region, or a collection of regions, not a country like France or the Netherlands. It does not have a history in the sense that these lands have a distinct history, but it did have a unique blend of economic experiences which shaped the political and social habits of its people. This is also true of twentieth-century Scotland, and may help solve the problem of a national consciousness which should, in the eyes of many, have faded away, but which seems in fact to be growing stronger.

I am deeply indebted to the many friends and colleagues who have taught me most of what I know about Scottish economic history and in

particular that most amiable and generous of biennial phenomena, the
Scottish Economic Historians, whose meetings have been a source of
contacts and intellectual stimulus to me for years. None of them must be
blamed for the sins of error and omission in this book. Those are all mine.
To my wife and family, who bore with the burdens of my authorship so
nobly, and to Mrs Marjorie Nield, who typed my text, I am deeply grate-
ful.

St Salvator's College,   Bruce Lenman
St Andrews

THE COUNTIES AND MAIN TOWNS OF SCOTLAND

0 10 20 30 40 50 ml
0   20   40   60   80 km

ZETLAND

Lerwick

ORKNEY

Kirkwall

SUTHERLAND

CAITHNESS

Wick

TO
ROSS
&
CROMARTY

Stornoway

ROSS &
CROMARTY

INVERNESS-SHIRE

NAIRN

MORAY

BANFFSHIRE

Inverness

ABERDEENSHIRE

Aberdeen

KINCARDINE
SHIRE

ANGUS

Montrose

Arbroath

PERTHSHIRE

Dundee

Perth

KIN

FIFE

St Andrews

ARGYLLSHIRE

Oban

Inverary

STIRLING
SHIRE

CL

Stirling

Grangemouth

DUNBARTON

DUNBAR

WEST
LOTHIAN

Leith

Edinburgh

EAST
LOTHIAN

Dunbar

BUTE

Dumbarton

Paisley

Glasgow

Motherwell

MIDLOTHIAN

BERWICK
SHIRE

Berwick-on-Tweed

Peebles

LANARK
SHIRE

Galashiels

Ayr

PEEBLES

SELKIRK

ROXBURGH
SHIRE

AYRSHIRE

WIGTOWN
SHIRE

KIRKCUDBRIGHT
SHIRE

DUMFRIES-SHIRE

Dumfries

ULSTER

ENGLAND

1

The Physical Setting

Hector Boece (1466–?1536), the first Principal of King's College Aberdeen and author of a Latin history of Scotland, has not fared well at the hands of modern critics. They jib at his florid humanist latinity and rage at his patent disrespect for truth. Nevertheless, it is not inappropriate to start a study of modern Scottish economic history with a quotation from Boece's history, in the 'braid Scots' version produced by John Bellenden in 1536. In it Boece is made to say that 'cosmographie maist necessar to the knawledge of history is'. Translating 'cosmographie' into its modern equivalent 'geography', we have one of the basic truths about any kind of Scottish history: much of it is meaningless unless set in the very unusual context of Scotland's geography. Scotland is not a big country, but if allowance is made for the Orkney and Shetland Islands, formally annexed to the Scottish Crown in 1471, it stretches from latitude 60° 51′ to 54° 38′ north. Thus the tip of Unst, the most northerly of the Shetland Islands of any size, lies north of the city of Bergen in Norway, while the south-western tip of Scotland, the Mull of Galloway, lies well south of a large part of the North of England and of a great part of Ulster. Aberdeen, the regional capital of the North-East, is one of the largest cities in the world, for its latitude. It has no rival in America, Asia or Western Europe and only in the Baltic can be found cities like Stockholm and Leningrad lying in or beyond its latitude, and matching or exceeding its importance.

Scotland has in fact a much more temperate climate than say Labrador, which lies in roughly comparable latitudes, due to the warming influence of the waters of the Gulf Stream. There are however, significant climatic

11

variations between the different parts of Scotland due mainly to the extremely varied nature of Scottish topography. For a start, although the largest part of Scotland is a peninsula at the northern end of the mainland mass of Britain, Scotland also encompasses a very large number of islands of very varied sizes. There are a mere handful of islands off the east coast of Scotland; two substantial archipelagoes in the north; and a whole world of islands off the west coast. The exact number depends very much on the point at which a sea-girt rock becomes an island but it is worth quoting the total of islands given by the 1861 Census of Scotland, which was 787. Even in 1861, 602 out of these 787 Scottish islands were uninhabited. The Northern and Western Isles can conveniently be grouped into four: Orkney, Shetland, the Outer Hebrides, and the Inner Hebrides. Each group differs markedly from the others, partly because of climatic factors, but mainly because of underlying geological differences. An extreme example of this is the contrast between Orkney and Shetland. Orkney is composed mainly of sedimentary rocks of the Old Red Sandstone or Devonian system covered unevenly with 'till' or soil debris deposited by Ice-Age glaciers. It possesses an impressive acreage of land of high agricultural and pastoral value, and its people have always been farmers with only a subsidiary interest in fishing. Shetland has a far more complex geology. Its 'back-bone', stretching from the north of Unst to the southern tip of Sumburgh Head is a ridge of metamorphic rocks much older and harder than the Devonian sedimentary rocks of Orkney, and producing a much less fertile, hilly, peat-covered landscape with only occasional pockets of limestone or sandstone. The Shetlander has always been a fisherman first, a farmer second.

Broadly speaking mainland Scotland falls into four major geological divisions separated sharply from one another by major faults, that is by great fractures due to the straining of the rocks beyond their breaking point. From north to south the divisions can be listed as follows:

(1) *The Northern Highlands*: these consist of very ancient metamorphic rocks, i.e. rocks which were originally laid down as sediments but which have been altered by the heat and pressure of major earth movements into a hard crystalline form. The southern boundary of the Northern Highlands is formed by the Great Glen Fault, south of which lie:

(2) *The Grampian Highlands*: consisting of somewhat younger metamorphic rocks than those of division (1). These Grampian High-

land metamorphics decrease in age towards their southern boundary, the Highland Boundary Fault, south of which lies:

(3) *The Midland Valley*: consisting of layered rocks of the Old Red Sandstone and Carboniferous systems gently folded and much younger than those of (2). The southern boundary of the Midland Valley consists of the Southern Uplands Fault, south of which lie:

(4) *The Southern Uplands*: consisting of tightly folded fossiliferous rocks older than those of (3) but younger than those of (2).

All four divisions contain contemporaneous volcanic lavas and ashes as well as underground injections of igneous rocks, i.e. rocks which have crystallised from a molten state.

The fundamental distinctions between highland, lowland and upland are not just distinctions in height but also distinctions in soil and human opportunity. Thus in the Outer Hebrides especially in the Long Isle which comprises Lewis and Harris and between Glenelg and Loch Eriboll along the North West Highland coast, there are extensive outcrops of some of the most ancient rocks in Scotland. Patches of hard Torridonian sandstone form mountain masses as they lie unconformably on a partially exhumed ancient land surface of Lewisian gneiss. This gneiss appears in the form of ice-abraded knobs and hills between which lie peat moorland and thousands of small lochans and bogs. In North Uist, just to the south of the Long Isle, there are so many lochans in the glacial hollows between the gneiss hillocks that over one tenth of the land is covered with water and the environment has been described as semi-aquatic. Obviously, the agricultural potential of such a terrain was, is and will remain limited.

The reason why the great bulk of the population of Scotland had by the start of the twentieth century concentrated itself within the Midland Valley was basically twofold. The sedimentary rocks of Devonian and Carboniferous age which form the floor of this downfaulted corridor, along with their covering of glacial till, give rise to soils of vastly greater potential fertility and offering much greater scope for improvement than can be found on any scale to the north or south. Secondly, economically significant coal deposits, an essential pre-condition for sustained and massive industrial development in the nineteenth century, are found in Scotland only in the Midland Valley. These coalfields fall into three groups. One stretches from the mouth of the Firth of Forth east of Edinburgh to around Girvan in Ayrshire and contains the greatest thickness of workable seams. The second group includes the south Fife, Stirlingshire, Dumbartonshire and north-east Lanarkshire deposits, while the third and thinnest group of seams comprises the deposits of north Ayrshire, Renfrewshire and the other coal-bearing parishes of Lanarkshire and Dumbartonshire. A few outlying mines like the small one in Jurassic rocks at Brora in the Northern Highlands are of purely local significance.

South of a fault line running from Girvan to Dunbar lies the dissected plateau known as the Southern Uplands. This consists of metamorphosed Ordovician and Silurian strata with volcanic intrusions of a later period, and granitic masses, like the Merrick and Cairnsmore of Fleet in Galloway and Criffel to the south of Dumfries, which were originally underground but which have been revealed by subsequent erosion. This rolling countryside is, with the notable exception of the fertile lower valley of the Tweed, better suited for pastoral than for arable farming. In the high Middle Ages the abbeys of the Scottish Borders used great areas of the Southern Uplands for commercial sheep-farming geared to the international wool trade. In the late thirteenth century Kelso Abbey had in all 7,700 sheep; Melrose Abbey some 12,500 and the abbeys of Glenluce and Dundrennan each owned between 3,000 and 4,000 sheep. All four houses exported wool to Flanders and to Italy.

With the deterioration in Anglo-Scottish relations after 1296 much of the Southern Uplands had the dubious distinction of being organised as the Scottish Marches, for the defence of a much fought-over border, but perhaps we exaggerate the impact of these wars on the pastoral Border economy. The wars were hard on burghs like Roxburgh, which had been burned five times over by 1398, or Peebles, which was burned by the English in 1403 and 1549 and looted by Scots in 1583. They were hard on the great abbeys, nearly all of which were devastated by the armies of Henry VIII of England. However, the Borderers held mobile wealth, and well-defended lairs, usually in the shape of a fortified tower house fronted by a barmkin or defensible enclosure capable of holding stock. Raiding was a seasonal activity concentrated in autumn and early winter, wherein gains balanced losses, at least to some extent, overall. Invading armies crushed anything on their usually well-trod routes, but passed on. The Scottish Borderers were latterly keener on trading with their English counterparts than on seriously fighting them, and it would be wrong to think of the pastoral economy of a large part of the Southern Uplands as permanently blighted by war in the centuries before the

Union of the Crowns in 1603 brought a ruthlessly-enforced peace to the Borders.

It is equally wrong to think of the division of the Scottish Mainland into four great regions separated by three major geological faults as other than a convenient over-simplification. The Highland Boundary Fault does run out to the North Sea just south of Stonehaven, but there are several significant Lowland areas north of that point. The whole of the North-East, that great shoulder of land comprising the Lowland parts of the counties of Aberdeen and Banff, is one example of this. Until well on in the eighteenth century its fertility was restricted by the geological accident that covered its fields with vast amounts of rock detritus from vanished glaciers, but it demonstrates the fact that the Highland Line is only partially synonymous with the Highland Boundary Fault. Around Inverness the Moray Firth is fringed with lands emphatically Lowland in nature, be they the coastal plain of the old Province of Moray to the east, or the fertile peninsulas of Easter Ross, such as the Black Isle, to the west. Finally, in Caithness there lies a society and agriculture based on the same Devonian rocks as occur in Orkney, and emphatically beyond the Highland Line, with its roots in a Norse rather than a Gaelic tradition.

That cultural contrast is a reminder that Scotland is an amalgam of cultures as well as a complex of regions. Around 1660 Norn, a derivative of Old Norse, could still be heard on the lips of the farmers of the Northern Isles, and Shetland, Orkney, and Caithness formed a distinctly Scandinavian culture-province in contrast with the strong and vital Gaelic culture which lay behind the Highland Line to the south and west. The Midland Valley and most of the Southern Uplands formed the Lowlands, with a Scots speech derived from northern dialects of Anglo-Saxon, in contrast to the Gaelic Highlands. In the late seventeenth century Gaelic was still being spoken by a few of the humbler classes in Galloway, historically a complex and isolated pocket of Gaelic culture dating from the Dark Ages.

Even within the major divisions of Scotland there are sharp variations and contrasts. In the Gaelic Highlands and Islands, for example, so much of the land is difficult and infertile that the occasional area of moderately good soil tended to be disproportionately important. Thus limestone where it is present in quantity as in the islands of Lismore and Islay or on the west coast of the peninsula of Kintyre is agriculturally valuable and explains why Lismore became the seat of a bishopric, Islay the headquarters of the Lordship of the Isles, and Kintyre a much fought-over territory. Some of the islands of the Inner Hebrides, like Canna, derived historic significance from the presence of moderately good soil derived from the lava flows of volcanoes active there relatively recently, in geological terms. The high lime content of the machair lands—stretches of consolidated shell sand on the Atlantic seaboard—makes them still vital for the growth of grain and grass in the Outer Hebrides.

Geographical position and relative height are two other sharply differentiating factors. The abrupt rise of moist winds off the Atlantic when they strike the Western Highlands ensures a heavy rainfall on these western mountains, usually of the order of 60 inches per annum (152 cm.). This rainfall steadily decreases eastwards until along much of the eastern seaboard of Scotland the rainfall is under 30 inches per annum. On the west coast lies Scotland's highest mountain Ben Nevis, which at 4,406 feet is the highest mountain in the British Isles. Between 1884 and 1903 an observatory was maintained on its summit and it produced some quite unique high-altitude meteorological data for this period. Two basic facts from this data are highly significant. First, from October to April the mean monthly temperatures never rose above freezing point, and the July temperature on Ben Nevis was, on average, a mere 3° Fahrenheit above the January temperature in Fort William, the town which nestles near its foot.

The Scottish climber Hugh T. Munro (1856–1919) selected those main summits and other distinct peaks over 3,000 feet high (c.900 metres) as the supreme challenges of Scottish climbing, thus immortalising not only the magic 3,000 feet, but also the summits and peaks as 'Munros' and 'Tops' respectively. These are, obviously, the higher points in the Highlands, but a very great many summits do lie between 2,000 and 3,000 feet. Geologists see this as evidence that the gnarled topography of the Highlands may well represent the dissected surface of an ancient plateau, stripped of its original sedimentary cover. Here it suffices to point out that much of Scotland's land surface is high enough to experience much severer weather than it would if it lay at sea level.

Such is the infinitely varied physical setting for economic activity in Scotland. It was, needless to say, no less varied on that day in spring 1660 when the cannon salutes rang out and the spouts of Edinburgh Cross ran with wine to celebrate the restoration to the throne of his ancient kingdom of Charles II.

2

The Scottish Economy
c. 1660–1690

Self-sufficiency with commerce—the agricultural foundation

The foundation of Scotland's economy and life in the late seventeenth century was the land. Probably eight or nine Scotsmen out of ten lived and worked in the countryside, and it is natural to ask whether any generalisations can usefully be made about something as dispersed and varied as agriculture in seventeenth-century Scotland. Climate and terrain varied from region to region and indeed very often there were sharp contrasts within regions. Nevertheless, there is at least one generalisation which is not only defensible, but also fundamental to an understanding of the subsequent development of the Scottish economy as a whole. This is that around 1660 most of rural Scotland was still recognisably a peasant society, bound by customary law and practising a relatively undifferentiated mixed form of agriculture.

There was, of course, a tendency for the balance of agricultural activity to differ from region to region. Most of the Highlands were better suited for pastoral than for arable farming. Every Highland community would try to raise as much grain as it conveniently could, but there is no doubt that the Highlands as a whole had a more or less permanent need to import some grain, balanced by an unusually large surplus of pastoral products. The interregional trade which was the natural consequence of this situation was catered for by a series of frontier settlements on the Highland Line such as Dingwall, Inverness, Kirriemuir, Dunkeld, Crieff, Dunblane and Dumbarton.

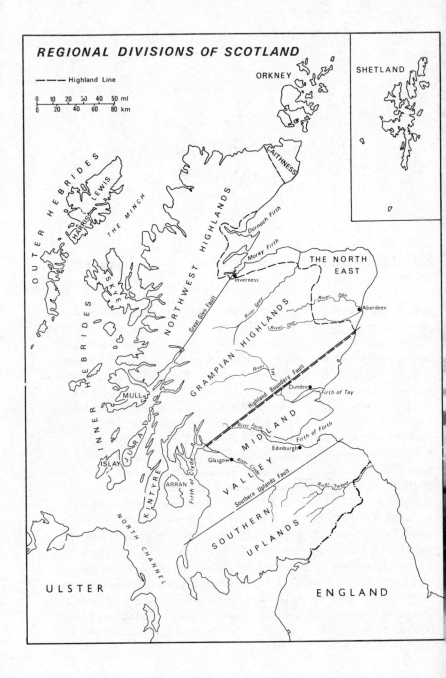

REGIONAL DIVISIONS OF SCOTLAND

- - - Highland Line

0 10 20 30 40 50 ml
0   20   40   60   80 km

ORKNEY

SHETLAND

CAITHNESS

OUTER HEBRIDES

LEWIS

HARRIS

THE MINCH

NORTHWEST HIGHLANDS

SKYE

INNER HEBRIDES

Dornoch Firth

Moray Firth

Inverness

Great Glen Fault

THE NORTH EAST

River Spey

River Don

Aberdeen

GRAMPIAN HIGHLANDS

River Dee

River Tay

Highland Boundary Fault

Dundee

Firth of Tay

MULL

JURA

River Forth

MIDLAND

Firth of Forth

Edinburgh

ISLAY

Glasgow

River Clyde

VALLEY

KINTYRE

ARRAN

Firth of Clyde

Southern Uplands Fault

River Tweed

SOUTHERN

NORTH CHANNEL

UPLANDS

ULSTER

ENGLAND

It is still true that the average seventeenth-century Scottish farmer, in all regions, practised a far higher degree of self-sufficiency than his modern counterpart. Take, for example, the records which survive of the barony, village and parish of Stitchill, which lies in the border county of Roxburghshire, three miles to the north of Kelso. Beneath the landlord lay a structured but apparently not very complex rural society referred to comprehensively as 'the haill tennants and Coatters within the said Barrouny'. The tenant would farm enough land to keep himself and his family, whereas the Cottar needed employment by the tenants at such periods as harvest to supplement what he produced from his much smaller holding. It is clear from surviving judicial complaints against 'them and ilk ane of them' for not maintaining adequate dykes to keep their stock off the corn ground, that all tenants both raised corn and ran cattle on the grazings. Crops mentioned include bere, a coarse four-rowed barley; 'aits' or oats; and pease. Transport requirements were met by the ubiquitous 'naig' or riding horse, while the Border speciality of sheep-raising is reflected in complaints from tenants that 'herds and others' were stealing wool by pulling it from grazing sheep. A fine imposed on all tenants and cottars for laying 'Green Lint' or retting flax in lochs, burns and running water in 1695 is a reminder that most households produced from their own resources most of the woollen and linen clothes they wore. Fuel was provided by cutting whin, digging peats or buying the latter by the load from nearby peat banks. Specialists like the 'cordiner' or shoemaker existed, but he also followed agricultural pursuits.

Wherever we look in later seventeenth-century Scotland we are liable to find a similar pattern. Thus in the barony of Urie in the county of Kincardine and parish of Fetteresso, not far from the county town and port of Stonehaven, we have records of the management of the property by the Barclay family. There is a heavy emphasis on grain, which clearly formed a significant part of the landlord's drawing from the estate. His tenants were, of course, thirled or bound to the barony mills, where they paid substantial multures or dues to have their grain ground, and where, through the miller, the landlord could further tax the tenantry. A decree of the baron court of 18 May 1674 shows David Barclay of Urie pursuing his mill tenants for back payment of meal due on the crop of 1673. Significantly 'Alexander Wyis in Woodheid' is ordered, within fifteen days and under pain of seizure of goods, to make payment 'at such rate and pryce as the said David Barclay, his said maister, gettis for the rest of his meal'. So it is obvious that the laird habitually marketed at least a proportion of the grain rents he received. Nevertheless, Urie was clearly an area of mixed farming with a relatively self-contained economy. There are references to sheep grazing on the common pastures, distinguished as belonging to specific tenants by a system of clip marks in their ears, and the growing scarcity of the vital peat fuel is underlined by a decree of the baron court of 28 January 1684 forbidding all tenants to 'carry with horss or otherwayes any peats to Stonhyve (modern Stonehaven), under the falzie of tenn pounds, without libertie of the maister'.

In Shetland, *Ultima Thule* to many contemporaries, the same sort of picture emerges from a study of Shetland life under the successive administrations of Earl Patrick Stewart and Bishop Law in the first half of the seventeenth century. The grazing lands of twentieth-century Shetland are dominated by sheep but at this earlier period there was far more of a balance between sheep and cattle. On Mainland Paul in Houff in Whiteness had at least 11 cattle but only 21 sheep while Nicol Thomasson in Veensgarth in Tingwall had 27 cattle and 45 sheep. In the island of Fetlar most families had from four to six cows and two oxen, but the number of sheep per family was often no more than this total. It is true that Fetlar is a green island well-suited to cattle, but even in Yell, an island with extensive moors, the average household seems to have had about ten cattle and a little more than twice that number of sheep. Fishing was naturally an important activity for many households, but it was nowhere developed as a deep-sea commercial fishery such as flourished in Shetland in the second half of the eighteenth century. On the contrary, it was an inshore fishery which supplemented what could be gained from the land.

The emphasis on grain production in the self-sufficient husbandry of late seventeenth-century Scotland was natural. A given area under grain produces far more food than the same area under pasture. Yet yields would be, by modern standards, poor, for a ratio of 1:4 or 1:5 represented the sort of relationship expected between seed and crop. Usually 25 to 30 per cent of the average annual harvest was retained for seed; another 30 per cent or so went to the landlord to be eaten by his household or marketed, and the rest was eaten or sold by the tenant. Dearth was a recurring phenomenon. Between 1550 and 1660 there were some seventeen years when the harvest failed over a wide area and grain prices were forced up to heights from which they only partially receded after each crisis. This was, of course, a common phenomenon in Western and Central Europe. In southern England one result was a 60 per cent fall in farm labourers' purchasing power between 1500 and 1610–19, while the value of German farm wages in terms of rye fell by 33 to 50 per cent between 1491–1500 and 1591–1600. Nor was the period between 1600 and 1660 a particularly happy one for Scottish agriculture, since fifteen to twenty seasons of extensive harvest failure can be identified. After 1660 years of severe dearth were of much less frequent incidence. They occurred in 1674–5 and 1695–1700. There was in fact a significant shift in Government policy after the Restoration, probably as a consequence of changing circumstances, away from protecting grain consumers and towards encouraging the producer. In 1671 imports of grain were forbidden, except by specific Privy Council permission in a period of high prices. In 1695 the Scots Parliament passed a Corn-export Bounty Act, and it is significant that this bounty system was extended by an Act of the Westminster Parliament after 1707.

The fact is that the relatively unspecialised agriculture of Restoration Scotland did not serve society badly, and there was really no alternative to it. The increasingly specialised and commercialised agricultures which did exist in South-East England and the Noorderkwartier of the United Netherlands in the later seventeenth century were the product of quite abnormal stimuli and opportunities. The market offered by London was unique in that no other city in Europe had anything like the proportion of the total population of the state concentrated in it as was to be found in London. In the Northern Netherlands that circle of cities known as the Randstad in modern times was already highly important and there had developed a crucially important grain trade with Eastern Europe which liberated Dutch agricultural resources for dairying and industrial crops. This is not to suggest that there was no significant change in the Scottish agricultural scene in the seventeenth century. It is clear that large-scale liming was increasing the area and yield of arable land in the Lothians from the 1620s. Edinburgh, like Glasgow, doubled or trebled its population between 1560 and 1700, and on both sides of the Forth the latter part of the seventeenth century saw the rapid growth of small urban centres like Alloa, Wemyss and Methil, Prestonpans and Bo'ness, all dependent on coal and salt production and shipping. As all early modern European cities tended to be insanitary to the point where death rates easily exceeded birth rates, this expansion must signify a movement of rural population into these towns.

Yet the central reality of rent seems to have remained remarkably

stable. Neither grain nor stock prices appear to have been notably buoyant and we do know that rents in the barony of Belhelvie in Aberdeenshire remained unchanged from 1662 to 1704. At Mains of Panmure
in Angus rent was unvaried from 1612 to 1700. On the estates of the
Campbells of Breadalbane in the Central Highlands the same story of
extreme stability in rent occurs. The exceptions which are known to us at
present often involve unusual circumstances. Thus, there was a significant increase in rents on the Campbell estates in the peninsula of
Kintyre on the west coast in the later seventeenth century. Farms there
were described as consisting of so many 'merklands'. This was the area of
land which could originally be rented for an annual sum of a merk or
thirteen shillings and four pence Scots. With inflation the merkland rental in Kintyre had risen to £32 Scots by 1650. By 1681 the merkland rent
was over £60 Scots, but the area was unusual in that a substantial
number of Lowlanders had been settled in Kintyre by the Earl of Argyll
to replace expelled followers of the Macdonalds of Dunnyveg. Recovery
after warfare plus new tenants from the Lowlands were both factors
likely to lead to enhanced production. No doubt further work will reveal
more exceptions, but stable rents seem to have been very common and
this is what one would expect at a time when grain prices were not particularly buoyant.

We know that this subsistence-orientated agricultural economy made
many of its rent payments in kind rather than cash, and this has been
used to explain the 'uproarious hospitality' of many Highland chiefs.
The Macleod of Macleod in Dunvegan Castle in the 1680s was in annual
receipt of 9,000 hens and from Skye alone 400 stones of butter. Not much
wonder that he maintained a substantial 'tail' of followers and kept open
house. However, for many landlords rent payments in kind were a highly
commercial proposition, especially in the case of grain. The landlord
would collect the grain in great girnals or granaries as a prelude to marketing it. It could be marketed locally, which helps explain the very large
increase in the number of non-urban markets authorised by the Scots
Parliament in the late seventeenth century. It could be marketed in a
substantial Scottish urban centre accessible by means of the comparatively cheap freights offered by coastal shipping. The Earl of Sea-
field shipped victuals from Buchan to the Firth of Forth, and Fife lairds
naturally shipped grain to Leith for the Edinburgh market. Some
records survive which enable us to reconstruct the revenue accruing to
the Fife barony of the family of Hope of Craighall between 1663 and

1679. It is clear that there was heavy dependence for cash on sales of grain. In addition grain tended to increase its percentage significance amongst all other sources of income, averaging some 20 per cent of total income by value in 1663–6 and over 30 per cent for the period 1671–7. There was an increase of the quantity of grain returned in the rentals of the order of 20 per cent for bere and 50 per cent for oatmeal between 1663 and 1675. Most of it was sent to Edinburgh where 'falling of mercats' was bad news for the laird of Craighall.

Finally, grain rents and other victuals could be exported across the North Sea from the many Royal Burghs whose harbours conducted a busy foreign trade. This was a significant trade, but its profitability was limited by two basic facts. First, European population was not buoyant in the second half of the seventeenth century. Overall estimates contain massive guess-work but it has been estimated that due mainly to war, famine, and plague, and especially the latter, European population fell from perhaps 118 million in 1648 to perhaps 102 million in 1713. Secondly, as all European societies, with rare exceptions, were predominantly agricultural, there was no natural price-enhancing scarcity of agricultural products. Harvest failure was never universal, for 'Europe' was very much a geographical term for a spectrum of very loosely-connected societies, and in the event of significant failure merchants, and especially the Dutch, derived profit from moving grain surpluses from favoured regions to stricken ones. However, with low contemporary yields, very special social structures and abundant land were necessary to produce large marketable surpluses, and Scotland had neither.

Perhaps the most significant movement in long-range trade in seventeenth-century Scotland lay in the growth of cattle exports to England. The number of Scottish beasts paying toll at Carlisle in 1663 was 18,574 (the toll was 8d. a head) and subsequent developments drew both official complaints to Westminster by Yorkshire graziers (to the effect that they were being ruined by cheap imports of Scots cattle); and official encouragement by the Scots Privy Council, which in 1680 set up a Commission charged, among other duties, with the encouragement of cattle exports. Here the growth of the London market combined with the traditional surplus of cattle in parts of Scotland to produce a growing trade. Black cattle formed a substantial part of the rental of many Highland lairds, but the last quarter of the seventeenth century saw a highly significant experiment in non-traditional cattle raising. Sir David Dunbar of Baldoon in Wigtownshire started to enclose land on a large scale for cattle grazing. He is said to have formed a park two and a half miles long by one and a half miles broad and capable of holding 1,000 beasts, some his own, others brought in. Reputedly he sold to drovers or sent to England himself some 1,600–2,000 head of cattle annually. Sir David was a straw in the wind; no more. Around 1690 the bulk of even the substantial commercialised element in Scottish agricultural life was geared to a recognisably traditional society.

The physical appearance and social structure of the countryside

Appearance

The appearance of the countryside, at least in Lowland Scotland, was quite different in the seventeenth century from the modern 'norm' which itself became predominant from the later eighteenth century, as the ideas and methods of the Improvers spread. In place of a pattern of fenced or dyked fields, seventeenth-century Scotland lay open, with occasional broom or gorse thickets but virtually no tree cover and no artificial field boundaries apart from the important earthwork 'head dyke'. Beyond the head dyke lay grazing land little different from moorland to modern eyes, as there was no cultivation of grass as a crop. Within the head dyke lay human settlement and its associated arable land. No attempt should be made to over-simplify the pattern, least of all by envisaging a series of distinct units comprising a grazing area and a central block of arable surrounding a nuclear settlement. Apart from the Lothians and indeed the south-east part of Scotland in general, with its strong Anglo-Saxon cultural tradition (it had been the northern province of the Anglo-Saxon kingdom of Northumbria) Scotland was not a land of substantial villages. Rather was it a land of hamlets, known as fermtouns in the Lowlands and clachans in the Highlands. Emphasis on pastoral farming may partially explain this, but only partially, for the basic units of land-measurement which had evolved in late medieval Scotland were all emphatically connected with arable farming. In the area south of the Forth the notional unit, or rather measure of capacity, was the ploughgate, the infinitely variable quantity of a given soil which a notional team of eight oxen could plough in a year, and of which an oxgang was an eighth. North of the Forth the notional nature of the unit and its arable nature is even more patent for the unit was the davoch. Davoch is a Gaelic word implying a vat, tub, or large measure of volume, here clearly of grain. The davoch is clearly pre-Gaelic in origin, going back probably to the Dark-Age kingdom of the Picts in eastern Scotland. It had an astonishingly long run as a living term of measurement, for it is referred to as the standard unit for the measurement of Inverness-shire farms in Sir John Sinclair's *General View of the Agriculture of the Northern Counties and Islands of Scotland*, published in London in 1795.

It is more realistic to see the scattered nature of much Scottish rural settlement as a product of the arable, as well as the pastoral, methods of pre-Improvement Scottish farming. Much low ground was waterlogged and could not be efficiently cultivated until tile drainage became commonplace in the early nineteenth century. A light but fertile soil on a moderate slope was self-draining and therefore ideal for arable farming. This is why the best grain lands of Angus in the seventeenth century were the braes of the Sidlaws and other southward-facing lands sloping gently to the sea. Similar light soils, often associated with raised beaches, account for an earlier Scottish king's description of Fife as 'a beggar's mantle fringed with gold'. This was accurate description, not dramatic hyperbole. A great deal of central Fife remained, until well into the eighteenth century, unimproved moor, or undrained loch, or bog. The latter category would include 'raised bogs', which were self-sustaining and water-retaining domes of sphagnum moss and associated plants, often of substantial dimensions. A few examples are now preserved as specimens of a vanished habitat, for they have been swept away from the Lowland landscape.

In the seventeenth century, however, arable land in the non-coastal Lowlands necessarily lay in scattered patches, separated by moor and moss. No doubt the nucleus of the arable of substantial towns in, say, landward Berwickshire, lay in communal fields associated with the original Anglo-Saxon settlement in the sixth or seventh century, but thereafter arable would spread by a complex process of assarting, or breaking-in land to arable, mainly in response to population pressure. This was an opportunistic process. Pre-Improvement field names indicate that very often arable was developed on slopes or well-drained hollows sheltered from the salt winds off the North Sea. Even in these favoured areas it was necessary to facilitate drainage and this was done by ploughing the land in such a way as to produce the 'lang rigs' or long raised strips which were typical of Scottish husbandry. The plough varied infinitely in detail, as did the composition of the plough teams, in response to local conditions, but the majority of Lowland ploughs were heavy mouldboard ploughs of wooden construction apart from their share, coulter and 'cheek-rack' or bridle, all of which would be of iron. They were pulled by teams of oxen or oxen and horses, while bing managed by a scarcely less numerous team of men. It was possible to plough in such a way as to heap the soil towards the centre of the rig where the roots of planted crops would enjoy natural drainage. Water shed by the rigs ran down the weedy baulks or balks which separated the rigs and were therefore like them perpendicular to the slope.

It would be false to suggest that there was a sharp contrast and constant relationship in size between two parts of the arable, referred to respectively as the infield and the outfield. What is clear is that the better-quality arable lying closer to the settlement was referred to as infield and more carefully husbanded than the poorer, remoter outfield. Where arable was limited, close to the settlement and of high quality, it might be all infield. Elsewhere there might be a rough equality between infield and outfield and in areas where the quality of the land was low the outfield could be several times more extensive than the infield. The infield was kept constantly under crop, usually in the form of oats and bere, and was regularly dunged, albeit at lengthy intervals. Outfield tended to be cropped until the yield became miserable, whereupon it was allowed to revert to pasture. Time plus the dung of grazing stock then restored enough heart to justify cultivation. Even this is an over-simplification for we know that it was common to 'fold' stock or enclose it overnight within temporary turf enclosures in order to dung more intensively specific parts of the outfield.

What can one say about the early modern Scottish countryside with confidence is that, on the whole, it had a bad contemporary press. Travellers who recorded their impressions tended to range from the patronising to the abusive. Scotland was not in fact a very convenient country to travel in if you were a stranger. The easiest way to move was often by water. As each of the many royal burghs monopolised the import-export trade in a finite landward area, merchants did not normally traverse the realm. Gentry moved from one castle to another. Humbler folk who had to travel, from drover down to tinker, tended to camp out. Inns were therefore few and poor. As late as 1724 it could be said of the ancient parish of Keirn in the Aberdeenshire district of the Garioch that: 'The Kings highway passes by the Church from the highland country to

Aberdeen. Here are no Inns for lodging, save a common Ale house . . .'
Far more colourful illustrations of this point can be found than this sober
quotation from *Macfarlane's Geographical Collections*. Sir William Brere-
ton, a future English Parliamentary general, visited Scotland in 1634
recording that on a forty-mile ride across the moors from Ayrshire to
Galloway there was no hostelry and one of his party nearly collapsed
from exhaustion and hunger.

There was a network of routes covering most of Scotland. These were
rights of way rather than modern metalled roads. Water barriers were
crossed by ferry or ford, rather than by bridge, though bridges did exist
on many rivers. Such a route system was essentially designed for seasonal travel. People did not travel in winter if they could avoid it. Apart
from snow, continuous heavy rain and spates made travel dangerous as
well as difficult. Spring and summer were the travelling seasons and the
only sensible time to move goods in any bulk by land. In inclement
weather over-use of such routes merely churned and damaged them. Yet
travellers from abroad repeatedly tried to traverse Scotland without
adequate local knowledge and at inappropriate times. The extreme
example is perhaps a fifteenth-century one. Aeneas Sylvius Piccolomini,
the future Pope Pius II, crossed to Scotland amid winter gales on the
North Sea, which nearly drowned him. He then made a barefoot pil-
grimage of thanksgiving from Dunbar to Whitekirk, to a shrine of Our
Lady. This meant ten miles over ice and snow which left him with
rheumatic pains in his legs and feet for the rest of his life; a state which an
Italian physician of the day later described as neither redounding to the
glory of God, nor particularly useful.

As such travellers squelched across the boggy, treeless, wind-swept
Scottish countryside, they tended to form the lowest opinions of the land
and its people. The latter are normally described as squatting in misery
in filthy hovels. In fact they were making the best of their environment.
Their cottages were constructed of local material. The walls would be of
turf, wattle, stone or mud-mortared stone, depending on the district.
Thatching was turf or heather. Cruck-frame construction, whereby the
roof rested on pairs of stout curved timbers or couples set in the walls,
was normal. The couples were valuable, as countless inventories and tes-
taments show. When a man moved house he took his timber couples with
him. That cattle and hens shared the building with humans was no more
shocking to a seventeenth-century Scot than it is to a twentieth-century
Alpine farmer. A central hearth with a peat fire not only served for cook-

ing and direct heat, but also heated up the beaten clay floor. To a traveller a moss or bog meant a soaking or a detour. To the locals, it was a source of fuel. When John Ochterlony of Guynd wrote his description of the shire of Forfar (modern Angus) *c.* 1682, he described 'Meikleloure' (modern Meikleour), a house of the Earl of Northesk as 'a good house, and well planted, with an excellent moss, good cornes, and well grassed'. Clearly, the nobility needed its peat as well as the lower orders.

The countryside was, of course, studded with the residences of the nobility and gentry. Compared with, say, England, these classes formed a high percentage of Scottish society. They clustered particularly thickly in parts of Lothian and Fife where the normal resident leaders of rural society were reinforced by Edinburgh lawyers and bureaucrats. When the latter achieved major office in royal government or a place in the Court of Session, they underlined the noble status they had won by settling down in suitable style on a small estate not too far from the capital. Fife land being, on the whole, cheaper than Lothian land, Fife was notably full of lairds. They occurred there at intervals of a few miles and quite a small remote parish like Creich in the North Fife Hills had no less than three baronies in it. In addition to the seat of the baron every barony boasted its doocot or pigeon house, a useful source of fresh meat in winter when the absence of winter feed for stock normally meant that only heavily-salted meat was available. However, as the doos were parasitic on the arable farmer, the right to a doocot was restricted to those of baronial status, a status which every laird of consequence inherited or had conveyed on himself by royal grant. The residences of the lairds varied a great deal. In the late seventeenth century a few mighty medieval fortresses with gatehouse, curtain walls, and flanking towers were still inhabited. Good examples are Doune in Perthshire and Kilchurn at the north-east end of Loch Awe in Argyll. By far the most numerous type of laird's seat at this time would, however, be the tower-house, in which stores, kitchen, hall, chamber and bedrooms were set on end, served by one or more turnpike stairs. Erected as early as the twelfth century and varying infinitely in detail and size, these tower-houses were still being built in a relatively simple form in the 1640s. They were the basic element in the more elaborate complexes of building which in the later sixteenth and early seventeenth century marked the brilliant apogee of the vernacular castellated tradition in Scotland. Such complexes as the kindred North-East castles of Craigevar, Crathes, Fraser and Midmar; Angus castles like Glamis and Claypotts; and Amisfield in

Ayrshire, all embody a remarkable and distinct aesthetic and social tradition, which arguably experienced a crucial loss of self-confidence in the Civil Wars of the mid-seventeenth century. After 1660 Sir William Bruce (c. 1630–1710), introduced a fairly well-developed neo-classical style into Scottish prestige building. His achievement culminated in his extension and remodelling of the royal palace of Holyroodhouse in Edinburgh, and in his own superb mansion at Kinross before he handed on the torch to what was to become an apostolic succession starting with his pupil James Smith and stretching through William Adam to the latter's illustrious sons.

The Highland landscape was necessarily more dominated by grazing land than that of the Lowlands. A much higher percentage of the total Scottish population than in modern times lived in the Highlands, but poor soil spread human settlement much more thinly even in the late seventeenth-century Highlands. Where the dwelling of magnate or peasant occurred, it did not differ in kind from those of their Lowland counterparts. Human life was even more strikingly attached to the rhythms of nature than in the Lowlands. Transhumance was widely practised in the Highlands. This involved moving the cattle and a section of the population up to the high mountain grazings in summer. The people lived in temporary dwellings or shielings before they moved the stock down again at the beginning of autumn. There are plenty of place-names including the element 'shiel' in the Borders, so it is clear that the shieling system was not originally confined to the Highlands. In the Borders the practice probably died out as a result of the establishment of exclusive grazing rights by lay and more particularly ecclesiastical landlords, greedy for the profits of commercial wool production in the medieval period. Though doubts have been cast on the efficiency of the system in the Highlands, it was almost certainly the only effective way to utilise the high grazing, producing a flow of cheese and butter to the settlements in the summer, and well-fed cattle, some of which could be driven to market in autumn.

Apart from topography, the single most striking physical difference between the Highlands and Lowlands in the late seventeenth century was probably the presence of extensive forest cover in the Highlands. Numerous Acts of Scots Parliament from 1424, encouraging planting and discouraging irresponsible felling, had failed to preserve Lowland forests. Felling, burning, and above all consequent destruction of seedings by grazing, especially by goats, were eroding Highland forests too, but even so, more timber survived there. That the Lowlands usually imported timber, very often sawn timber, from Scandinavia or elsewhere in the seventeenth century is well known and generally misunderstood. It was not so much that Scots lacked the technology and transport systems to exploit their own resources: it was more a function of relative costs. In his *Description of the County of Angus* originally published in Latin in 1678, Robert Edward, Minister of Murroes, tells us that when, as in time of war, the inhabitants of Angus could not import Norwegian timber: ' . . . they supply themselves with any quantity of planks and logs from the neighbouring woods, on the west of the Grampians; where they have water-mills, which, unless obstructed by frost, are constantly employed in sawing the timber.'

Social structure

The social structure of rural Scotland in the early modern period was more complex than modern historians have been prepared to admit. This is curious because the evidence is voluminous and significant parts of it are in print, such as a long run of the *Registrum Magni Sigilli Regum Scottorum*, the Register of the Great Seal which records crown land grants. If one analyses non-baronial grants from this source in any given area, say a relatively well-favoured stretch of land from Newton of Falkland, along the Howe of Fife, to the Grange of Lindores, one finds a fairly numerous class of men designated 'portioners' and constituting a solidly-based emergent rural middle class resting on a substructure of cottars and subtenants. Though not barons, these portioners could have directives in their grants from the Crown which resembled directives normally included in baronial grants 'to maintain a mansion with plantation and necessary policies'. Some of these men were local burgesses from small burghs like Auchtermuchty, other were lawyers or doctors, and a few were Edinburgh merchants. They invested money in land, becoming portioners and holding 'in free tenantry'. The incidence of portioners varied from parish to parish, but it is possible to argue that there were certain general trends which account for such 'middling people' in Scottish rural society.

There were, of course, many tenants protected only by the customary usage of the barony within which they lived. However, the picture of the average Scottish tenant as purely a tenant-at-will daily haunted by fear of eviction, though propagated by such publicists as John Major, Provost of St Salvator's College in the University of St Andrews from 1534 to

1550, is misleading. Even custom was not to be laughed at in a society which regarded the baron himself as subject to the law of his own baron court, but there were much more formidable means of security for a tenant. To hold land in feu-ferme was one. In exchange for a lump sum and an annual charge, fixed in perpetuity, the tenant holding in feu secured absolute security, indeed virtual proprietorship. In an era of inelastic rents feuing was one of the few ways in which a landlord pressed for cash could quickly raise it. Feu charters were highly formulaic but there is real significance in the fact that most examples from the late medieval or early modern period start with a statement to the effect that the charter is being issued for the augmentation of the landlord's rent. James IV managed to increase his rents from Ettrick Forest, which was feued in the early sixteenth century, by some 500 per cent. This Border property had ceased to be of much value as a hunting preserve, and the king could not foresee the long-term erosion, even of enhanced rents, by sustained inflation.

More significant than Crown feus, in many ways, was the extensive feuing of ecclesiastical land which went on both before and after the Scottish Reformation-Revolution of 1560. Here again legend has been busy, creating a picture of the 'gearking gentillman' who used his superior financial resources to take over the land of the poor tenants in feu. Such gentlemen existed, but modern research has shown that very often feus were granted to existing tenants, many of whom held tenancies which had been in their families for generations, and therefore the feuing process could confirm the existing pattern of smallholdings. Nor did land have to be feued in small portions to reflect pre-feuing patterns, for tenants of long standing often held sizeable holdings which they sublet to smaller tenants.

It is clear that the Earls of Eglinton in Ayrshire built up their great territorial holding partly by acquiring feus from former ecclesiastical tenants. Yet in the same county on the barony of Kilwinning the Garvens of Auchenmaid, one of five tenant families there to take feus in the first half of the sixteenth century, were still in possession in the seventeenth. Nineteenth-century landowners of some substance like the Watsons of Sauchton, can be shown to be descended from tenants of an ecclesiastical institution, in this case Holyrood Abbey, who feued land they farmed in the sixteenth century. Interestingly, in the barony of Strathisla in Banffshire, the feuars of Kinloss Abbey, a numerous class, had turned themselves into small landlords or 'bonnet lairds' complete with tower-houses by the seventeenth century. Yet by the end of that century Alexander Duff of Braco, ancestor of the earls of Fife, had pulled most of these small properties into his own hands. On the other hand, it is easy enough to find a county where any long-term consolidation of holdings in the hands of a few proprietors is conspicuous by its absence. Kinross, even in the late eighteenth century, was remarkable for the number of its farms which were feus in the hands of the farmers themselves.

In the Highlands power broadened down from the landlords and clan leaders through a collateral gentry to a lesser, but still highly-esteemed gentry known as the tacksmen, before it reached the basis of society, the peasantry. Tacksmen held great tracts of land on tack or lease and lived on the difference between the not very heavy rents they paid to the proprietor and the sums they could raise from their peasant subtenants. Two considerations accounted for the existence of this intermediate strata in Highland society. One was the need for lieutenants to mobilise the usually reluctant fighting men in what was still a military society. The other was that same need for cash which affected the landlord in the Lowlands. This need could be satisfied by various expedients. Lands could be leased for lengthy periods in exchange for a lump sum as well as an annual payment. They could be wadset. This was a species of mortgage whereby lands were allocated as security in exchange for a lump sum and a low annual payment. The redemption of such lands necessarily involved repayment of the lump sum, which is why it was relatively easy, in exchange for further payment, to persuade impecunious landlords in the Highlands to turn wadsets into feus. Throughout the Highlands, well into the eighteenth century, it was common to find men holding their land in exchange for specialised hereditary service to their chief, be it as bard, piper, harper, armourer, armour-bearer, or some other prized function in this ancient and complex society.

There was therefore nothing simple, nor static about rural society in early modern Scotland. At its peak under the crown stood the great earls (later usually translated through marquisates to dukedoms). Some of these were held by very old families like the Campbells who turned the earldom of Argyll into a mighty power in the Highlands, and who were themselves almost certainly of ancient pre-Gaelic British stock from the kingdom of Strathclyde. Other earldoms, like that of Atholl, though of Dark-Age origin, passed rapidly through a whole succession of families. All, however, were effectively regional princes wielding regal powers in Scots feudal law. Under them lay a very complicated society remarkable for the way in which successive layers of nobles and gentry faded into substantial 'middling people', themselves of many different kinds and origins, who in turn rested on a complex society of subtenants; cottars who held only a scrap of land near their cottage and lived by hiring their labour; and hynds or farm servants. It is fashionable amongst historians to quote a speech made by Oliver Cromwell to his Parliament in 1658 in which he categorised Scots into 'the meaner sort' and 'great lords' and claimed that his rule had freed the former from the tyranny of the latter. Cromwell was a reluctant imperialist with respect to Scotland, but like all imperialists, he was quick to claim that his conquests really set people free. It was not as simple as that in Scotland: nor was Scottish society the stark polarisation Cromwell implied. It is true that the Restoration regime inaugurated in 1660 rested ultimately on an understanding between the nobility and the Crown but it was precisely the multiplicity of the links between the nobility and the rest of society which gave the nobles their political and social significance. If this was pre-eminently true of rural society, it was by no means irrelevant in the urban context to which we must next turn.

The burghs, trade, manufactures and fishing

Despite the small percentage of the population living in them, Scottish burghs were numerous and they played a very important part in the economic life of the country. We have a fair idea of the appearance of the more important Scottish burghs in the 1680s from the work of the Dutchman John Slezer who published in 1693 his *Theatrum Scotiae*, with beautifully drawn views of the more important Scottish towns. The original sketches for these must mostly date from the 1680s and they show, on the whole, compact and visually pleasing urban settlements whose skylines are dominated by the spires of their kirks. What Slezer's picture cannot convey is the stench, which modern noses would undoubtedly find excessive, and which in the case of Edinburgh even contemporary travellers found excessive. Stench in moderation was, of course, standard in all early modern European cities, Venice, Queen of the Adriatic, sat malodorously on canals which were open sewers. Edinburgh was much the largest Scottish city with perhaps 30,000 indwellers at the end of the seventeenth century. This made Edinburgh roughly comparable with Bristol, the second city of England. London was by this time a quite abnormal phenomenon, approached in terms of absolute size by only a couple of cities like Paris or Naples, and unique in terms of the percentage of the population of a major power concentrated within it. Edinburgh was therefore quite large, relatively speaking, and unlike virtually every other substantial Scottish town of the period it was not built on flowing or tidal water, so it sat on its cramped ridge site and stank to high Heaven.

In the middle of the seventeenth century Aberdeen, Glasgow and Dundee came next amongst the Scottish burghs in terms of size, with perhaps 10,000 or so inhabitants apiece. Aberdeen and Dundee seem to have declined in the second half of the seventeenth century, while Glasgow expanded to 12,000–14,000. Perth alone amongst other burghs may have had a population as high as 5,000. Smaller regional centres such as Inverness, Stirling or Ayr must have had only a thousand or two inhabitants. Many burghs numbered their inhabitants in hundreds, quite a few in scores, and several remained 'paper burghs' throughout their theoretical history, which reflected the optimism of a prospective developer rather than reality. Such speculations emphasise the value of the nexus of charter-guaranteed legal rights which in Scots law alone could constitute a burgh. There was, however, a fundamental distinction between two kinds of burgh.

First came the royal burghs, a privileged group of 66–70 in the seventeenth century. As well as representation in the Convention of Estates, the Scots Parliament, these burghs had their own constitutional organ in the shape of the Convention of Royal Burghs. Indeed membership of the latter body was the crucial test of status. Confusingly five old and important burghs of regality or barony were treated as if they were full royal burghs. The royal burghs were granted charters giving them a monopoly of overseas trade within a defined landward area, in exchange for services to the Crown, mainly in the shape of shouldering a share of national taxation, and collecting the customs dues, largely on exports, which were an important source of royal revenue. Thus enrolment in the Convention of Royal Burghs was followed inevitably by assessment and stenting, or taxation for an appropriate proportion of burghal taxation. The system was a classic illustration of symbiosis between the Crown and self-governing corporate tenants in chief, which was the legal status of royal burghs. Inevitably there were disputes about the precise boundaries of specific royal burgh monopolies. Thus Dumbarton and Glasgow fought legal battles for control of the Clyde, just as Perth quarrelled with Dundee over the commerce of the Tay. Nobody disputed the fact that Leith, the most important port in Scotland, lay within the monopoly area of Edinburgh, though this and the financial leverage Edinburgh merchants usually could exert on the Crown reduced Leith to colonial status. Other landlocked royal burghs had their own vassal ports. Linlithgow, which like Edinburgh contained a great palace of the Stewart kings, had its port of Blackness, just as Haddington, the main corn market for East Lothian, had Aberlady.

Those addicted to the interpretation of early modern Scotland as a land in which a vicious and irresponsible clique of magnates habitually abused a powerless Crown, a prostrate peasantry, and cringing burgers, should reflect that the royal burghs enforced the monopolies granted them by royal charter against the highest in the land for centuries. Part of the explanation of their ability to do this was the fact that the nobility of Scotland had a vested interest in the system of chartered burghal privilege, notably through the burghs of barony of which as many as 210 came into existence before 1707. Many were small but others throve to the point of being promoted to the status of royal burgh, Glasgow itself being a case in point. The century between 1560 and 1660 saw the creation of 19 new royal burghs and 75 burghs of barony. The principal function of the latter was to provide markets for the internal trade of the country. To some extent they served as intermediate gathering centres for commodities ultimately destined to enter international trade through a royal burgh, but we must not underestimate the significance of, and potential of, internal markets in the seventeenth century. It just was not true that growth in a seventeenth-century European economy had to be export-led. Before the disasters of the Thirty Years War overtook it, the economy of the Kingdom of Bohemia was exhibiting an impressive rate of growth based largely on the exploitation and development of internal trade markets rather than on expensive and hazardous long-range trade. In Scotland even royal burghs were often heavily dependent on landward trade.

Dumbarton, situated at the confluence of the Leven and the Clyde, is a good example. It had overseas trade. In 1666 five Dumbarton ships were entered in customs records: the *James* and *Providence* with cargoes from Ireland; the *Speedwell* from Veere in Zeeland; the *Rainbow* with French wine from La Rochelle; and the *Swan* from Barbados with tobacco, indigo and sugar. Nevertheless Dumbarton was probably more significant as the capital of the earldom of the Lennox than as a centre of

overseas trade. There were three main Dumbarton fairs, at Patrickmas, Midsummer and Lammas, when the produce of both Highland Dumbartonshire and Lowland Dumbartonshire was concentrated for sale. The town was very closely involved with the county community of lairds. Lairds held office in the burgh, and they held land of it. Many lairds, like MacFarlane of Arrochar, Colquhoun of Luss, Darleith of Darleith, and the Earl of Glencairn, had town houses in Dumbarton. The town herd daily took the cattle of the townsfolk out to the common grazing while the burghal authorities regarded it as part of their routine duties in 1658 to arrange for the spreading of 50 loads of muck on the unlet Meickle Acre of Overbog, prior to the sowing of a boll and two pecks of barley there.*
Nor was this heavy involvement in agriculture at all unusual amongst royal burghs. As late as the early nineteenth century the Reverend James Hall in his *Travels in Scotland by an Unusual Route* (London, 1807) remarked that the great support of the burgh of Crail in the East Neuk of Fife was agriculture and that it was striking to see cattle, corn and hay being moved through the streets to the barns behind the houses.

Overseas trade was, however, very important and one of the most interesting aspects of the late seventeenth century is the way in which access to overseas trade was systematically widened. In 1672 an act of the Scots Parliament, passed in the teeth of bitter opposition from the Convention of Royal Burghs, severely restricted the privileges of royal burghs. The export of all native commodities—livestock, coal, salt and skins—was made free to everyone, and burghs of regality and barony were allowed to export their own manufactures and to import timber, iron, soap, hemp and agricultural implements. Of the exclusive rights once enjoyed by the burgesses of royal burghs, all that was left was a monopoly of trade in wine, wax, silks, spiceries, wald and other dye-stuffs. In 1690 another act was passed which nominally restored the privileges of the royal burghs, but the exceptions allowed by this legislation gravely compromised the apparent victory for the old vested interest. The privilege of importing foreign goods was once again reserved for the royal burghs, but an exception was made in the case of cattle, horses, sheep and other livestock. On the export side the monopoly of the royal burghs was not to extend to corn, cattle, horses, sheep, metals, minerals,

---

* The boll was a measure of capacity which varied from place to place, but in 1696 it was standardised at a weight equivalent of roughly 140 pounds avoirdupois. There were four firlots and sixteen pecks to the boll.

coals, salt, lime or stone. To cap it all inhabitants of burghs of barony and regality were specifically authorised to buy and sell the native commodities of the country.

Of the total volume of seventeenth-century Scottish overseas trade we cannot speak confidently. There exists a contemporary document surveying all Scottish exports in 1614. It probably represents no more than an informed guess by circles close to King James VI but there is no reason to doubt the accuracy of the broad pattern of exports and re-exports which it gives. It shows an economy exporting a surplus of primary products like, skins, hides, wool, salmon and other fish, coal and in good years grain. Manufactured exports were of the simplest—salt (produced in coal-fired coastal pans) and coarse woollens. The Scottish lead-mining industry was a very fluctuating one, so the fact that in 1614 it was reckoned that Scottish lead exports nearly matched the value of coal exported is probably a freak. Normally coal was a very important export indeed. After 1660 when a Book of Rates was issued listing duties on imports, a more serious attempt was made to collect and record customs and excise revenues. However, smuggling, rights of exemption, and sharp practice on the part of the entrepreneurs who took tacks or leases of the customs were so rampant that these records can only be treated as guides to minimum values and relative proportions.

Scots imports consisted of raw materials, luxuries and manufactured goods. From the northern parts of Europe came timber, tar, iron, flax and hemp, and in years when the Scottish harvest was poor, grain. During the Middle Ages and after Norway was the chief source of timber imports to Scotland, for it was cheaper to ship timber from the fjords than to extract it from Scottish forests. The Norway trade accounted for three ships out of ten reaching Scotland between 1680 and 1686, and in a few areas like Dundee and Montrose the figure was five or six out of ten. Tar, an essential preservative for ships, houses and sheep came from Trondhjem and Bergen. Timber came from a long stretch of the west coast of Norway from May to September or October. About two thirds of Scots timber imports went to the Firth of Forth, a fifth to the Clyde and the rest to the Tay or further north. Not all of this material was Norwegian, though most was. From the early sixteenth century the Scots had developed a trade with Sweden, originally in timber, but by the later seventeenth century overwhelmingly in iron. Though only one ship reached Scotland from Sweden for every six from Norway between 1680 and 1686, the value of the malleable iron bars or 'gads' which the ships from Sweden carried may well have equalled that of the Norwegian timber.

Further east in the Baltic Scottish trading connections were largely concentrated on the cities of Danzig and Konigsberg. The former was roughly twice as important to Scots trade as the latter, and both had long-settled Scots merchant colonies. The Sound Toll Registers, recording payments to the crown of Denmark by all ships entering or leaving the Baltic, enable us to say that flax and hemp were the staple Scots imports from the Baltic. A last was the equivalent of just under a ton and in the 1670s Scottish imports of Baltic flax and hemp averaged 430 lasts per annum. In the 1690s the figure was 212 lasts; and between 1700 and 1707 the annual average was 325 lasts. When Scotland was experiencing a grave subsistence crisis in the late sixteenth century, the Baltic was a major source of grain supplies, especially in the shape of rye. The subsistence crisis of the late seventeenth century saw an increase in grain imports from the Baltic, though not on the same scale because of increased reliance on English and Irish suppliers.

Between 1660 and 1689 the Scots employed one in ten of their vessels in the French trade. Indeed, on the Clyde half of all ship arrivals, excluding ones from Ireland, came from France. Imports were dominated by the young wine from the Gironde, shipped mainly through Bordeaux. This claret was the traditional drink of the lairds. In 1681 the tacksmen of the customs estimated the average import of wine per annum to be some 1,600 tuns. It appears that Leith received 60–70 per cent of wine imports, Glasgow a little under 20 per cent and no other port as much as 5 per cent. After 1660 a new trade in brandy from northern Biscay reinforced this large and lucrative traffic. Moralists were less disapproving of the Scots import of salt produced by solar evaporation on the Biscay coast. It was superior as a preservative to Scots salt. Especially in wartime, Spain and Portugal acted as alternative sources of both wine and salt.

Some manufactured goods reached Scotland from Normandy, but the two great sources of more sophisticated imports were the Netherlands and England. The Dutch Republic was a very important trading partner for Scotland and although England's Dutch wars of 1652–4, 1665–7 and 1672–4 dragged an unwilling Scotland into belligerency, they did not permanently wreck Dutch–Scottish trade. Nor did the decline of the ancient Staple system after 1661 have much real significance. Under it Scottish trade with the Dutch Republic was supposed to be concentrated on a Staple or single port which agreed with the Convention of Royal Burghs to grant special privileges to Scots merchants, privileges supervised by a Conservator appointed by the Convention. Increasing Crown interference with the system and the erosion of the overseas trade monopoly of the royal burghs led to a situation where by the 1680s over 80 per cent of Scottish ships sailing to the Netherlands headed for the great and growing port of Rotterdam. Imports included fine textiles of all sorts; a great range of metalwork; all sorts of military and industrial equipment; various forms of glass, paper, toys and paint; not to mention soap, sugar, spices and all the other wares of the emporium of Europe. From England, mainly by coastal shipping routes, came similar, if less varied categories such as textiles, mainly cotton and calicoes; masses of metal goods and a lot of glassware; plus products of the English colonies, notably tobacco.

The exports with which Scotland tried to pay for this formidable list of imports were overwhelmingly agricultural. By the last quarter of the seventeenth century the relative importance of different elements in the pattern of exports was different from what it had been in say 1614. In good years grain was much more important. For example in 1685 over 103,000 bolls of grain were shipped from harbours between the Tay and Dornoch Firths to foreign markets, and this may have been worth upwards of a quarter of a million pounds Scots. Even divided by twelve to give Sterling value, this was a large sum. It reflected a large increase in tillage in Scotland plus bounties for grain exports. Grain had always been the principal Scots export to Norway and, to a lesser extent, to Sweden. However, it was an uncertain trade. In years of dearth the Scots exported no grain. Bumper crops did not necessarily mean high prices unless, as in 1685, the Baltic grain harvest failed. Cheap Baltic grain shipments usually kept the price of Scots grain, mainly oats and bere, low on the Netherlands markets.

As we have seen, cattle were being exported on the hoof to England in ever-increasing quantities after 1660, but hides and skins were still an important, if declining, element in Scottish exports. About 93,000 skins a year were exported to the Baltic, of which 98 per cent appear to have been lambskins and the balance largely fox skins. The skins of wild animals were also exported but goat skins were the only other really valuable component of skin exports. Wool was an important export, going mainly to France, Holland and Sweden, and to a lesser extent Danzig. In the 1670s exports of wool to the Baltic averaged 45 shippounds or roughly 830 stone per annum. Thereafter the figure rose sharply, probably as in other markets, with the assistance of superior English wool smuggled to Scotland for re-export contrary to English law.

After 1660 Scottish coal mining appears to have resumed a pattern of expansion which, apart from the troubled years of the middle of the seventeenth century, had characterised it since the middle of the sixteenth century. Much coal was exported—it had been the most important commodity shipped to the Staple of Veere before the Civil Wars. Significantly, after 1660 the harbours at Methil in Fife, Port Seton in East Lothian, and Saltcoats in Ayrshire were all improved to provide more berthage for colliers. The high standard of mining technology typical of the Culross enterprises of Sir George Bruce of Carnock in the very late sixteenth century, and more especially of his Moat Pit which ran under the Forth and was drained by a chain of buckets driven by a water wheel, appears to have been abnormal. However, the tradition of technical superiority may explain why, in 1663, the Culross Chalder was made the standard measure for weighing coal in Scotland. A chalder contained 16 bolls. Export of coal in 1614 was said to be 6,308 chalders or roughly 30,000 tons. In the 1660s annual exports may have been a little below this, though by the 1680s they had certainly recovered. The main overseas markets were the Netherlands, both Spanish and Free; France; Scandinavia; Ireland; and England. Tariffs and competition were grave problems. Even in Holland, though Rotterdam was supplied with Forth coal, Amsterdam burned English Tyne coal.

In 1670 the annual output of 15 mines in the Forth was estimated at 50,000 tons, and valued at about £173,000 Scots, so most Scots coal must have been burned at home. A fair quantity of this coal was used to produce somewhat inferior salt in the great iron pans which have left their names studded on the Scottish coast. This was a valuable outlet for 'small coals' or dross difficult to sell because of the contemporary consumer's mania for 'great coal' lovingly cut and shipped in large pieces prior to being smashed by the hammer in many a domestic cellar. After 1660 salt exports were insignificant, except to the Baltic. The once important Norwegian and Dutch markets had been lost to superior Biscay or English salt and the latter destroyed any hope of growth in Scots salt exports to Ulster. The only other Scots export based on mining was that of lead ore and smelted lead. It appears to have varied wildly from year to year. By the 1680s we can say that probably 80 per cent of such exports came from two sites—Leadhills in south Lanarkshire and Wanlockhead in Dumfriesshire. Recurring bouts of speculative prospecting for minerals, originally touched-off by the copper-mining boom in Elizabethan England, yielded no other significant results in seventeenth-century Scotland.

Fish featured prominently in the diet of most Scots. Salmon and trout abounded in inland waters, while white fish and herring were caught at sea. Interestingly enough, salmon and herring also contributed substantially to Scots exports, with salmon perhaps a third in value of all exported fish and herring making up nearly all the balance. The main outlet before 1689 was France and the ban on all imports of foreign salted herring to France in that year was a serious blow, forcing the Scots back on the Baltic, their second-biggest market for fish exports. The fishery was not sophisticated. It was conducted from open boats manned by a few hands and never venturing much beyond ten to fifteen miles offshore. The great and highly-capitalised herring fishery operated by the Dutch off the east coast of Scotland was a source of revenue to the inhabitants of Shetland, who supplied many of the needs of the Dutch fishermen. The Scottish government, eager to increase the few thousand lasts of fish exported for Scotland, twice sponsored over-ambitious fishing companies to challenge the Dutch, and the Royal Company for the Fishery of Scotland, founded in 1670, was as unsuccessful in this enterprise as its predecessor, which was futile.

Another field where the bombast of the Stewart state on matters economic failed to produce significant results was that of manufactures. Manufactures were widespread in both countryside and burgh. Textiles, mainly woollen and linen cloth, provide the outstanding example. They were produced everywhere on a domestic basis usually from local material and were normally used by the household producing them, though the North-East counties of Aberdeen, Banff and Kincardine were known to export coarse woollens in quantity, mainly to northern Germany. Textile craftsmen were prominent in the Incorporated Trades, each a self-governing craft body headed by an elected deacon, into which burghal craftsmen were organised. However, the hand-loom of the weaver was the most sophisticated machinery involved and most of the cloth produced was, like the products of the cordiner (shoemaker) or the wright (carpenter), destined for home consumption. The sett or constitution of most Scots burghs allowed the craftsmen a subordinate role in burghal government but the emphatic ascendancy of the Merchant Guild underlined the extent to which trade rather than manufactures was the lifeblood of the burghs. There was, of course, no necessary contradiction between manufacture and trade as the history of Glasgow, the most rapidly-expanding of major Scottish burghs in the Restoration period, shows.

By 1670 Glasgow was easily the second city of Scotland after Edinburgh. In 1667 Glasgow had begun to develop a good harbour further down the Clyde at Port Glasgow, to compensate for her own shallow moorings at the Broomielaw Quay. The expanding Clyde fishery and a circle of coal pits close to the city provided export cargoes for Glasgow merchants, who already traded with the Americas. During the Restoration era Glasgow also developed soap manufacture; sugar refining and rum distilling; a big woollen manufacture and in 1690 the first cordage works in Scotland. Nor was the Edinburgh–Leith area wholly outstripped by Glasgow in enterprise, for in 1675 the first Scots paper works were founded at Dalry on the Water of Leith, and Leith itself had an expanding glass industry by 1664.

However, the attempt to force industrial development by a policy of banning the import of many foreign manufactured goods after 1681 was wildly unrealistic. It was sponsored by James, Duke of York, or Albany as he was known in Scotland where he was virtual viceroy for his brother Charles II. Retaliation by other countries inflicted harm well beyond possible gains. The success of joint stock companies set up under government aegis, such as that at Newmills near Haddington tended to be transient. By 1683 the Newmills venture was producing 12,000 ells of woollen cloth per annum (an ell was roughly equivalent to 37 English inches—i.e. just over a yard) but production costs were high and the dependence of the company on government orders and protection such that when they were eventually withdrawn the company just faded away. Scottish craftsmen could reach very high technical standards indeed in certain fields. Silversmithing is one example. From 1617 onwards superb ecclesiastical silver vessels were being produced. After 1660 this tradition continued alongside the production of fine secular silverware for the Restoration nobility. Edinburgh tended to dominate this trade whereas the production of luxury firearms, especially pistols, was surprisingly dispersed in places like Dundee and villages along the Highland Line. Such was the quality of these decorated weapons that they were literally fit presents for kings, even kings of France. However, the general pattern of Scottish trade rested on a sensible exchange of the products of agriculture and mining for those of different climates or more sophisticated manufacture.

Scotland was a fairly typical north-west European country. It had a rich and complex social structure sustained by an economy at once self-contained and part of the international economy. From the doldrums produced by war, famine, plague, taxation and confiscation in the Cromwellian era the Scottish economy recovered to vigorous prosperity for most of the period 1660–1690, with a peak in the later 1670s. Above all, it continued to exemplify the real strength of traditional Scottish society by functioning as a series of regional units relatively impervious to the misconceptions and follies of its central government.

3

Crisis, Union and Reaction
1690–1727

By 1690 the high hopes of prosperity which had attended the early decades of Restoration Scotland were fading. Under the post-Glorious Revolution government of William and Mary late seventeenth-century Scotland passed through a decade of indescribable anguish, both physical and psychological. By 1700 there was universal agreement in Scotland that the Union of the Crowns of 1603 was a proven disaster. As to the remedy, there was deep division. When in 1707 the Act of Union selected the path of total political incorporation with England as the way ahead, it was widely argued that here alone lay the route to economic recovery and growth. Much of the liveliness of Scottish politics in the two decades after 1707 derives from the extent to which these hopes were disappointed.

The Scottish economy of the late seventeenth and early eighteenth centuries was not a particularly big one, compared with other European states. Population is one convenient way of demonstrating this, but before the middle of the eighteenth century when Scotland suddenly became the third European country after Sweden and Austria to publish a comprehensive census, it is necessary to use indirect evidence to produce estimates of Scottish population. Modern demographers have had difficulty finding a single large parish sufficiently closed and documented for them to indulge in techniques of family reconstitution. In any case, baptismal records are erratic, and marriage records confused by two factors. One is the Scottish habit of being married by a favourite clergyman who is not necessarily the parish minister. The other is the nature of Scots law which does not regard a formal ceremony as an indispensable part of marriage. There exist Poll Tax Returns for 1694–5 and Hearth Tax Rolls for 1683–4, but the most complete records are burial registers and bills of mortality which allow of aggregation and the identification of crises of subsistence. These records suggest nil population growth between 1695 and 1755, which would give a 1695 population of roughly a million and a quarter.

Such a population was naturally dwarfed by the 20 million or so people who made the France of Louis XIV the most populous of European states. It was outclassed by the approximately five to six million inhabitants of late seventeenth-century England. More significantly, it was inferior to the population of the Republic of Venice, even if that state be defined as simply the city of Venice and its Italian mainland territories which together in 1700 had some 1,700,000 inhabitants. The population of Scotland in this period was roughly comparable to that of Switzerland and only slightly larger than that of the island of Sicily. This fact was highly significant in a world where the major European powers were increasingly inclined to regulate economic life within their jurisdictions in accordance with a variety of economic nationalism often referred to as mercantilism. In the mercantilist mind mercantile profit and state power were two sides of a single coin. Much mercantilist policy was ineffective, more ill-conceived, but through much of it ran an obsession with improving the balance of trade by encouraging exports and actively discouraging imports by means of protectionism. Thus Scotland faced a widespread policy of beggar-my-neighbour against which her smallness hardly permitted effective retaliation.

Crisis was the keynote of most contemporary discussion of the late seventeenth century economy. It is therefore logical to probe the nature of this crisis before going on to discuss its two consequences. The first of these was the Act of Union of 1707, which was seen by many as a solution to the crisis. The second was the disillusionment which set in when the immediate consequences of the Union became apparent.

The crisis of the late seventeenth century

The 1690s were distinguished by a major subsistence crisis in Scotland. It was deeply ironic that Scottish agriculture should pass through this experience just when it was beginning to become the subject of a literature devoted to the theme of improvement. Scotland had nothing comparable to the group of sixteenth-century writers on agriculture in England, and even in the seventeenth century the Scottish record is very bare before 1697, consisting of a brief manuscript 'Of Husbandrie' produced by the Midlothian laird John Skene of Hallyards sometime before 1666. Then in 1697 came James Donaldson's *Husbandrie Anatomiz'd*, published in Edinburgh and suspiciously literary in flavour. In 1699 a short treatise entitled *The Countrey-Man's Rudiments : or, An Advice to the Farmers in East Lothian how to Labour and Improve their Ground*, by A. B. C. The author is thought to have been John Hamilton, second Lord Belhaven. Tragically, the agriculture which these writers wished to improve had been passing through acute crisis since August 1695, when the harvest failed unexpectedly. By June 1696 victual imports from anywhere were being admitted free of duty and in August an unprecedented bounty was offered on such imports for two months. Despite this grain prices rocketed, dearth was widespread even in areas like the Lothians noted for corn production, and the two grim consequences of dearth—disease and mass displacement of population—were prominent. Sir Robert Sibbald, physician and geographer, was one of many who painted harrowing word pictures of death by the roadside and in the faces of the wandering poor, while the stern patriot laird Andrew Fletcher of Saltoun wondered whether forced labour might not be the answer to the problem of vast numbers of wandering, destitute, and potentially dangerous people.

Yet it is important to place this dreadful experience in a wider context. Jacobite propagandists successfully labelled the catastrophe 'King William's Seven Ill Years'. The phrase conceals two truths. First, out of anxiety to establish an analogy with a Biblical Pharaoh, it conceals the real chronology of the crisis, which ran for four years from 1695, with peaks of severity in 1696 and 1699 and a relative respite in 1697–8. Secondly, the phrase suggests a specific Divine Judgement on the Scottish nation for the sin of dethroning James VII and II in the Glorious Revolution of 1688. Nothing could be further from reality, for this agrarian crisis was widespread. It harrowed the fair fields of France with mounting severity from the summer of 1691, despite the manifest blessings of indefeasible hereditary right embodied in Louis XIV's absolutism. By 1693–4 France was deep in an appalling famine from which it began to emerge just as Scotland entered on a similar experience. Fletcher of Saltoun's alarmist reaction to the wandering destitute hordes of Scotland can be exactly parallelled by the reaction of a Mexican professor, Don Carlos de Sigüenza y Góngora, to rioting Indians in Mexico City in 1692.

The hunger gnawing at the hearts of Scots and French peasants and Mexican Indians alike was rooted in a global cycle of bad weather. There is now a formidable weight of direct and indirect evidence, from direct weather and crop records; to the absence of reports of observations of the normal cycles of sunspots; to precipitation temperature analyses of New Zealand stalactites; which suggests a significant fall in the energy output of the sun in the seventeenth century leading to crop failure on earth.

Another relevant point is that almost certainly this was not the worst Scottish famine of the century. Like virtually every other early modern European agrarian economy, that of Scotland was subject to recurring cycles of dearth, more punishing in the seventeenth century than in the two or three previous centuries but not unprecedented, and of these famines that of 1623 may well have been the most lethal. Certainly such evidence as we have for mortality suggests that the crisis of 1623, which was preceded by two consecutive harvest failures, was much more serious than any subsequent crisis and unusual in its very general impact. In 1634–36 there was a regional dearth in the north of Scotland. From the summer of 1644 until 1649 the burghs of Scotland and many rural parishes were ravaged by bubonic plague which rose and fell in intensity until early 1649 when it vanished from the realm for two and a half centuries, to reappear in a transient visitation in Glasgow in August 1900. 1650 saw dearth in the Highlands. High grain prices in 1674–76 formed the background to widespread reports of disease; no doubt the result of weakened resistances due to malnutrition. The crisis of the 1690s was grave, but it was far from unprecedented or unique and it was the last of its kind.

Famine was, however, only one of four major crises affecting the late seventeenth-century Scottish economy, and of these three were political in nature. First we can consider the impact of war. This was a consequence of the Glorious Revolution of 1688, but not a necessary consequence. Dutch William was lucky to be able to drag England and its political satellites Scotland and Ireland into a series of great Continental wars. Indeed, without massive assistance from the arrogance and folly of Louis XIV it is difficult to see how he could possibly have succeeded. The English ministers of Queen Anne had to violate the express terms of Scottish legislation of 1696 to hijack Scotland into the war of the Spanish Succession by illegally postponing the meeting of the Scots Parliament in 1702 until the tame Scots Privy Council had declared war on Louis XIV. These French wars which lasted from 1688 to 1697 and then from 1702 until after the Union were far more disruptive of Scots overseas trade than the Dutch wars of the Restoration. Conscription for the King's ships—1,000 men in 1692—was a serious drain on a small seafaring community. It did in fact provoke riots. Embargoes on trade with hostile powers were often enforced with a high hand by the English Royal Navy and they closed many harbours to the Scots. Above all the activity of French privateers was deadly. Not only were many ships lost, but insuring and crewing others became vastly more difficult. The Scots navy was tiny and the English navy did not over-exert itself on behalf of Scottish shipping. The situation was offensive as well as ruinous. Decisions were taken in London. The Scots merely paid the price for them.

The second politically-determined problem facing the Scots economy was that of trade prohibition, or rising tariff barriers all over the Atlantic world. Most contemporary European states were striving to increase their degree of self-sufficiency and all the European-based Atlantic empires tried to operate as self-contained economic units. Even before 1690 direct trade with England had suffered from the imposition of tariffs on Scots coal and salt exports and by 1698 Scots linen exports were similarly affected. Between 1697 and 1702 it was possible for Scots to trade legally with France but such trade was hampered by absolute bans on the importation of wool and fish into France and by very heavy duties on coal. In order to stimulate its own developing coal-mining industry, the government of the Spanish Netherlands (roughly modern Belgium) placed prohibitive duties on coal imports, thereby destroying a developing Scottish trade. In the same way the Danish government of the twin kingdoms of Denmark–Norway imposed tariffs on corn imports in the 1680s with a view to securing the Norwegian market for Danish grain producers. The Atlantic empires of Spain, Portugal and England were run in as exclusive a manner as circumstances would permit, and it was particularly galling for the Scots to watch in the late 1690s a deliberate tightening of the English Acts of Trade and Navigation of the Restoration period which themselves virtually confined the English colonial trade to merchants and ships of the English empire.

What one must recall is that late seventeenth-century governments, including that of France, which as late as 1680 was arguably the most sophisticated state machine in the European world, could seldom effectively enforce their more drastic trade policies. Spanish colonists traded with any foreign shipping which could reach them. The saints of Puritan New England gleefully disregarded the Acts of Trade and Navigation save during brief periods of unwonted zeal on the part of the hard-pressed officers of the English government. So far from being capable of effectively stopping specific export trades from Massachusetts or Ireland, the English government was utterly incapable of preventing its subjects in the southern parts of England from conducting a massive and complex smuggling industry. Thus the follies of governments were modified by the practical common sense of peoples.

It was perhaps the most unfortunate feature of the third great politico-economic crisis which afflicted late seventeenth-century Scotland that government and people united in that act of folly, the Darien scheme, or 'our African and Indian Company' as it was known to contemporary Scotsmen. The origins of this enterprise were threefold. First there was a long-standing Scottish interest in the creation of an overseas colony for Scotland. As early as 1621 Sir William Alexander of Menstrie had received a grant of 'the Nova Scotia in America' from James VI, though he had met with little success in turning his charter rights into reality in the face of French opposition. Later colonising enterprises in Carolina and East New Jersey underline the extent to which interested Scottish opinion was thinking of fairly typical North American settlement and plantation colonies. Despite some overlap in personnel, such as Principal William Dunlop of Glasgow and Bailie Robert Blackwood of Edinburgh, with the Company of Scotland Trading to Africa and the Indies, neither the strength nor the continuity of this colonising zeal should be exaggerated.

Equally uninfluential in the supreme crisis of the Darien scheme was the second originating impulse in the shape of the zeal of a group of Edinburgh merchants for the development of Scottish trade to Africa. Men like Bailie Robert Blackwood, a director of the Newmills Cloth Company, were convinced that an African trade would stimulate the Scottish woollen industry as they were sure it had the English woollen industry. In fact the only successful venture ever conducted by the Company of Scotland was the voyage of the *African Merchant* which anchored in the Road of Leith at the beginning of July 1700 with a cargo of gold, ivory and rice which eventually yielded a clear profit of £46,668 Scots.

The spectacular débâcle which is the centrepiece of the whole history of the Darien venture was rooted in two abnormal phenomena. The first was the unsatisfactory relationship which had existed between England and Scotland since the regal Union of 1603. Long before the King's Commissioner in Parliament Hall in Edinburgh on the 26 June, 1695

touched an Act for a Company Trading to Africa and the Indies with the
Sceptre of Scotland and thereby gave it the final royal consent, English
merchants and financiers had been interested in the new Scottish company. The act named 20 Directors, of whom ten were Londoners, seven it
is true London Scots, with only two Englishmen and the Jew D'Azevedo,
but there is no doubt that many English businessmen saw the Scots
company as a legal way of outflanking the monopolies of trade in the
hands of the English African Company and, more significantly, the
Honourable East India Company. The Scottish company was meant to
be Anglo-Scottish in practice and it was the London Directors who
started to raise the stakes. Thirty Edinburgh merchants guaranteed capital to the tune of £13,600 sterling as soon as the act was passed. When,
however, a delegation of three Scots Directors, led by Lord Belhaven
went down to London in November 1695 they were shaken to find that
the London Directors were thinking in terms of a total capital fund of
£600,000 sterling, half to be raised in London, half in Edinburgh. The
Edinburgh men had envisaged £360,000 sterling as the upper limit, but
they gave way, and it looked as if all was well when half the larger sum
had been offered within a fortnight of opening the subscription book.
Then an offensive by the Westminster Parliament, stirred up by such
vested interests as the Honourable East India Company, forced the
English and Anglo-Scottish merchants to withdraw. All the neuroses
bred in Scotsmen by a century of disastrous Union focused on this one
issue. The heroic and fatal decision was taken to raise £400,000 sterling
in Scotland. With a subscription list headed by the remarkable Anne,
Duchess of Hamilton, for £3,000 sterling, and including such humble
figures as pages, the whole guaranteed capital was raised. Contemporaries believed this to represent half the capital of Scotland. The
phrase is meaningless and uncheckable, but the commitment was clearly
staggering.

   While the systematic attempts by King William's agents to under-
mine Scottish appeals for aid from the Netherlands and Hamburg kept
Scottish opinion very much on the boil, the second disastrous influence
on Scottish policy asserted itself. This was William Paterson, born in
Dumfriesshire but a long-standing London resident and businessman,
hitherto best known for his important part in the founding of the Bank of
England. Paterson had traded in the Caribbean. He knew the Brethren
of the Coast, the buccaneers who prayed on the Spanish empire. From
their tales and his own over-fertile imagination he had shaped a vision of

the Isthmus of Darien—very roughly modern Panama—as 'this door of the seas, and the key of the Universe'. By means of an overland route at this isthmus, secured by a Scottish colony of Caledonia, the Cape of Good Hope route was to be superseded. Spanish legal claims in the area were very dubious: Spanish power feeble, as buccaneers like Sir Henry Morgan had shown. It was not Imperial Spain which ensured the catastrophic failure of the two expeditions sent out by the Scots in 1698 and 1699 respectively. Nor was it the English diplomatic boycott enforced by King William himself lest the meddling Scots generate a crisis undermining his complex arrangements with Louis XIV about the future of Spain and its empire. Rather, was it the basic folly of the concept.

Scotland did not have the power to protect an empire of monopolistic trade or settlement against rival European powers, all predatory, most much larger. The only worthwhile objective for her in the colonial field was other nations' colonists. Trade with these was feasible and could be so lucrative as to easily cover the marginal risk of its technical illegality. Glasgow in the late seventeenth century was flourishing partly because of a brisk illegal trade with the English Empire. A fraction of the capital thrown away in Darien, applied to honest smuggling to semi-independent American colonists would have yielded solid dividends. Paterson combined in one charismatic personality two disastrous traditions. He had all the pretentious futility of the late Stewart fishery schemes which quite failed to challenge the Dutch but did tax the inshore fisheries which the Dutch left alone. At the same time his career looks forward to that of another Scot, John Law, who in early eighteenth-century France generated a major financial crisis by recklessly creating an unsound mania for investment in a state-sponsored company controlled by himself. Paterson rallied support by means of patriotism rather than by an appeal to greed, which was Law's method, but the upshot was not dissimilar. Nobody paid a higher price for Darien than Paterson, who went there and lost his wife as well as his reputation in the unhealthy rain-sodden and feud-ridden Scots colony.

It was not just the money which was lost. More important were the wasted opportunities to do something constructive with it, and there is no doubt that by the late seventeenth century large sections of the Scots nobility and gentry were avid for the economic growth which alone could increase their disposable incomes. Increasingly, the Scottish aristocracy was attracted to and assimilated by the vastly wealthier nobility of England. Only a very few seventeenth-century Scots peers like the Earl of

Dysart and the Duke of Lauderdale actually took up residence in England. It was very expensive to do so. The classic example is that of the Duke of Hamilton who was the leading Court Scot of his generation and a favourite of Charles I. His estates were all in Scotland. He held well-paid office at Court and yet his career was remembered with something like horror by the next generation of his family, less because of his death on the scaffold after Cromwell defeated him at Preston than because his expenditure so exceeded his income as to bring the mighty Hamilton estates to the verge of ruin. Around 1700 roughly one Scots peer in seven was marrying an English bride. It was one way of trying to bridge the financial gap, for English dowries were vastly fatter than Scots ones. Here was one expedient, no different in substance from such devices as trying to levy rent in grain rather than cash. It has been shown that in particular baronies like that of Skirlin in Peebleshire the latter device did secure a substantial rise in the value of rent at a time when the 'siller' or money rent was virtually static. However, grain was like English brides; in relatively short supply outside favoured areas and subject to unpredictable vicissitudes.

Increasingly the ruling classes of Scotland were ready for drastic, nay revolutionary change. It was very much a revolution of frustrated expectations. What satisfied their fathers satisfied them no more. The regal union whetted appetites it did not satisfy and the only question around 1700 was how the ruling classes of Scotland would try to break out of what they saw as a vicious circle. Their opening for the operation was obvious—the crisis over the succession to the Crown.

The Union of the Parliaments of 1707

Proposals for a uniting of the legislatures of Scotland and England had been repeatedly advanced ever since James VI of Scotland succeeded to the English throne in 1603. James assumed the title of King of Great Britain, but in reality he was simply the occupant of two distinct thrones, and his attempts to secure a fusion of the two states and their legislatures foundered on the stolid hostility of both. The English legislature was particularly unenthusiastic about the idea, yet it was first implemented in response to a purely English initiative. After the Cromwellian conquest of 1651 Scotland was eventually incorporated by the Instrument of Government of December 1653 into a 'Commonwealth of England, Scotland

and Ireland'. To the unicameral legislature of this Commonwealth the Scots had the right to send 30 MPs and they were naturally given freedom of trade within the Commonwealth and its dependent imperial possessions. In general the Scots had no great reason to value either their MPs or the new common market they were part of until the Restoration of 1660 restored the old order including their independence. Restoration governments toyed with the idea of a legislative union between England and Scotland for purely political reasons. It would, for example, have well suited Charles II to swamp the Westminster legislature with all the existing members of the Estates of Scotland, loyal and penurious as the latter tended to be. Needless to say, neither the Lords nor the Commons of England relished the prospect.

On his death bed William III urged his English ministers to effect a legislative union with Scotland. Here again the motives were entirely political. Though arguably the most intelligent man to sit on the English throne since Tudor times, William had been an abysmally bad king in a Scotland he never visited nor even faintly cared for. To him Scotland's function was to supply money and troops and keep quiet. Faced with mounting mutiny by the Scots political nation, the king's dying instinct was to obliterate them as an obstacle to Government by incorporation in a legislature of which they would only form an insignificant part. His successor Queen Anne pursued the scheme.

In the winter of 1702–3 Commissioners from England and Scotland met at the Cockpit in Whitehall to discuss possible legislative union. The discussions proved abortive. England and Scotland by 1703 seemed to be moving apart rather than together. Realistically, the English ministers decided to concentrate on the essential issue of the succession and as late as 1704 would have been quite prepared to accept the enactment of a Scottish measure parallel to the English Act of Succession of 1701, which settled the throne on the House of Hanover, as a satisfactory outcome to the crisis. Behind the succession lay very real fear about English security if the thrones were separated, yet the Scottish ministry, led by Lord Tweeddale quite failed to produce the desired settlement and had to accept an Act of Security which left the nomination of a successor to Queen Anne in the hands of the Scots parliament. Suddenly English politicians grasped that their minimal terms might only be obtainable by the extreme expedient of a union.

If English motives were consistently political, there is no doubt that economic considerations carried much weight with the Scots at this time.

In 1703 the Scottish legislature had passed a Wine Act which allowed trade with France in the traditional Scots import of wine despite the fact that Queen Anne was at war with Louis XIV. The revenue generated did help the hard-pressed Scots Treasury but the main point to the legislation was protest against forcible involvement in ruinous war. Nor was Darien forgotten, for in 1705 occurred the ghastly judicial murder in Leith of the English Captain Green of the ship *Worcester* along with two of his crew, on trumped-up charges which made sense only in terms of Scottish spleen and hysteria over the Darien disaster. It was therefore a shrewd move by the Westminster legislature to open its campaign for a union with measures of open economic blackmail. In March 1704 the Alien Act was passed in England, placing before the Scots the choice of either negotiating a parliamentary union or accepting the House of Hanover with no change in the existing relationship between England and Scotland. The latter was a bogus option, for it was universally agreed in Scotland that the union of the two crowns had worked badly and was strangling the smaller kingdom. If Scotland enforced her Act of Security and chose a separate monarch, all Scots, with few exceptions, were to be treated as aliens in England and the principal Scottish exports to England—coal, cattle and linen—were not to be imported to either England or Ireland. Threats of force were made and the penalties of the Alien Act were to become operative on Christmas day 1705 if the Scots did not climb down.

Primarily, this was an attack on the Scots aristocracy. They alone amongst Scots resident in Scotland would find alien status in England unendurable, for many had estates and relatives there, and more had hopes. Equally, it was primarily the rent-rolls of the aristocracy which were swollen by the proceeds of the coal, cattle and linen trades to England. Often a tenant paid his rent by means of the money he received for the linen produced by himself and his family during the lengthy periods in the year when their labour was not fully exploited by agriculture. More important in the context of 1705 was the fact that most lairds were well aware of this fact. The great game was fairly begun. On the English side the goal was the political incorporation and therefore emasculation of Scotland. On the Scots side there is little doubt that the bulk of the self-conscious nation wanted to trade the Hanoverian succession for an improved political and economic relationship with England. Nobody could be quite sure of the outcome, so it is not surprising that as Mr Joseph Taylor, barrister of the Inner Temple, returned in September

1705 to England from a trip to Scotland he met in the vicinity of Carlisle 'a prodigious number of Scotch Catle, coming from the Mountains to be sold, before our Act of parliament pass'd'.

Being inexperienced, the Scots politicians had really overplayed their hand and roused the ire of a still formidable England. Furthermore, English money could and did work wonders. It is difficult otherwise to explain the extraordinary behaviour of the worthless fourth Duke of Hamilton who was nominal leader of the anti-Unionists in the Scots parliament, but who, in a thin house, suddenly stood up, proposed and carried a motion which destroyed any chance of serious negotiation by handing the nomination of the Scots commissioners for negotiating the terms of a union into the hands of Queen Anne. Thereafter it was certain that the Treaty of Union would be a pre-arranged package concocted by Anne's English ministers with a view to railroading it through the Scots legislature and securing not the consent but the acquiescence of the Scottish nation. Nevertheless, the Scots did hold a lively debate on the issue of the Union which, if politically marginal, does tell us a great deal about the prospects which intelligent Scots saw for their economy around this time.

The first point worth making about this debate is that it concerned itself hardly at all with the question of access to the English colonies. Indeed a strong school of thought deprecated the significance of the imperial dimension. In reality there were limits to Scottish capacity to raise the capital for large-scale participation in such a trade in the early eighteenth century, and in so far as Scots could raise the capital there was very little the English government could do to stop them. The last point was particularly appreciated in Glasgow, which had a rapidly increasing stake in Atlantic trade but whose overwhelmingly Protestant and Whig merchant community remained very hostile to the Union. The crux of the debate lay in traditional trades and especially in the trade with metropolitan England.

Arguments in favour of the Union were pressed by a school of writers headed by that remarkable Englishman Daniel Defoe who had been sent to Scotland by the English government to make propaganda for the Union, but he was backed by a whole school of Scottish pamphleteers including Thomas Coutts, John Clerk of Penicuik, William Seton of Pitmedden, and the Earl of Haddington. The central argument advanced by this school of thought was that Scotland suffered from chronic balance of payments problems which drained the kingdom of coin, and that the only trade where Scotland enjoyed a positive balance, with some prospect of increasing that balance, was the trade with England. Defoe was prepared to quantify that positive balance at £100,000 sterling per annum. His figures are almost certainly as worthless as his forecast that the Scots could easily and rapidly double their exports of coal, cattle, corn, linen and salt to England, but his main point was probably correct. There does seem to have been a positive balance even in such a difficult year as 1704 when there was a drastic currency shortage in Scotland and the Bank of Scotland stopped cash payment temporarily. The fact that a great deal of the currency circulating in Scotland was usually foreign was not in itself a sign of weakness in this bullionist age. A great deal of England's eighteenth-century currency consisted of Portuguese gold coins. What was significant and depressing to contemporaries was the chronic shortage of specie in Scotland.

The opponents of the Union were led by the uncompromising and incorruptible Andrew Fletcher of Saltoun but he too was supported by many other writers including John Spreul, a Glasgow merchant, David and William Black, Lord Belhaven and others. Necessarily, these writers had to contradict flatly most of the propositions advanced by their opponents. They were almost certainly right that men like Defoe grossly exaggerated the benefits of the English trade, but unconvincing when they tried to argue that there were no benefits. As the anti-Union school strongly disapproved of both the spending of Scots rents in stylish living in London by Scots peers and of luxury imports from London, they tended to take a dim view of the massive importation of wines and spirits from France to Scotland. They denied that trade with the Netherlands involved an unfavourable balance for Scotland and, more convincingly, extolled the virtues of the Norway and Baltic trades and the potential for the expansion of Scottish traffic in such places as Iberia and the Mediterranean.

Apart from the unavailability of statistics, which very often meant that neither side in the debate really knew what it was talking about, the disputes between the two sides were rendered more complex by the fact that no serious opponent of the Union wished to preserve the existing situation. Fletcher of Saltoun, for example, stood for a very drastic reshaping of Scotland's government and foreign policy which would inevitably have affected the development of the Scottish economy, for Fletcher's decentralised near-republican Scotland would certainly have aimed at the benefits of neutrality in England's wars, though it would also have cultivated sincere good neighbourliness with the adjacent realm. This drive for change extended to specific aspects of the contemporary Scottish economy. Thus opponents of the Union, while granting the importance of the cattle trade to England, argued that the Scots derived surprisingly little profit from it compared with English middlemen. After a long trek, the weary Scots cattle or 'runts' would be sold to English graziers at such places as St Faith's, a well-known cattle mart in Norfolk. The local graziers then fattened the 'runts' into the finest beef cattle in England on their own pastures, supplied the needs of Norwich and Yarmouth, and sent weekly consignments of cattle to the London market throughout the winter season. It was suggested by opponents of the Union that it would be better to fatten the cattle in Scotland before exporting them as barrelled beef and hides to the Netherlands and elsewhere. In view of the fact that the kingdom of Ireland in the second half of the eighteenth century was exporting some 60,000 cows a year as barrelled beef, much of it destined for France or the Caribbean market, this suggestion was not without point. Yet the prospect of the impending enforcement of the Alien Act was a daunting one, for it would clearly disrupt existing trade patterns before new ones could be formed in a hostile world. The Earl of Roxburgh was not the only contemporary observer convinced that reasons of trade were the most significant factors creating support for the Union.

It would have required stronger will and nerve than the Scots leadership possessed to sit out the crisis and see if England really was foolish enough to hazard war on her northern frontier when she was deep in a great conflict in Europe. Led by the nobles the three estates of the unicameral Scots parliament all voted for the Treaty of Union in 1706–7. The key remained the nobility, and although some of the very greatest magnates such as the Duke of Atholl, opposed the Union, conviction, self-interest and the usual lubrication of patronage, swayed a decisive majority for the measure. Given the closely interwoven nature of Scottish society, the nobles could be relied upon to carry the gentry or lairds, and even to exert substantial pressure on the burgesses who in January 1707 voted 30–20 for the Union. Opposition increased steadily from nobles to lairds to burgesses. The Convention of Royal burghs voted to petition against the measure 24–20, with 22 abstentions, and one quarter of the burghs including Edinburgh, Glasgow, Perth and Stirling petitioned individually against it, making nonsense of Defoe's bland line that no serious interest opposed so beneficent a measure. In fact very few Scots wanted the incorporating Union which emerged. A federal settlement was as far as the nation was prepared to go and the pro-Union politicians showed that they too thought the measure desperately unpopular by arranging for the elections to the first British parliament in Scotland to come not from the constituencies but from the old and discredited Scots legislators.

Economic arrangements were a crucial part of a Treaty of Union whose principal authors relied more on the force of inertia than on force of conviction to make it palatable. Many clauses of the Treaty of Union were therefore devoted to matters economic, starting with Article 4 which guaranteed complete freedom of trade and navigation to all subjects of the United Kingdom both within that kingdom and with 'the Dominions and Plantations thereunto belonging'. The Scots were now partners in the English empire. Article 5 allowed Scottish ships which were foreign built though owned by Scots at the time of the ratification of the Treaty to rank as ships of Great Britain, if so registered after oath taken. All Scottish ships in 1707 were thus to come within the privileges of the English Navigation Laws. Articles 6 and 7 unified the customs and excise services of the new state according to the English system. Article 8 made the concession that for the first seven years after the Union Scotland should be exempt from the much higher English duty on imported salt (vital as a preservative for meat and fish) provided it was used domestically, while receiving the same rebates as England on foreign salt used to cure fish for export. Under Article 9 an attempt was made to work out an equable distribution of direct taxation, given the relative wealths of England and Scotland. In Scotland direct taxation took the form of so many months' cess or tax at £6,000 sterling a month, £5,000 being paid by the landowners and £1,000 by the burghs. It was now specified that eight months Scots cess (£48,000) should be treated as equivalent to an English tax of 4s. in the £ yielding a little under £2,000,000. Contemporaries appear to have regarded the ratio of these two lump sums (1:42) to one another as a roughly accurate measure of the relative wealth of Scotland and England.

The next four Articles specifically exempted Scotland from existing temporary English duties on stamped paper, windows, coal and malt. Indeed Article 14 in words which turned out to be ironic not only relieved Scotland of 'any Imposition upon Malt during this present War' but also expressed the conviction that the new united legislature would distribute future fiscal burdens with equity and understanding. After this burst of optimism Article 15 buckled down to the most complex piece of financial horse-trading in the entire Treaty. The problem was that Scotland's financial structure before 1707 bore little relationship to the financial system which was absorbing her. English customs and excise yielded £2,289,161 per annum while the Scots customs were farmed at £30,000 sterling and the Scots excise at £33,500 per annum. However, the Scots had no National Debt, having had the good sense to keep their rulers so poor that they lacked the credit to start accumulating one. After 1 May 1707 they were to shoulder their share of the English National Debt servicing charges, since the English debt became a British one. At a little over 15 years' purchase £398,085 10s. was deemed the capitalised Equivalent of this new burden and was assigned to the Scots in compensation. It was expected that the Scottish revenue yield would increase and part of this increase would be used for servicing the British Debt, so the Scots were also to receive a Rising Equivalent amounting to the whole increase in Scotland's customs and excise revenue for the first seven years of the Union and thereafter such part of the increase as was devoted to debt servicing.

Highly significant were the four objects to which the funds of the two Equivalents were to be devoted. Much the most pressing of these was the complete compensation for loss of all who had invested in the Company of Scotland Trading to Africa and the Indies. The Scots would have preferred to keep the company alive. The English were determined to kill it but they grasped that those who had lost money through Darien constituted such a substantial cross-section of the Scottish ruling classes and their dependants that there was no prospect of securing the passage of the Treaty of Union without massive financial compensation to these people. The last act touched with the Sceptre of Scotland regulated the repayment of capital plus five per cent per annum interest to investors in 'the African Company'. Calculated to a nicety at £232,884 5s. 0⅔d., this was much the biggest bribe offered at the time of the passage of the Treaty. It was all paid within two years. The second object to which Equivalent funds were to be dedicated proved more troublesome. This was the compensation of private individuals who lost by the provision in Article 16 of the Treaty that the coinage be standardised on the English model. The recall of the old Scots coinage, to the amount of £411,117 10s. 9d. sterling, proved protracted. It was interrupted by a liquidity crisis which in March 1708 forced the Crown to restore Scots coins to circulation by proclamation, and was only completed after two years and eight months.

The other two objects allocated Equivalent moneys were a very disparate pair. One was the payment of the public debts of the Scottish Crown. Though Scotland had no funded National Debt, there had been an imbalance between revenue and expenditure for some time. In 1682 it was reckoned that revenue amounted to £91,477 sterling per annum and expenditure to £93,718. At the time of the Union Scottish revenue was not more than £110,000 sterling per annum and the pay of the army alone, excluding its equipment and clothing, £66,000 per year. Figures like these have been quoted to uphold the thesis that 'in 1707 an independent Scotland was not financially viable'. This argument is itself non-viable. The bulk of Scottish expenditure was for a military establishment which an independent Scotland would not have maintained if it could have withdrawn from England's wars. Besides pro-Union men like Clerk of Penicuik and anti-Union men like Fletcher of Saltoun and Lord Belhaven all agreed that Scottish administrations before 1707 were, to an offensive degree, mere tools of English ministers, so Scottish reluctance to pay taxes to such men no more indicated a fundamental weakness than American reluctance to pay taxes to Westminster precluded an independent United States of America. The last object to be financed from the Equivalents—£2,000 per annum for seven years to encourage wool manufacture and thereafter to promote fisheries and other manufactures—yielded no immediate political benefits, so no effective action was taken to carry theory into practice after the passage of the Union.

Apart from Article 17 which standardised weights and measures on the English model, the rest of the Treaty was legal and political in nature. Scots weights and measures in practice only faded very slowly from the scene, while Scots money survived as a unit of account until well into the nineteenth century. At local level, Scotland went on governing itself much as before. The heritable jurisdictions in the hands of the nobles and the rights of the royal burghs were specifically guaranteed. It remained to be seen how far the Union fulfilled its promise.

Scottish Reactions to the Union 1707–1727

Those Scots who had fought hardest to secure the passage of the Treaty of Union undoubtedly justified their policy on two main grounds apart from pure political expediency. The first was that the terms were reasonable: that the great surrender of legislative autonomy was balanced by generous access to the English world-state and that much that was particular to the Scottish way of life was secured by specific guarantees in the Treaty, which was a permanent piece of fundamental law at the very basis of the new state. The second ground was that Scotland would soon experience, in the words of Article 15 of the Treaty, 'the Increase of Trade and People (which will be the happy consequence of the Union)'. In practice the first generation after the Union was mainly remarkable for the extent to which both these assumptions were cruelly falsified.

The only bonanza enjoyed by Scots merchants immediately after the Union was brief and peculiar. Because the Union was certain by February 1707 but did not take effect until May, it proved possible to import large quantities of such commodities as French wines and spirits, which could then be despatched to England, without any trouble from the usual fiscal barriers, after 1 May. The new united legislature registered its indignation but the exercise was unrepeatable. A new customs and excise service on the English model was rapidly established in Scotland. Contemporary Scots were given to saying that it was staffed exclusively with rogues from England. This was just not true, though there were plenty of Englishmen among the Scots in the new service. What Scots objected to was the very existence of an institution to which their previous history offered no parallel. The old Scots customs and excise were a tiny charge on the wealth of the nation, and farmed out to speculators who could be relied upon to wink conveniently for a relative or a consideration. In relation to the central state, pre-1707 Scotland was not playing the English game badly, as Englishmen then and now assume; it was playing a quite different game, nor was it keen to abandon it. Smuggling became and remained for much of the eighteenth century a national sport in Scotland; one which a despairing customs and excise service fought against with its own inadequate strength and with such meagre and provocative assistance as the British Army and the Royal Navy could offer. The situation was well epitomised by the experience of Montrose, an east-coast port with an entrenched merchant class of notoriously Jacobite views, where the King's Warehouse was looted by local mobs, bent on recovering confiscated smuggled goods, so often that the local customs and excise were frightened to store much in it. Their policy was to ship confiscated goods to Edinburgh rapidly before their owners organised a mob to repossess them.

Nor were the years immediately after the Union particularly prosperous for Scotland. There was a bad harvest over much of Scotland in 1709. Though it did not produce a subsistence crisis like that of the 1690s it bred much suffering and, in so overwhelmingly agricultural a land, necessarily lowered the general level of economic activity. When there was a surplus of grain for export, Scots lairds were exasperated to find that grain prices were low. Nor did the much-heralded huge expansion in the linen trade to England occur. It had never been very likely that it would. What one may describe as the osmotic theory of economic growth—that if you join a rapidly-growing economy your economy will grow rapidly too—is as common now as it was then, but that does not make it correct in every case. It came very easily to the lips of eighteenth-century politicians anxious for purely political reasons to eliminate the spinosity of the Scots by losing them in a larger entity. Such men tended with great sincerity to argue that provided the Scots acceded to their will all other benefits spiritual and temporal would be added unto them. However, in a common market which behind its external tariff did operate mainly on straight capitalist market principles, the quality and pricing of Scottish products were crucial factors in deciding their fate after 1707, and Scottish linen was, by and large, inferior in quality. In the late seventeenth century the Huguenot refugee Nicholas Dupin, strongly supported by the old Scots parliament, had tried through the medium of the privileged Scots Linen Manufactory to raise the efficiency and product quality of the Scots linen trade. Partly due to the failure of the royal burghs to honour pledges of financial support, he failed to make any significant impact. By 1710 Scots linen was in the doldrums. A great deal of what was produced was for domestic use and it proved very difficult, in the face of a vigorous English linen trade, to expand sales in England.

It seems that a similar period of relative stagnation was experienced by other Scottish industries. Coal is a case in point. The second half of the seventeenth century had seen rapid expansion in coal output. It was estimated that by 1700 Scotland's salt pans alone were using 150,000 tons of coal per year at six tons of coal for every one ton of salt produced. The export of coal, especially to the Netherlands, was levelling off, but it was much greater in 1700 than it had been in 1600. Above all, the second half of the seventeenth century saw a massive increase in the demand for coal from the cities of Scotland, both for domestic and for industrial purposes. The heavy cost of land transport for coal was to a large extent offset by the proximity of the markets. Both Edinburgh and Glasgow were sited very close to major coalfields, as were lesser centres such as Haddington, Linlithgow, Falkirk, Stirling, Dunfermline, Kirkaldy, Renfrew, Paisley and Ayr. Shallow pits could cost as little as £50–60 sterling to sink. However, after 1700 and more particularly after 1707 neither home nor export markets were notably buoyant, partly because of a vigorous competition from English coalfields. The Tyneside mines and salt pans were old rivals of the Scots, but the Midland coalfield in England was expanding rapidly. Between 1700 and 1760 its annual production may have risen from 1 million to 2½ million tons. As Scots mines went deeper the drainage problem made them more expensive. A new pit, with pumping machinery, at Carden in Fife cost £600 sterling in 1705. It is significant that very few of the new steam pumping engines evolved in England through the work of Thomas Savery and Thomas Newcomen were installed in Scotland before the second half of the eighteenth century. The first steam engine to be installed in a Scottish mine was one at Elphinstone colliery near Stirlingshire in 1720, but it was not until 1763 that they reached Glasgow collieries.

The absence of investment in steam engines is a pointer to relative lack of expansion in coalmining, nor was the salt-producing industry likely to provide an independent stimulus for the mines. Scottish salt simply could not compare with solar salt in quality and it is no accident that the terms of the Treaty of Union presuppose that the Scots will be importing substantial quantities of foreign salt for the curing of fish. Curiously enough, the one trade with England which held up well after 1707 was the long-distance trade in cattle which was of particular interest to the districts north of the Highland Line where about half the population of Scotland lived and where hostility to the Union was especially strong. The trade was temporarily gravely interrupted by the 1715 rebellion, but drovers were exempted from the provisions of the, admittedly largely ineffective, Disarming Acts of 1716. Even so, it was in the period after 1730 and more especially after 1739 (when demand for salted meat for the armed forces soared due to the outbreak of war) that the droving industry entered its halcyon period.

To some extent droving, like other industries, was held back by the shortage of cash credit in the Scottish economy. Prior to 1695, with gold coins scarce, silver becoming scarcer, and too much poor copper in circulation, bills and bonds had become commonly used as credit instruments in the Scottish economy and Edinburgh goldsmiths acted as clearing houses. When the Bank of Scotland was established in 1695 one of the purposes it was meant to serve was a measure of credit creation, but once it had secured a 21-year monopoly in its founding legislation, it chose to pursue an extremely conservative policy. It had a modest capital of £100,000 sterling. Its liquid resources when it started business were a mere £10,000; the product of the first call on shareholders. Branches in Glasgow, Aberdeen, Dundee and Montrose were promptly closed after a year as unprofitable and all business concentrated in its head office in Parliament Close in Edinburgh. No money was received on deposit. Customers were borrowers, strictly on security of heritable and personal bonds, or discounters of bills, for the Bank of Scotland was in many ways little more than a clearing house. Only in 1704 did it descend to the level of issuing a note of as low value as £1 sterling or rather 'twelve pounds Scots' as the face of that note continued to say long after the demise of the pound Scots. It hardly mattered, for the Bank of Scotland was sparing of its note issue. The Company of Scotland briefly dabbled in banking before Darien ruined it, but apart from this episode the Bank of Scotland remained unchallenged, profitable, and therefore undynamic until the London government chartered the Royal Bank of Scotland in 1727.

Against such a background of disappointment, stagnation and frustration, the occasional Scottish outbursts of emotional and or physical fury against the Westminster regime become perfectly comprehensible. By 1715 Westminster had come within an ace of creating a revolution of frustrated expectations in Scotland. Partly this was due to a whole series of unilateral breaches in the letter and spirit of the Treaty of Union which came as a great shock to the Scots who like many others then and since failed to grasp the arbitrary and absolute nature of the power wielded by that very English beast the King in Parliament. In 1712, for example, it was proposed to raise the level of taxation on ale in Scotland to something like the English level by imposing a tax of 6d. per bushel on malt despite the explicit prohibition in Article 14 of the Treaty of Union of any malt duty 'during the present war', which had not ended. Faced with a general mutiny by Scots MPs and peers, in the course of which a motion for the repeal of the Union was lost in the Lords by only four votes, the ministry abandoned the scheme. However the Scots had been unable in 1711 to prevent the imposition of an export duty on linens which was regarded as a national grievance since linens were much more important in Scottish exports than in English textile exports, where woollens were traditionally the main staple. All in all, had anyone less paralytically incompetent both as a strategist and a tactician than the

Earl of Mar led the 1715 rebellion, there is little doubt that it would have fulfilled the gloomy prophecy of Dean Swift in his poem 'On the Union', that:

> Tossing faction will o'erwhelm
> Our crazy double-bottom'd realm.

Even after the rebellion fizzled out in 1716 Anglo-Scottish economic relations remained emotion laden and potentially explosive. In 1725 what were known as the Shawfield riots erupted as a result of the decision of Sir Robert Walpole to impose a tax of 3d. a bushel on Scottish malt. This was half the English rate and in any case represented an attempt to modify and soften a back-bench proposal to tax Scots ale at 6d. the barrel while withdrawing the bounty on exportation of grain. The new malt tax was nevertheless only imposed after savage rioting in Glasgow, aimed at the property of Daniel Campbell of Shawfield, MP for the Glasgow burghs, who was supposed to have shown too much enthusiasm for the tax. Virtually condoned by the Glasgow burgh authorities by virtue of their failure to take any vigorous action against the rioters, this disturbance was eventually put down by a substantial military force under General Wade. Nor was this the last episode of its kind. In 1736 Edinburgh was the scene of the extraordinary Porteous Riot. This episode had its origin in the execution of a smuggler called Wilson. 'Black Jock' Porteous, the captain of Edinburgh City Guard, felt obliged to fire on a threatening mob during the execution and was himself subsequently lynched by a large and disciplined mob. Westminster, whose grasp on the realities of Scottish politics had never been strong since the abolition of the Scots Privy Council in 1708, was beside itself with rage and quite wrongly assumed that the civic authorities of Edinburgh must have connived at the murder of Porteous. Strong opposition from the Duke of Argyll alone reduced the penalties to a heavy fine on the city and the deposition and exclusion from office for life of its provost.

Just when the depressing history of mismanagement and stagnation in post-Union Scotland comes to an end is not easy to decide. Political and administrative failure continued on a surprising scale until they culminated in the 1745 rebellion. Basic restructuring of Scottish society began with the abolition of the heritable jurisdictions in 1747. Dramatic re-organisation of agricultural or industrial production came much later. However, there was at an earlier stage a definite trend towards relative prosperity within a largely traditional social and economic context, and, if one arbitrary date has to be chosen as indicating the arrival of the first few swallows of this particular summer, 1727 is as good as any. In that year the establishment of the Royal Bank of Scotland marked an important stage in the elimination of the financial constraints on the development of the Scottish economy. Equally significant was the establishment in the same year of the Commissioners and Trustees for Improving Fisheries and Manufactures in Scotland, commonly referred to as the Board of Trustees. While one must not exaggerate the role of this body if is a fact that the linen trade, in which it displayed a very lively interest, was one of the sectors of the Scottish economy which experienced early, sustained and significant growth. If the Union had failed to produce either political stability or satisfactory economic growth within a generation, it was still possible for economic growth to render the Union tolerable.

4

The Beginnings of Radical Industrial and Agricultural Change 1727–1780

The previous chapter covered a period during which many Scots began to doubt whether they would ever see that sharp acceleration in economic growth for which they longed. Between 1727 and 1780 the economic climate completely changed, for by the latter date it was clear that the Scottish economy was experiencing significant growth and change and that the rate of growth and change was accelerating. It will be argued that this historic transition owed less to the highly publicised activities of the state and those men known as Improvers, than to the vigorous exploitation of comparative cost advantages in a few sectors of the economy by a host of relatively unknown men, most of them rooted in the traditional social structures of pre-industrial Scotland. Nor was the transition to growth instantaneous. If 1727 saw the arrival of a couple of significant swallows, it by no means marked the start of high summer, for some key growth-areas in the Scottish economy were far from booming in the 1720s and 1730s. Cattle production and export is a good example. Prices were not particularly buoyant until well after 1740. Thereafter there was a rapid rise in the market price of cattle which indeed increased fourfold over the period 1707–94. However, the great bulk of the increase came between 1740 and 1794, and even within that half-century the later decades were more satisfactory than the early ones for Scottish drovers who had to cope with the potentially ruinous hazards of cattle plague (rinderpest) which broke out in England in 1745 and remained endemic, if with decreasing virulence, until 1757. Scottish cattle did cross the English border in steady and significant quantities even during the '45 rising. In the same way Scottish sheep from the Borders were being driven into England to meet the rising demand for wool from the expanding English woollen industry. It so happened that the woollen and worsted industry of the West Riding of Yorkshire was expanding steadily and was unusually concentrated, so Scottish wool could supply the industry while Scottish mutton helped feed its workers. Yet prices were fairly stable between 1730 and 1760 and the Scottish woollen industry in the Borders and Lothians simply failed to survive in the face of shipments from the traditional West Country strongholds of the English woollen manufacture, supplemented by Yorkshire woollens arriving mainly by pack horse.

That droving, overall, paid is clear by reason of its continuation and gentle expansion, but before 1740 there was no chance of profit on a scale massive enough to effect major consequent changes within Scottish society, and it was always easy to lose money on a particular drove. The exception to this picture of a still very stable rural society is Galloway, and Galloway is the exception which proves the rule. In the late seventeenth century this extreme south-west tip of Scotland was an unenclosed countryside with a traditional farming in which the main contrast lay between the low-country people with an economy based on cattle, barley, and long-bearded oats, and the 'moor men', living in smaller settlements, herding sheep, and cultivating plots of rye. Sir David Dunbar of Baldoon, with his great enclosed cattle park, was an exception. Yet there were certain factors which, by the early eighteenth century, undoubtedly offered the nobles and lairds of Galloway opportunities for making profits in the English market.

First, this south-west corner comprising the counties of Wigtown and Kirkcudbright, or the western two-thirds of the modern Dumfries and Galloway Region, was naturally well endowed for cattle grazing and had been noted for its 'store of bestiall' from the sixteenth century. Secondly, it was close to the English border, thereby eliminating the expense and loss of condition incurred by say a laird north of Inverness by the time his cattle had arrived within sight of England. Thirdly, it was in a strategic position to import cheap Irish cattle across the 20-mile-wide North Channel separating the Rhinns of Galloway with its harbours such as Stranraer, Portpatrick and Port Logan, from Ulster. Fourthly, its landowners were active through the old Scots Parliament to fix and maintain traditional drove roads through the south-west hills and moors to Dumfries and by Solway Sands or Sark Bridge over the Western March into England. Fifthly, and crucially, these same lairds set about the consolidation and enclosure of grazing land for commercial stock fattening and raising early and on a big enough scale to convulse traditional rural society.

The reaction was dramatic. The Levellers of Galloway were the most significant Scottish rural protest movement before the Crofters' War in the Highlands in the 1880s. These eighteenth-century Levellers seem to have consisted of smaller or tenant farmers threatened with eviction. In bands they roamed Galloway breaking the dykes of enclosed parks and fields where cattle destined for southern markets grazed. From 1723 through 1724 and 1725 a virtual rising involving groups of up to 2,000 men led usually by tenants under notice to quit raged over the area. It was crushed by the gentry, aided by troops and its demise was confirmed by heavy fines imposed by the courts. Despite sympathy from some ministers, some merchant burgesses, and even a few radical lairds, the Levellers had failed decisively. Galloway moved to a ruthlessly commercial agriculture two or three generations before most other Scottish regions. Market opportunities due to abnormally favourable production costs explain the move, and it left a practical heritage as well as a precedent. Dry stone walling, or 'dry stane dyking' as Scots call it, was the basic tool of Galloway enclosure. It was to become very common elsewhere in Scotland when similar changes came.

Comprehensive dry stane dyking was first undertaken on the lands of the McKies of Palgown in the west of the Stewartry district of Kirkcudbright around 1710. A skilled dyker could build a rood of dyke a day (six yards in granite or whinstone districts and seven yards in more favourable limestone country). As enclosure spread, thousands of miles of dry stane dyke were constructed in Galloway alone. Specialist forms developed. The average stock-controlling dyke was 4½–5 feet tall. March dykes between estates could be 6 feet high. About 1730 Hamilton of Baldoon invented a combined dyke and thorn hedge known as a 'sunk fence' or 'Galloway hedge', it was copied extensively by Lord Selkirk of St Mary's Isle, and became common on sloping ground. Once the thorns were fully grown it would turn even those athletic and venturesome jumpers, blackfaced sheep. Another device for coping with those animals which evolved in eighteenth-century Galloway was the Galloway dyke, a dry stane dyke, the top 22 inches or so of which were laid with big rough stones firmly interlocked, but with light showing through the interstices in such a way as to convince sheep that it was precarious and too risky to attack.

Nothing is more revealing of the limited impact of those market forces breeding basic social change in pre-1750 Scotland than a contrast between Galloway and the Highlands. Though Highland regions were major participators in the long-range droving trade, Highland society, with rare exceptions, remained traditional and armed. In such a society a certain amount of cattle thieving was inevitable. Indeed it was a sport as well as a necessity. William Mackintosh of Borlum argued in 1742 that the parts of the country most infested with cattle thieves were the western parts of Inverness, Perth and Stirlingshire and the northern part of Argyll. Nor is it generally appreciated how late large-scale cattle thieving flourished in the Highlands. It increased rather than decreased in the troubled times after the '45, reaching something of a peak in 1747 or so, after which it was finally suppressed with the aid of standing military garrisons and patrols. The scale and effects of such thieving before 1745 are easily misunderstood. It did not stop the droving trade. Drovers were armed and the great cattle fair or tryst at Crieff was originally guarded by the military vassals of its noble patron. Violence had positive, as well as negative functions. It kept English middlemen out of the Highlands in any number until after 1747, thereby reserving a large economic niche for the enterprising Gael. It helped keep the military muscle of Highland society in decent trim at relatively small cost, and it spared the Highlander the full rigours of a legal system which stressed the rights rather than the obligations of property.

Rob Roy Macgregor, a legendary Jacobite figure of this period, was in fact a bankrupt drover who defaulted on debts due to the Duke of Montrose. Far from being excluded from economic activity, he continued to play a prominent role in the Highlands, drawing on a great fund of native wit and homespun philosophy, as well as a rare dexterity with a yard of cold steel. The blackmail he levied on his cattle-owning neighbours was of course a protection racket, but arguably no more so than some schemes sponsored by modern insurance companies. His premiums were tolerable and his capacity for recovering stolen goods impressive. When Daniel Defoe spoke of Galloway in the appropriate section of *A Tour Through The Whole Island of Great Britain* which he published between 1724 and 1726, the height of his praise was to remark that it was 'no uncommon thing for a Galloway nobleman to send 4,000 sheep and 4,000 head of black cattle to England in a year, and sometimes much more'. When Defoe visited Perthshire what seems to have impressed him most was 'The Duke of Athol . . . lord, I was almost going to say king of this country'. Defoe was intrigued by the duke's mighty 'tail' of vassals. From the point of view of the majority of Highlanders there is no doubt that the emphasis on men rather than beasts was to be preferred, and was sustained and safeguarded by the military nature of their society. Contained violence, the by-product of the fighting potential of the area, was not incompatible with gentle economic growth and was a socially conservative force. Unbridled economic growth geared to a market economy was, as Galloway proved, socially disruptive in its consequences. The great bulk of Scotland lay somewhere between the extremes of the Highlands and Galloway in 1726 but it is quite clear from entry after entry in the *Statistical Account* of Scotland published in the 1790s that, except in abnormally favoured areas, consolidation and enclosure in agriculture were of no great account much before 1760. Most of Scotland was still a traditional society.

Yet it had clearly passed a highly significant economic milestone by the early 1740s. After a poor harvest in 1739 a bitter winter was followed by an even worse harvest over much of the western seaboard of Europe in 1740. In Scotland the ground lay frozen until April and air frosts persisted until July. From the autumn of 1739 to the summer of 1741 there was great scarcity of victuals and high prices until the mercifully good harvest of 1741 relieved the situation. There were food riots. Typhus ravaged a weakened population and measles became epidemic as a killer disease in Edinburgh. At any other previous point in Scottish history this concatenation of events would undoubtedly have set off a major subsistence crisis accompanied by demographic collapse, economic debility and a long slow painful recovery to the previous level of population. Harrowing though the years 1739–41 were, they saw no such fundamental collapse, despite the fact that the activities of the British state seem to have exacerbated rather than helped the situation. An ill-advised plunge into aggressive war in 1739, followed by the usual ruthless use of the press-gang to secure crews for the undermanned Royal Navy, had caused a severe crisis in Scottish coastal shipping with consequent dislocation in the vital inter-regional grain trade.

The explanation for the relatively happy outcome of the crisis lies at two levels. Immediately, the crisis was staved off by much more efficient importation and distribution of grain than had ever been seen before. More corn was probably imported into Aberdeenshire alone in 1742 than into the whole of Scotland during the dreadful crisis of the 1690s. The Edinburgh magistrates sold imported grain below cost price at the

height of the dearth in 1740, but it does seem that due to increased prosperity and a stronger balance of payments position, Scotland was capable of importing unprecedented quantities of grain and Scotsmen, one
way or another, could afford to buy it on a scale unprecedented in previous dearths. It is interesting that in December 1742, when the social
consequences of the subsistence crisis were still very visible, the burgh
authorities of Kirkcaldy resolved to employ suitable persons 'to furnish
the poor who are not in the session roll with lint to spin, and to receive
that yarn and pay them sufficiently for it, and one other fit person to be
employed by the Kirk Session to furnish the poor upon the roll in the
manner aforesaid'. The assumption was that a certain measure of self-
help was possible in the context of contemporary demand for linen yarn.

This fact points to long-term factors at work in abating the impact of
the 1739–41 crisis. Before discussing these it is worth looking at the size
and distribution of the society which weathered this last threat of general
famine. Alexander Webster's *Account of the Number of People in Scotland*
estimated the population in 1755 to be 1,265,380, and such efforts as
mid-twentieth-century Edinburgh historians have been able to make to
check his estimates suggest that they are surprisingly reliable. The distribution pattern for these million and a quarter or so people was quite
different from that produced by the impact of Victorian industrialism.
Roughly 51 per cent of the population lived in the counties north of the
Tay; 37 per cent in the central belt or triangle between Glasgow, Dundee
and Edinburgh; and the remaining 11 per cent in the southern uplands.
Whereas London in 1640 had about 450,000 inhabitants, which was
approximately 8 per cent of the population of England and Wales, Edinburgh and Leith together in 1751 had not more than 57,000 people,
which was a little over 4 per cent of the Scottish population. Of other
burghs, only Glasgow (approximately 31,700), Aberdeen (approximately 15,600) and Dundee (approximately 12,400) had populations in
excess of 10,000 and only eight burghs altogether had more than 5,000
inhabitants apiece. Here was fairly convincing proof that Scotland was
still a rural society in which no very drastic restructuring had yet
occurred. It remains to be explained why such a society had been able to
avoid demographic disaster and economic relapse in the early 1740s,
when all previous history suggested that such a recession was the natural
end of two generations of recovery from the previous low point of the
1690s. The answer is best sought by first examining the traditional
explanation—the improving state and landlord—and then by trying to

create an explanatory model which copes with at least some of the major inadequacies of the traditional explanation.

The improving state and landlord before 1780

Mainly as a result of the recurring Jacobite rebellions in early eighteenth-century Scotland, the Westminster government became involved in a series of enterprises designed to modernise some of the more archaic regions of Scotland. In contemporary language the London politicians set out to encourage, especially in the Highlands and Islands, the Protestant religion, loyalty to the House of Hanover, and a spirit of industry. For them, the integration of politically recalcitrant areas of Scotland into the increasingly commercial society of Great Britain was a means of obtaining long-term military security. Security and commercial habits were thus two sides of one coin.

One often-quoted example of this is the programme of road construction which began under the aegis of General (later Field Marshal) Wade as a typically belated response to the '15 in 1726. Eventually these military highways, constructed by troops, constituted a significant network in the Grampian Highlands and the North-East, with a couple of extensions beyond the Great Glen, and an unrelated but substantial outlier in the South-West designed to facilitate troop movements to and from Ireland. From the very start it was believed that these roads would have a dual function. In a letter to Lord Townshend, written from Killichiumen in Lochaber and dated 16 September, 1726, Wade wrote:

> The work is carried on by the Military with less expense and difficulty than I at first imagined it could be performed; and the Highlanders, from the ease and conveniency of transporting their merchandise, begin to approve and applaud what they at first repined and submitted to with reluctancy.

This was with reference to a 60-mile stretch of road up the Great Glen on the south side of its numerous lochs and designed to link Inverness with Fort William by a route capable of use by wheeled carriages and artillery. By 1728 Wade was reporting to his political masters that he was currently employing 300 soldiers on a work which he deemed of major significance to His Majesty's Service viz. 'the new road for wheel-

carriages between Dunkeld and Inverness, of about 80 English measured miles in length'. Wade's own roads were essentially a system
whereby the strategic road along the Great Glen could be approached
through the central Grampians from either Dunkeld or Crieff, the latter
route passing by Aberfeldy to converge with the road from Dunkeld at
Dalnacardoch. Of an eventual 1,100 miles of military road, Wade was
directly responsible for about 260 miles. Most of the rest of the system
was constructed under the supervision of Edward Caulfield, who started
out as a surveyor under Wade and rose to be Inspector of Roads. By 1757
Caulfield was reputed to have spent £130,000 on his roads, but by then
the strategic imperative behind their construction and maintenance was
weakening.

By 1784 Lieutenant-General Mackay, the Command-in-Chief Scotland, was urging the Treasury to look at the system with a view to
economies. Arguably the only person who ever derived massive advantage from the central parts of the military road system was Bonnie Prince
Charlie, who found the Hanoverian roads very useful for the purposes of
a Jacobite army. The roads were not designed for normal commerce,
either in terms of their gradients, or their routes. Cattle could not be driven on them for any distance without damage to their hoofs. Significantly, the only two sections of the system which Mackay thought
could be offloaded onto 'the gentlemen of the county' in 1784 were the
peripheral Galloway and North-East roads. Military roads were an
expensive marginal event in the economic history of the eighteenth-
century Grampians. In the military history of the region they were a
rather sour joke.

Nor can it be argued that elsewhere in Scotland before 1780, road
improvement was one of the spearheads of economic development.
There existed legislation which made provision for the improvement and
maintenance of roads. Acts of 1617 and 1661 directed Justices of the
Peace to mend roads leading to market towns, seaports and parish
churches. Neither Act was effective. JPs fitted awkwardly into traditional Scottish society, being little more than an alien device imported
by the Crown, so in 1669 a more comprehensive Act made the Sheriff and
one of his landowner deputies, plus the JPs, the local road authority.
They could call on tenants, cottars, and servants for up to six days labour
for a man and a horse per year, in the months of June and July. Theoretically they could stent or tax landowners up to 10s. in £100 valued Scots
rent per annum and they also had power to levy tolls on roads, bridges,

and ferries. In practice they seldom used their powers of taxation, which after all hit their own pockets, while the statute labour they could call on was notoriously grudgingly and badly done. Further legislation of 1686, 1715 and 1719 merely exacerbated an already serious crisis in the statute labour system.

Over most of Scotland roads were scarcely recognisable as such. Essentially they took the form of traditional rights of way traversed by three or four collateral tracks. Each track was in turn abandoned when churned excessively by traffic and this habit could be carried to the point where nobody was very clear exactly where the public highway lay. In 1723 the Commissioners of Supply for Banffshire exercised a prerogative bestowed on them by the 1686 legislation, which conjoined them with the JPs in road administration, and ordered heritors or landowners to stop byways running through their lands in order to prevent travellers from straying from the highway. Even in so advanced a county as East Lothian in 1740 carts were a rarity and none of them were used over any distance. This was very sensible for suitably prepared road surfaces hardly existed. The odd magnate who sought prestige by travelling significant distances in Scotland by coach usually became the centre of a muddy and inglorious pantomime whose dreary immobility was relieved by squads of workmen and underlined by successive broken axles. Simon Fraser Lord Lovat did travel from Inverness to Edinburgh by coach in the summer of 1740, but his progress was paralytic, and his language, always colourful, must have scaled new heights of expressiveness. When in 1760 that great Ulster magnate the Marquis of Downshire tried to traverse Galloway by coach he took with him a squad of labourers to heave him out of ruts, mend axles, replace wheels, and so on, but he still ended up stuck and benighted with his family in his coach near Creetown. Sensible men rode or walked. If they had to send goods any distance by land they sent them by pack horse, and for short haulage of heavy goods, say stone on a farm, nothing could beat a sled. It was common sense rather than invincible ignorance which ensured that nobody in the town of Selkirk possessed a cart before 1725, or in the royal burgh of Campbeltown in Kintyre before 1756.

The state did provide legislative encouragement for the turnpiking of Scottish roads. Under this arrangement a group of men undertook to construct or improve a highroad up to a standard suitable for the regular passage of wheeled vehicles. In recompense for their efforts and expenditure they were authorised to levy tolls, on an agreed scale, on traffic using their stretch of road. The first Turnpike Act of which any evidence survives was passed in 1713 and related to Midlothian, but thereafter there was a long gap until the next Scottish Turnpike Act was passed in 1751. There may have been important activity by Commissioners of Supply in the 1770s in the field of bridge building. Three significant bridges were built in that decade in Lanarkshire, for example, improving access between Clydeside and the south. Nevertheless, almost every account published between 1791 and 1799 in the *Old Statistical Account of Scotland* makes it clear that good roads for wheeled vehicles, where they existed, were all comparatively recent. This is true of remote parishes and of surprisingly central ones. The minister of Kirkwall and St Ola, the Reverend George Barry, who later published a *History of the Orkney Islands*, recorded that there were only three roads of any consequence on the Mainland of Orkney. They had been constructed in a fit of zeal in the 1760s using stenting, donations of money, and statute labour. They had since simply crumbled and turnpikes were still unknown. The post road through the Carse of Gowrie between Perth and Dundee was built in the 1790s. Turnpike roads did by that time link Dundee over the Sidlaw Hills with the great valley of Strathmore. However, the author of the *Statistical Account of Dundee* records that they were only recently completed. Well he might, for an Act of 1789 authorising landowners to improve the road system in the large county of Forfar (re-christened Angus in 1928) which lies north and east of Dundee, and to recoup their expenses by the erection of turnpikes and toll houses, describes the existing road system as ruinous and dangerous. State-sponsored improvement of the road system clearly does not go far to explain the changed economic status of Scotland before 1780.

Nor can much weight be given to the two great surges of Westminster interest in modernising estates confiscated from convicted Jacobite rebels after the '15 and '45 rebellions. Of these two episodes the one which followed the '45 was much the most ambitious in scope, but the earlier episode is interesting in its own right. After the collapse of the rebellion in 1716 it was hoped that widespread confiscations would bring profit to the central government and deter future rebels. Partly due to deliberate obstruction by the Scottish courts, neither expectation was fulfilled, for it proved extraordinarily difficult to secure convictions and enforce confiscations. Despite this, a very substantial block of estates belonging to leading rebels was by a new statute of 1717 vested in Commissioners of Inquiry who were to sell them by auction. By the autumn of

1719 the Commissioners, who had each been pocketing the staggering salary of £1,000 per annum since 1716, were in a position to offer estates for sale. This was the age of the South Sea Bubble with its mania for speculation and a group of English financiers used the shell of the Company of Undertakers for raising the Thames Water in York Buildings as a vehicle for raising £1,200,000 sterling for purchasing forfeited and other estates in Great Britain by means of a fund which was also meant to grant annuities on lives and to finance life assurance. The York Buildings Company duly acquired an enormous landed property in Scotland in the shape of forfeited estates in the counties of Aberdeen and Banff, Forfar, Perth, Linlithgow, Haddington, Berwick and Stirling. In 1712 the rental of Glasgow, with a population of 14,000, was £7,840 2s. 6d. sterling. In 1719 the clear rental from the York Buildings Company's Scottish estates was about £13,700. Ironically, after payment of administrative charges, debts chargeable on forfeited estates, and Crown grants, the total gain to the Exchequer from 50 forfeitures and nine years' expensive service from the Commissioners was a paltry £1,107.

The York Buildings Company itself was in deep financial trouble almost at once. Its most lucrative activity was puffing its own stock which became unsaleable in the general collapse of the speculative mania. Devices ranging from loans to lotteries to watering the stock merely put off the day of reckoning. Meantime the company leased estates to, amongst others, such notable improvers of agriculture as Sir Archibald Grant of Monymusk and his brother-in-law Alexander Garden of Troup. Sir Archibald has been virtually canonised by modern scholarship, as one of the fathers of modern Scottish agriculture but he appears in a much less admirable light as the head of a legion of relatives and connections who penetrated the York Buildings Company and manipulated it, much more to their own advantage than to that of the company. The company also bought and exploited woods on Speyside from 1728; started an iron works at Abernethy; worked coal mines and salt pans on the attainted Earl of Winton's estate at Tranent; and pursued lead and silver with very little success on the Panmure estates in Glen Esk and with more success but no profit at Strontian in Ardnamurchan. The process whereby the company's creditors squeezed it out of existence was immensely protracted. A vital stage came in 1764 when four of the forfeited estates were bought back by the attainted families, on very easy terms. Later sales were made at better prices but the brutal fact is that the York Buildings Company, for all its furious energy, progressive economic ideas, and inspired dishonesty, never could raise a big enough revenue from its landed property to stave off gradual dissolution. As an agent of permanent economic transformation it was a fiasco.

It is commonplace to think of the much more direct intervention by the Westminster government on the estates forfeited after the '45 as more significant. Forfeiture was more extensive after the '45 than after the '15 and the legal manoeuvres indulged in by the Scottish lairds and lawyers to obstruct the '15 forfeitures were simply not tolerated after the '45. Furthermore there was a deliberate policy of retaining some forfeited estates as crown property to be run as models of progressive administration converting the surrounding countryside by sheer example from rebellion and barbarism into a hive of industry, trade and manufacture. In 1752 legislation annexed 13 forfeited estates 'unalienably' to the Crown. All rents and profits were to be used for 'Civilising the Inhabitants upon the said Estates and other Parts of the Highlands and Islands of Scotland, the promoting amongst them the Protestant religion, good Government, Industry and Manufactures and the Principles of Duty and Loyalty to his Majesty, his Heirs and Successors and to no other Use or Purpose whatsoever'. The Forfeited Annexed Estates constituted a large area of Scotland. Apart from an interruption in the shape of the unforfeited estates of the Campbell Earl of Breadalbane, they were said to stretch in a swathe some 30–40 miles broad from just north of Stirling to Inverness. In addition to this central area of the Grampian Highlands, they comprised the estates of Barrisdale, Kinlochmoidart, Lochiel and Ardshiel in the Western Highlands, while north of Inverness the Earl of Cromarty's forfeited property stretched from the east to the west coast. Here was a potentially formidable instrument of change.

In practice the Westminster government's interest in the venture cooled almost as soon as it became clear that there could never be a serious recurrence of Jacobite rebellion in the Highlands. A board of commissioners to manage these estates was therefore nominated only in 1755 and so dilatory was the government in clearing up certain legal problems relating to some of the western estates, notably that of Lochiel, that their rents, to the tune of £1,200 sterling per annum, were denied to the new commissioners until 1770. Such members of the board as did regularly attend the meetings of that body were well-intentioned, serious and active. Yet the lack of acknowledgement or reply from the Crown to their numerous communications had by 1760 so discouraged the commissioners that they threatened to suspend all operations pending some sign from Westminster that somebody was reading their letters. By the reign of George III minimal recognition from London was available, and the commissioners continued to perform their duties until 1784.

They included amongst their active members several leading figures amongst those Scots famed for a devotion to the improvement of industry and agriculture. Amongst the earliest appointments were John Marquis of Tweeddale and James Earl of Findlater—both keen agriculturalists as well as members of the Board of Trustees for Fisheries and Manufactures. They were subsequently joined on the board by other eminent Improvers such as Lord Kames and Lord Gardenstone. These distinguished and progressive gentlemen did not see it as part of their duty to tour the estates. Administration was strictly by remote control from Edinburgh. It was not a cheap or a quick system. Factors were liable to be summoned to the capital at great expense, sometimes to face complex charges brought against them by a lawyer acting for the tenants on the estate they administered on behalf of the commission. In order to encourage a loyal attitude to the House of Hanover, the commissioners had a set policy of going easy on tenants. Combined with the presence of many lawyers on the board, this could make a factor's life a difficult one.

The commissioners never made a great deal of headway with their attempts to stimulate industrial development in the Highlands. A few small firms flourished on subsidies, but attempts to encourage craftsmen and settle labourers met only modified success. Their plans for establishing colonies of former regular soldiers in the Highlands proved abortive. Years in the army had given the old warriors a taste for liquor only matched by their distaste for hard work, and the carefully-planned settlements evaporated in a largely alcoholic haze. The board was deeply committed to agricultural change through the medium of long leases for tenants, which would encourage the tenantry to embark on schemes of improvement by giving them substantial security of tenure. However, the commissioners only gained control over all their estates as late as 1770 and in 1774 the Treasury suggested that no more leases be granted on the forfeited annexed properties. The reason for this was that in 1774 the Lovat estates had been returned to the son of the Jacobite Simon Fraser; the son being then a British major-general. By 1784 the rest of the estates were returned to the heirs of the original proprietors. No heir was likely to be pleased with long leases on gentle terms for his tenants, though it is to the credit of the commissioners that they did persist in granting leases of up to 41 years after 1774. All the same, after 1775 the board embarked on no new initiatives involving expenditure because its income was completely committed (much of it to administrative charges) and it could not raise its rents, which were controlled by statute. Arguably the sharp increases in rent imposed by most restored proprietors were more likely to effect change than the expensive surveying and administration and well-meaning cajoling of the commissioners. Lord Kames described the large sums of public money expended on the Highlands and more especially the forfeited estates as 'no better than water spilt on the ground'.

Underlying much of the policy of the government was a concept of the feasibility and desirability of substantial improvement in the organisation and functioning of the Scottish economy. This concept was of course widespread outwith the magic circle of power at Westminster, which in any case seldom displayed any enduring commitment to any set of principles other than the maintenance of its own power by the most expedient short-term opportunism. It is therefore important to look at that much-studied segment of the Scottish ruling class before 1780 which aspired to the title of the Improvers, and to assess the significance of the private actions of men who were very often also public dignitaries. Improvement was, after all, a pervasive concept in the intellectual world of eighteenth-century Scotland. Nor was it purely secular. Having named and read his text, the minister normally shaped his sermon in the form of a lengthy exposition of The Word after which he would direct his earnest hearers towards 'the practical improvement of this subject'. Improvement was therefore something from the vocabulary of evangelical appeal. No wonder that in secular guise it often retained its evangelical fervour.

In June 1723 there was established in Edinburgh the 'Society for Improving in the Knowledge of Agriculture'. Its first president was Thomas Hope of Rankeillor who had studied progressive agriculture in England, France and Holland, and other leading figures included the Marquis of Lothian, the Earl of Kinnoul, Lord Elibank, the Earl of Hopetoun, the Earl of Stair, the Earl of Islay, Lord Cathcart, Lord Drummore and Cockburn of Ormiston. Its secretary, who was also to some extent its driving spirit, was a Galloway laird Robert Maxwell of Arkland. Significantly, when in 1724 the society issued a publication (largely thought to be the work of Thomas Hope and Robert Maxwell), its title was not purely agricultural, for it announced itself as a *Treatise concerning the Manner of Fallowing of Ground, Raising of Grass Seeds, and Train-*

ing of Lint and Hemp, for the Increase and Improvement of the Linnen Manufactures in Scotland. Only the first two chapters dealt with the cultivation of arable land, though they are important for two reasons. They contain the earliest known advocacy of the sowing of grass seeds in Scotland and they also included an elaborate demonstration of the profitability of efficiently-organised dairy farming in contemporary England. From 1724 a steady stream of improving treatises on Scottish agriculture flowed from the press. Two of them, with a heavy emphasis on the need for fallow, enclosure, and tree planting, were written by Brigadier William Mackintosh of Borlum during his lengthy (1719–43) imprisonment in Edinburgh Castle on account of his Jacobite activities in the '15 and '19. They do rather belie the theory that all Jacobites were backward-looking champions of an archaic society. In 1733 Patrick Lindesay, Lord Provost of Edinburgh, published a book whose brief title was *The Interest of Scotland* and whose importance hinges on the fact that it is the first all-out attack on the older agriculture and in particular on its central features of runrig or the distribution of arable land in strips, and common grazing.

Throughout this literature there is much stress on the example of England, perhaps at its height in the lengthy appendix on modern Scottish agriculture attached to the translation of Vergil's *Pastorals* and *Georgics* published by James Hamilton, schoolmaster in East Calder in Midlothian, in 1742. Hamilton was not a man of high social standing but by the 1750s and 1760s an important laird like Sir Archibald Grant of Monymusk in Aberdeenshire was expressing his zeal for agricultural improvement, often on the basis of the practices of the best farmers of such English counties as Cheshire, Staffordshire, and Hertfordshire, in a series of publications. Indeed it has been argued that by about 1760 the literature on agricultural improvement in Scotland was passing beyond the pioneering stage into that of the systematisation of generally-accepted principles. The epitome of all this is *A Treatise of Agriculture* by Adam Dickson, minister at Duns in Berwickshire. Originally published in two volumes which appeared in turn in 1762 and 1769, the whole work went through new editions in 1770 and 1785. By the 1770s there were complaints that too many superficial treatises on agriculture were being churned out by hack writers devoid of real farming experience. This was not a description which could fairly be applied to Henry Home Lord Kames who published in 1776 *The Gentleman Farmer, being an attempt to improve agriculture by subjecting it to the test of rational principles.* By 1815 this work had passed through six editions. The lairds whom Kames addressed were by then wholly converted.

Only when we pause to analyse the financial record of the early Improvers and to assess the extent to which their ideas passed into common practice beyond the bounds of their own estates do doubts set in. Many of the early Improvers were very unusual people like John, Earl of Stair (1679–1747). He had a long run in very high military, diplomatic and political positions until his conflict with Sir Robert Walpole during the Excise Bill crisis in 1733 led to his dismissal from office. He spent his last dozen years or so as an innovating landlord on his West Lothian and Wigtownshire estates. He was one of the first to grow turnips and cabbages, a roadmaker, and an advocate of the enclosure, drainage and liming of land. He introduced an improved plough and he was a great planter of trees. All this made an admirable hobby for a superannuated politician and magnate. Whether it was profitable is a different matter. That it was fashionable in the sort of English circles from which Walpole's purge had forcibly retired Stair is demonstrated by the story of Henrietta Mordaunt, daughter of the Earl of Peterborough, who married the eldest son of the Duke of Gordon in 1706. Her father has been rather unkindly described as 'a muddle-headed busybody and braggart' by a modern historian. Certainly the bubble reputation he created for himself as a general in Spain during the War of the Spanish Succession burst before the end of that conflict. However, his daughter brought English ploughs and ploughmen to her new Morayshire home where she encouraged fallow, planted trees, and sowed grasses. It would be elegant to argue that her economic conquests were more enduring than her father's conquests in Spain, just as the donkey's conquest of Ireland has proved more lasting than the contemporary Iberian triumphs of the Duke of Wellington. The snag is that new fashions in farming were probably as much a question of style to her ladyship as the sophisticated architecture and expensively splendid formal gardens to which she was also devoted.

Such detailed evidence as we have of the financial history of one of the greatest of the Improvers, John Cockburn of Ormiston, does not encourage the view that their financial success was calculated to lead their neighbours to ape their ways at the earliest opportunity. John Cockburn succeeded his father Adam Cockburn, an enlightened landlord and Lord Justice Clerk of Scotland, as laird of Ormiston. Adam Cockburn had already tried, in 1698 and 1713, the experiment of granting long leases to selected farmers, so John Cockburn inherited a progressive tradition. A staunch champion of the Union, John Cockburn sat in the Westminster parliament from 1707 to 1741, thereby ensuring that he had a first-hand acquaintance with the most advanced agricultural techniques practised on the light soils of the south-eastern parts of England. After succeeding to his estate in 1734, John Cockburn rebuilt the village of Ormiston on spacious lines granting feus on generous terms to householders willing to build their houses according to certain minimal standards. He encouraged flax growing, spinning and weaving and sponsored, with the aid of the Board of Trustees for Fisheries and Manufactures, the erection in Ormiston of the second bleachfield in Scotland. A brewery and distillery provided a market for local barley. One of the aims of the Edinburgh Society for Improving in the Knowledge of Agriculture, of which John Cockburn was a member, was the establishment of similar bodies in other parts of Scotland. In 1736 Cockburn helped set up an Ormiston branch which eventually had a membership of 122. It was paralleled by similar branches in Buchan in Aberdeenshire and Ratho in Midlothian. Cockburn strongly advocated and practised enclosure, using embankments and hedges as field boundaries; extensive tree planting; systematic fallowing; the sowing of grass and clover seeds; and the planting of turnips and potatoes as field crops. Yet between 1747 and 1749 Cockburn had to sell all his land to the Earl of Hopetoun, for a total of £32,000 sterling. Cockburn inherited a debt and the heavy expenses which he too often incurred in the course of his improvements seem to have exacerbated rather than relieved the situation until liquidation became the only way to clear the Cockburn estate.

Nor would this story appear to be as unusual as it sounds. The Earls of Rothes in Fife were not as passionate Improvers as John Cockburn of Ormiston, but they have some claim to rank amongst the earliest innovators in the introduction of turnips as a field crop, with all that this implies for a more ample supply of winter feed for cattle and a more scientific rotation of crops, and they certainly pressed the need for all the major innovations of the new agriculture on their factors and tenants. Yet they can hardly be said to have made a fortune during the eighteenth century by means of this relatively enlightened management of their lands. When their principal seat, Leslie House, was burned down in 1763 the cash required for rebuilding it could only be obtained by selling off the Rothes lands on the northern shore of Fife, and though the policies and gardens normally gave Rothes House a high degree of self-sufficiency in food, it is clear that rents were not enough to accumulate large cash reserves. Arguably the Rothes family in the eighteenth century sailed very close to the wind financially, mainly because its heads failed to secure a substantial share of well-paid office in government service.

This is not to say that particular Improvers did not reap substantial financial rewards for their efforts. The classic example is Sir Archibald Grant of Monymusk, who ruled that small property some 20 miles from Aberdeen for the very long period between 1716 and 1778. Until 1734 Sir Archibald, though very interested in agricultural improvement, was often away in Edinburgh and London, being for a period an MP. In 1734 he returned to Monymusk heavily burdened with debt due to injudicious speculation. Thereafter he threw all his energies into making his property profitable. He was a great planter of trees. In farming he was deeply influenced by English precedent and his programme fell into two main divisions. First he aimed at changing the physical face of his fields by encouraging field clearance and enclosure. The two concepts were linked for the mass of stones cleared from the fields made excellent material for dykes. On occasion in Aberdeenshire there turned out to be too much in the way of stones and the 'consumption dyke' became a way of storing the surplus. The greatest of these, which was probably built by Alexander Jaffrey a friend of Sir Archibald Grant is on the estate of Kingswells in Aberdeenshire and is 500 yards long, 30 feet wide, and 6 feet high. Secondly Sir Archibald was anxious to change patterns of cultivation. He encouraged the adoption of the English fallow system and also the planting of new crops such as turnips, clover, and tye grass. Gradually he felt his way towards a system of rotation in which a cleansing root crop like turnips and a leguminous crop like clover alternated with cereals, rendering fallow unnecessary. Financially, the results were excellent. A rental of £3,586 Scots in 1733 became one of £9,709 Scots by 1767, though the victual rent of the estate did fall from 830 bolls of meal and 150 bolls of bere in 1733 to 318 bolls of meal and 29 bolls of bere in 1767. The real increase in revenue was nevertheless massive and was actually exceeded in percentage terms by specific farms.

Heavy investment had characterised the estate for decades. As early as the period of roughly 13 months between Martinmas 1718 and the beginning of 1720 Grant spent, out of a total rental of £7,663 Scots, some £1,198 Scots on improvements. After 1734 the laird was permanently resident, single-minded and ruthless in using his baron court or his power of eviction to discipline his tenantry in his own ways. Above all, Monymusk was near the city of Aberdeen with its market for produce and opportunity for export by sea. Not all lairds were so dedicated; not all estates so conveniently situated. Patrick Grant, Lord Elchies, was an enthusiast for new agricultural methods. We have the letters which he wrote from Edinburgh to Robert Grant of Tammore, who looked after his Morayshire estate and in 1733 Elchies wrote the following significant words: 'I'm glad to hear the good accounts of my beehives, but I'm afraid its a wood in a wilderness. I could have honey sent me sooner from Narbone than from Elchies by sea carriage.'

The simple fact is that Improvement on the grand scale was expensive and was liable to run into the open or tacit opposition of the tenantry. Where it was unlikely to produce quickly a substantial flow of saleable goods to accessible markets, it was equally unlikely to produce an increase in rent yields within what a normal landlord regarded as an acceptable time. Few were prepared to invest and struggle outside their own private policies, for nothing or very little. The obstacles could daunt even the very greatest magnates. Thus the second Duke of Argyll determined in the 1730s to eliminate the class of tacksmen on his estates and thereby enhance his revenues. Tacksmen held substantial grants of land, which they of course sub-let, at low rents in exchange for acting as officers in the clan army. In 1737 therefore Duncan Forbes, the Lord President of the Court of Session, visited the northern parts of the great Argyll empire and deprived the major tacksmen of their leases, granting instead smaller leases at enhanced rents to both sub-tacksmen and tenants. The result was extremely disappointing because the real rent collected proved much the same as before. The nominal increase assumed the form of ever-increasing arrears. To boot the effect of tossing loyal Campbell tacksmen aside was to unpick the once mighty Clan Campbell as a military unit and greatly facilitate the '45. The immensely shrewd third Duke of Argyll started to reverse his predecessor's policy from 1744—too late for military purposes but soon enough to restore a Campbell class of tacksmen even on the fringes of the Campbell empire by the 1750s. Improvement had to be feasible and profitable for the average absentee or semi-absentee proprietor before it was likely to become universal.

Until that day dawned, the significant evidence does not lie in the records relating to great Improvers like Maxwell of Arkland who as secretary of the Edinburgh society of Improvers lavished advice on everyone whilst going bankrupt himself, or even on Grant of Monymusk, an exceptional man as he proved by being expelled from the House of Commons for infamous fraud in connection with a charity, but on such unsung heroes as Lord Fife (1729–1809). Although described by a contemporary French biographical dictionary as 'un grand agronome', his letters to his factor from the Continent and England show him a keen planter of woods, but otherwise very orthodox. He was forever demanding his rents in order to cover his expenses. He indulged in prestige building and had a positive passion for extending the policies round his stately home, Duff House, and for excluding the vulgar and curious from them. One of his few positive orders concerning farming operations comes in March 1765 when he says that 'I wish you to dispose of all the Cattle that can be spar'd and take the time that you believe will be most advantagious'. It was a sensible, practical instruction and perhaps the best note on which to turn to the significant realities of Scottish economic growth before 1780.

Lairds merchants and bankers, and pre-1780 growth

Several features of pre-1780 economic growth are plain, even if the evidence for them is partial and indirect. For example, certain significant mileposts were passed surprisingly early on in the period. Scottish grain prices can be established, thanks to an almost complete set of local average prices kept for certain official purposes. Due to the considerable difficulty inherent in the overland transport of a bulk commodity like grain, it is scarcely surprising to find that regional grain prices varied widely and showed disparate movements. However the size of price regions steadily grew from the late seventeenth century until by the 1730s prices in all regions moved in close sympathy with no very striking regional disparities. In other words, there was now a national market for grain, well in advance of any commercially significant expansion in the national road system. The main explanation is twofold: more money must have been available to buy grain, and more efficient means of transporting it must also have been available. The latter necessarily implies more abundant sea transport, for coastal shipping was much the cheapest means of moving bulk commodities and the numerous firths and sea lochs provided deep penetration of the mainland. None of these ships can have been very big, if only because there were no docks as such anywhere in Scotland much before 1800. Probably the ship of 100 tons burthen which could reach Perth on the unimproved Tay represented a common upper limit. Precise figures are not available, but if we look at the Aberdeen records for about 1670 we are struck by the variety of types of ship—hoys, flibotts, yawls, frigots, skows, pinks, ketches and so on— visiting that port, and their varied ports of origin. From the northern parts of Scotland ships were coming from Newburgh, Peterhead, Fraserburgh, Pennan, the Moray Firth ports, and Caithness. Most Scottish ships came in fact from Leith, but others came from Limekilns, Bo'ness, Crail, Anstruther, Kirkcaldy, Arbroath, Montrose and Stonehaven. After the disasters of the 1690s, the early eighteenth century must have seen recovery and indeed increase in the flocks of small ships, Scottish and foreign, moving in and out of Scottish ports.

All this points a basic moral to our tale. Successful growth was achieved by exploiting low overheads and existing trends. No docks were needed for small wooden ships. Tidal harbours were good enough. Indeed, no specialised yard was needed to build them. They could be constructed above high tide on a convenient piece of beach and after they had been launched, no evidence of a permanent nature would need to remain. Profoundly different though the cattle trade was from the world of grain shipments by coastal craft, it shared the same basic characteristics that it was already well established and could be easily expanded without massive investment in permanent installations. Towards the end of this period the father of modern economics Adam Smith believed that the increase in the long-distance cattle trade was the greatest single immediate blessing bestowed on Scotland by the Union. It is time to turn to this topic.

The Highlands and Islands along with Galloway were the main reservoir of the black cattle which formed the bulk of the drovers' herds. Due to the anger and resentment roused by the Jacobite risings, it was fashionable for much of the eighteenth century to regard the Highlander as a 'savage' and his economic setting as 'primitive'. The first epithet is little better than a lie, while the second is at best a gross over-simplification. Highland society was not static, though it was never likely to try to match the patterns of Lowland or English development in every detail. Even in the late seventeenth century there are distinct signs of the increasing impact of market forces in the Highlands. In regions as physically remote as Harris evidence can be found of a tendency for produce rents to decline and for money rents to increase in the period before 1750.

It was a basic necessity of the trade that Highland cattle be cheap. Around 1707 the average price of cows in Scotland appears to have been between 20s. and 27s. sterling. Thomas Pennant, the English traveller and naturalist, was told during his Scottish tour that the price of cattle in the island of Colonsay in 1736 was still only 25s. a head and this is confirmed by a legal record of a Yorkshire drover buying 300 cattle in Colonsay and Jura for a total of £505 sterling. By the middle of the eighteenth century prices had risen. In 1763 a Yorkshire drover was paying 2 guineas a head for Skye cattle at Falkirk tryst. Ten years later Barra beasts were fetching only £1 7s. 6d. ther but in 1772 Pennant tells us that Skye, Islay and Colonsay cattle were worth £2 to £3 a head at the tryst, though Mull cattle fetched only £1 10s. 0d. to £2 10s. 0d. By 1794 the average price of beasts sold at Falkirk tryst was £4. At a guess these cattle were all three or four years old or more, if only because of their known slow growth rates. It is an equally safe conclusion from scraps of evidence that they were small by modern standards—perhaps under half the weight of a modern Highland beast, even when the figures taken are the fattened ones. The cost of the droving varied depending on the distance involved and the best figures we have are early nineteenth-century ones, but even then it was held that the cost of bringing a drove from Caithness to Carlisle was about 7s. 6d. a head, and the additional cost of the journey to, say, Norfolk for sale and final fattening would be of the order of £1 a head at the same time. In the early eighteenth century the cost was probably substantially lower. We have a Wigtownshire record of a figure of 7s. 1½d. a head for a drove to southern England in 1728, and the price was deemed steep.

The techniques employed in this far-flung trade minimised expense. Stout boats of 10 to 50 tons ferried cattle between islands and from the islands to the mainland. At other times they would carry bulk slate or lime and the bigger ones packed in up to fifty cattle loaded with little finesse off a rock or pier. Unloading was cruder still, for most cattle were thrown overboard, cleaning themselves as they swam ashore. A whole series of drove roads, largely if not exhaustively catalogued in A. R. B. Haldane's book on the subject, crossed the Highlands in the shape of broad rights of way with traditionally free grazing rights. There were local trysts or markets on most drove routes. Some were very old like 'The Chapel of Garioch' near Inverurie, authorised by the Privy Council in 1628. Argyll had five local trysts, while the tryst of Kilmichael-Glassary near Lochgilphead was a place where drovers and dealers came to buy the cattle of Islay, Jura, Kintyre, and Knapdale. Only near the great trysts, of which Crieff tryst was the most significant in the first half of the eighteenth century and Falkirk tryst the leading one after 1770, did drovers expect to pay significant sums for grazing for their animals.

However low the overheads, the total value of cattle involved in this trade was formidable. In 1747 it was estimated that the total annual loss suffered directly or indirectly from cattle thieves was of the order of £37,000 sterling; a loss which was simply not big enough in relative terms seriously to disrupt the trade. Financing such a trade was not easy in an economy like that of early eighteenth-century Scotland where cash was scarce and the only chartered bank, the Bank of Scotland, pursued a hyper-conservative policy on credit. Credit had to be created, and was created to some extent spontaneously, by the free use of the written promise to pay or the promissory bill. Bills could change owners many times before being cashed, so they served as virtual banknotes. When Dr Johnson and James Boswell visited Skye in 1772 they found that rents were usually paid in drovers' bills. The drovers obtained their original credit from merchants and goldsmiths in Edinburgh, or commercial houses such as Coutts and Company (founded in 1723). After 1727, when the Royal Bank of Scotland was founded, there was a rapid expansion in a cash credit system whereby any reputable person supported by two propertied guarantors could secure a cash credit. We know that in 1767 the British Linen Bank was giving advances, at Falkirk tryst, of £500 apiece to two Scottish drovers and of up to £2,000 to a well-known Yorkshire drover. However, the common pattern appears to have been for a Scots drover to receive a small amount of cash and much more credit. In the Highlands he would pay for cattle with a fraction of the value in cash and the rest in bills payable usually after three months, by which time he hoped to have sold his cattle at a tryst. Farmers normally needed to discount their bills, which provided the bankers with an additional cushion. Inevitably individual drovers went bankrupt. There were endless complaints about the instability of the system, but in fact overall it worked well.

The crucial role played by credit in the cattle trade provides a natural bridge to a third vital area of growth—linen. After considering this industry it should also be possible to begin to discuss the relationships between, and the relative significance of, lairds, merchants, and bankers in the expansion of the eighteenth-century Scottish economy. The importance of the linen trade can hardly be exaggerated. Between 1728 (the first year for which figures exist) and 1730 the amount of linen stamped for sale by officials of the Board of Trustees for Fisheries and Manufactures rose from (in round figures) 2.2 million yards to 3.7 million. By 1750 the figure was 7.6 million, by 1775 it was 12.1 million, and by 1780 13.4 million. The rise in the estimated value of this linen was from £103,312 in 1728 to £622,188 in 1780. While this expansion was general in Scotland it was most dramatic in the eastern area centred on Dundee where the quantity stamped rose from 817,416 yards in 1747 to 1,275,689 yards in 1759 and at Glasgow where production trebled from 625,000 yards in 1740 to 2,032,000 yards in 1757. There is a tendency to forget the importance of the linen industry in the west of Scotland throughout the eighteenth century because of the way in which by 1820 linen production had drastically slumped in Glasgow and the adjacent shires of Lanarkshire and Renfrewshire, mainly because of a massive transfer of effort and capital into the cotton industry. Without the expertise built up by a pre-existent linen trade, the rise of cotton in these western parts would have been much more difficult.

The expansion of the linen industry was based on the vigour of demand for its products. The figures quoted above do not include the probably very large element of Scottish linen production destined for domestic consumption within the producing, or a neighbourhood household. One can nevertheless safely assume that this figure does include a very high percentage indeed of all linen produced for the market, if only because of the need to have the guarantee of quality and access to premiums and other privileges which the stamp of the Board of Trustees conferred. The expansion in the production of Scottish linen destined for the market appears to have been almost entirely based on the growth of demand, for there was no reduction in the cost of the industry's raw material, flax, in the course of the century. On the contrary, it was said that Russian flax had risen in price from £25 per ton in 1736 to £50 in 1786, and Dutch flax had increased in price by a similar proportion. A great deal of Scots flax was exported directly to the American colonies or to the West Indies. Even more was consigned to London firms who in turn exported a good deal of the consignments. In the thriving linen trade of late seventeenth-century Glasgow it is easy to find individual merchants already involved in importing raw flax from the Baltic and Holland, in exporting cloth and yarn to England, and in branching out into the re-export of colonial produce. When cotton became a boom industry in late eighteenth-century Glasgow its expansion was sponsored by linen merchants, often master weavers of Glasgow and the surrounding district; men like David Dale, the Buchanans and the Monteiths. Their capital and knowledge made them the natural pioneers in a new product which could be manufactured largely within the familiar frame of reference of the linen trade, which thus served as the springboard for the second great advance in manufacturing industry in Scotland as well as being itself the first.

The linen trade required very substantial credit facilities, for it was a dispersed industry full of lengthy lags between the distribution of raw materials and the final sales. Here consideration has to be given not only to credit-creating institutions as such but also to such major commercial developments of the eighteenth century as the rise of the colonial trade, and more especially of the tobacco and sugar trades. Mostly these trades were centred on the Clyde. We know that by 1735 there were 47 square-rigged ships, mostly owned by Glasgow merchants, sailing out of Glasgow's harbours at Port Glasgow and of these 15 were trading to Virginia, 4 to Jamaica, 1 to Barbadoes, 1 to Antigua, 2 to St Kitts, 5 to London, 3 to Boston, 5 to the Mediterranean, 2 to Holland, 7 to Stockholm, and this in addition to many English and foreign-owned ships bringing in cargoes. Twenty smaller ships traded coastwise and to Ireland. The most spectacular growth in the period before 1780 lay in the import of tobacco from the North American colonies. In a sense this was all based on the artificial restrictions imposed by the English Old Colonial System which insisted that certain enumerated colonial products, of which tobacco was one, should first be shipped from a colonial to a British metropolitan port before re-export to foreign markets. Glasgow was in fact several hundred miles closer to the tobacco-growing colonies than most big English ports in terms of a North Atlantic run, so it was perhaps not surprising that Glasgow managed to emerge as the big city which the southern states of America never evolved in the colonial period. Charleston was the only city of any size in the entire south.

In 1755 Scotland imported in round figures 15.2 million pounds of tobacco. By the peak year of 1771 the figure was 47.3 million valued at £492,383, and most of this was imported into the Clyde. A very high percentage was re-exported, latterly mainly by means of vast deals with the managers of the state tobacco monopoly in France. In 1771 tobacco accounted for 36 per cent of the total value of all imports and for 51 per cent of all Scottish exports. Historians dispute the long-term effects of this trade on the Scottish economy. Probably its significance for developments after 1776 has been exaggerated. However, in the preceding decades of the eighteenth century its significance was clearly very great. It is true that the Tobacco Lords of Glasgow, as they were known, invested in landed estates near Glasgow, if they did not already own them, but this very seldom implied a major withdrawal of interest and capital from the original merchant house. Thus Thomas Dunmore, a pioneer of the early eighteenth-century Glasgow–Virginia tobacco trade, secured the estate of Kelvinside by an alliance with another Glasgow business family, the Peadies, and duly passed it on to his son Robert. Similarly the lands of Daldowie and Whiteinch became the property of another great family of colonial merchants, the Bogles, but as with the Dunmores, they provided a dignified seat for the head of an active merchant house. Such houses extended a web of credit over the North Atlantic to the point where most American planters were deeply in their debt and profoundly resentful of them and their local factors, despite the manifest necessity of the services they provided. In addition it is important to grasp that, partly to provide outward cargoes for their ships and partly to meet the clamant needs of the very specialised plantation agricultures of the West Indies or the southern American colonies, the Glasgow colonial merchants became heavily involved in industry, ranging from textiles, iron, and coalmining, to sugarhouses, ropeworks, glassworks, leatherworks, breweries and soapworks.

The main result of all this before the traumatic outbreak of the American War of Independence in 1776, as far as the Scottish economy was concerned, was a massive additional injection of liquidity. The early development of merchant banking in the Glasgow area, so vital for its linen trade, was largely dominated by the tobacco trade. If we look at the relative size of the two trades, it is clear why this was so. In the single year 1773 re-exports of tobacco from Scotland, which largely meant Glasgow, were officially valued at £965,196. The Glasgow linen trade was tiny by comparison. Its exports consisted mainly of cambrics, yet over the ten year period 1775–84 the total value of this cloth exported from all Scotland was only £158,578. In his essay 'Of the Balance of Trade', which he published in 1764, David Hume, the philosopher and historian, said that the precedents of easier credit facilities set by the two Edinburgh chartered banks in the late 1720s had been carried much further by Glasgow merchants in several local banks which they set up. Hume's reference would be to the Ship Bank and the Arms Bank, both founded in 1750, and to the Thistle Bank founded a few years later. All were dominated by

Tobacco Lords and together they constituted an important source of credit for the tobacco and other trades.

They were not, of course, the only new banks emerging in mid eighteenth-century Scotland. In 1746 the British Linen Company was founded specifically to help cope with the need for short-term finance within the Scottish linen industry. It bought and sold linen cloth and in 1747 took the first step towards the banking business which eventually became its sole activity by giving notes to weavers and manufacturers in exchange for cloth received. Apart from its initial capital of £50,000 sterling (soon raised to £70,000) the British Linen Company had a substantial cash credit with the Royal Bank, but the history of that credit underlines the unpredictable nature of the relationship between the two oldest Scottish banks and the newer ones. In 1766 the Royal Bank withdrew the credit to the British Linen Company and the Royal Bank and the Bank of Scotland both refused to accept British Linen Company notes between 1766 and 1771. It has been argued that this was an attempt to check depreciation of Scots money by excessive note issue, a practice which had certainly helped to bring on a severe balance of payments crisis in the Scottish economy in 1762. However, it seems more likely that less altruistic motives lay behind the embargo for it was lifted in 1771 just as the Scots economy was racing towards another major crisis culminating in a very sharp downward plunge of the Scottish business cycle. The most spectacular single episode provoked by this classic cyclical slump was the collapse of the Ayr Bank in 1772. That bank had been founded with the avowed purpose of increasing the supply of finance. It drew much of its capital from the counties of Ayr, Dumfries and Kirkcudbright and though Scottish and English merchants were among its shareholders, it leaned to an unusual degree upon the landed classes of whom its chairman, the Duke of Queensberry was the most prominent example.

Landowners participated in the financing of other banks. One example of this is the Improver Lord Milton, who made big loans to the British Linen Company, as well as being its largest shareholder. Generally, however, it was the local mercantile community which, often in cooperation with one of the chartered banks, sponsored new local banks. No less than six new banks were founded in Perth in 1763. They coalesced into the Perth United Company in 1766, a process assisted by the leadership of George Dempster of Dunnichen, a laird and MP whose family had been corn merchants in the early eighteenth century. George

Dempster's brother John Hamilton Dempster kept up the family tradition by being a merchant in Dundee, where he was active in the affairs of the Dundee Banking Company, founded in 1763, again with some help from George Dempster, who thereafter played no active role in its management.

The significance of these banks and of other less formal credit-creating devices was great, for the linen industry's primary need was for floating capital. It was not a capital-intensive industry for most of the eighteenth century, if one leaves out of account the bleaching and finishing sector, which did require substantial fixed investment. Its main resource was the reservoir of cheap labour represented by concealed or seasonal unemployment in the countryside. In his book on the principles of political economy published in 1767 Sir James Steuart remarked that preparing flax and spinning it was a process which enabled the cottar to utilise the energies of virtually every member of his household. In the *Wealth of Nations* published in 1776 Adam Smith, no admirer incidentally of his Jacobite predecessor Steuart, said the spinning of linen yarn in Scotland was carried on primarily by the families of cottars. If cottars, who were farm labourers, were prominent on the spinning side of the linen trade, rural weavers, who were more specialised craftsmen, continued to act as farm labourers at the busy periods of the agricultural year for a long time. It was difficult to secure a steady flow of webs to meet orders at harvest time.

Improvements in productivity did occur within this dispersed rural industry in the course of the eighteenth century. Thus the replacement of the rock spindle, or of the muckle (i.e. great) wheel, by the saxon wheel which was the treadle-operated variety usually illustrated in modern versions of *Sleeping Beauty*, did increase spinning rates. Even so, there was an increasing bottleneck at the weaving stage for it required several spinners to keep one weaver busy and it was perhaps just as well that piecemeal improvements such as Kay's flying shuttle, invented in England around 1733, did not increase weaving productivity by an even larger margin. Mechanical spinning of linen yarns was introduced into Scotland as late as 1790 by Sim and Thom who installed machinery invented by the Englishmen Kendrew and Porthouse in a small mill at Bervie in Kincardineshire. Before that date the equipment used in all departments of the linen trade other than the finishing process was cheap. Even looms and spinning wheels cost only a few pounds sterling a piece. The preparatory processes were equally inexpensive in terms of equipment, though the steeping and retting process needed to break up the structure of the flax stems to the point where the fibres could be extracted did require substantial quantities of water and labour. The hecklers who broke the woody fragments in the retted flax, extracted the fibre, and combed it out, were skilled workmen, but their tools were very simple. The Board of Trustees were therefore in a position to do a fair amount of good at comparatively small cost by offering prizes for better qualities of flax, yarn, and cloth; by introducing small numbers of skilled foreign craftsmen capable of demonstrating superior techniques or of making superior versions of small but vital parts of the manufacturing process such as the reeds used to firm up and pack the cloth as it was woven; or by distributing Dutch looms and other approved equipment to selected craftsmen in the hope that their success would influence others.

The field where the Board of Trustees can be shown to have made relatively heavy investments to good effect is that of the finishing trade. Here alone capital-intensive methods were unavoidable. A bleachworks required a substantial acreage of good, flat land with plentiful supplies of pure water and a lot of heavy water-powered machinery. The total outlay might run into thousands at a time when a weaver could set up in business for £10, a wright (or joiner-mechanic) for £20, a heckler for £20, a thread-manufacturer for £10, and a reed-maker for £16. In the last analysis mercantile capital carried the burden of creating bleachfields on the many sites offering abundant water power which could be found all over Scotland, though with notable concentrations of potential in such areas as the straths of the Tay and Almond near Perth. Landed proprietors such as Cockburn of Ormiston and Lord Milton spent money on bleachfields, but the Board of Trustees was ubiquitous in spending large and small sums to assist their erection. Thus Alexander Christie of Perth was granted £1,200 in 1735 for laying out a bleachfield. Another Perth merchant, William Sandeman, was granted £200 in 1750 for the enlarging of his bleachfield at Luncarty. Indeed by 1754 the Board of Trustees had spent no less than £11,000 on the improvement of bleaching.

It was perhaps just as well that this particular heavy investment came at the end of an already flourishing production process. The Board of Trustees were in this case backing a winner, in that the cheapness of Scottish labour and the inexpensive nature of most operations prior to finishing made Scottish linens competitive in the British market and the markets of the British Empire. Other heavy investments by the Trustees which were not geared to an already vigorous development had enjoyed little success. Their attempt to establish a cambric manufacture in Edinburgh, for example, was an expensive failure, while their attempt to introduce more highly capitalised forms of the linen manufacture into the Highlands has provoked the scorn of a modern historian for their 'ridiculously situated linen manufacturing stations'. By 1762 even the Board of Trustees was prepared to admit, if not in so many words, that its Highland enterprises were a flop. The landed interest did make some financial contribution to the linen industry, but the most valuable contribution which the lairds made was the spare time of their tenants. Furthermore, the tendency for rents to rise, especially after 1760, placed pressure on the rural population to pursue cottage industry in order to meet the mounting demands of the lairds. All this would still not have achieved the form of a major expansion in textiles without the organising ability of pre-existing mercantile élites, very often general import–export merchants from ports. A good example is the Wallace family of Arbroath. In 1738 the greatest of them, John Wallace, became Provost for the first time, while all the other magistrates of the burgh that year were also members of his family. It was not an unprecedented situation for a Scottish burgh. The ascendancy of the Traill family on Kirkwall Town Council provoked the local rhymsters:

Traills up the town, Traills down the town, Traills in the middle, De'il tak' the Traills' guts for strings tae his fiddle.

However, the Wallaces rendered great service to Arbroath and the county of Angus. They were shipowners and dealers in timber, grain and agricultural produce. In the course of their North Sea trading they became familiar with the coarse German linens known as Osnaburgs, which they began to imitate in Arbroath, thereby setting the Angus linen industry on its path towards specialisation in coarse linens and later jute.

Such men had the credit and connections needed to run a very dispersed linen industry, most of whose operations were conducted on a credit basis. Very often the merchant in Glasgow, or Montrose, or Dundee, who was distributing imported flax to his spinners, or yarn to his weavers, was himself operating on a substantial credit from a London firm, to whom he was likely to despatch cargoes of finished webs. It is not surprising that such men played a prominent role in using the older banking facilities of Scotland and in creating new ones. It is equally clear that they needed all the help they could muster and received it in significant amounts from the landed interest and from the Board of Trustees, though the latter made its main successful financial contribution in the specialised field of the finishing trade. More generally, one can argue that the pivotal position of the mercantile elites in mid eighteenth-century Scotland is insufficiently appreciated.

Too much emphasis has perhaps been laid on the role of the aristocracy in sponsoring economic growth. We have seen that the Improvers had only a very limited impact on society before 1780, for the very good reason that they failed to demonstrate consistent profitability on a large enough scale. Indeed, had the Scots lairds all become passionate Improvers overnight around 1750 the result would probably have been a major retardation in the rate of Scottish economic growth. Too much capital would have been locked up in ambitious schemes of dubious or negative profitability. To boot, Improvement tended to be a labour-intensive activity which might have competed with more profitable industries for the vital pool of underutilised rural labour. Historians of English agriculture are now tending to emphasise the extent to which innovation in the eighteenth century was disproportionately characteristic of the lighter soils of the south-eastern parts of England and industrial expansion the product of a symbiosis between those parts and the far more pastorally-oriented heavy-soil areas of that country. Only a very few areas of Scotland, notably the Lothians, were suitable for precocious Improvement on any scale. The main achievement of the Improvers was the tradition they established, which proved more relevant in later times. Perhaps the Gordon's Mill Farming Club which met in Old Aberdeen between 1758·and 1764 was, if an extreme case, not a misleading one, for it was in every sense of the word an academic body. Many of its members, like Principal Chalmers, or its secretary Thomas Gordon, Humanist (i.e. Teacher of Latin), were on the staff of King's College, the university of Old Aberdeen. Thomas Reid, father of the Scottish School of Common Sense Philosophy, was another member. They very often farmed college lands, but one does wonder how they would have fared without their academic incomes.

All this is not to deny that in certain areas of economic activity some landowners were very active indeed. These areas were usually those connected with the exploitation of the mineral resources and timber of their estates. Coalmining is a good example. There was undoubtedly a rising demand for coal in Scotland in the eighteenth century, though arguably this growth in demand was much more rapid after 1760 than before. Limeburning consumed large quantities of coal in numerous dispersed lime kilns. The third Earl of Marchmont was a strong advocate of the use of lime from the 1730s and Robert Maxwell, the secretary of the Edinburgh Society of Improvers, was busy disseminating information on the construction of draw kilns in the 1750s. Both men probably had only a marginal impact on a development which, being feasible in most places near a supply of limestone with access to supplies of coal, and profitable, was likely to spread fairly rapidly anyhow. There was increasing industrial demand for coal from non-metallurgical industries ranging from the Glasgow sugar refineries to the vitriol (sulphuric acid) works set up at Prestonpans near Edinburgh by two Englishmen John Roebuck and Samuel Garbett in 1749. Expanding towns burned more coal in domestic grates (Edinburgh in particular earned the nickname of 'auld Reekie' as a result) and indeed burned more coal for the lime needed in their building. After 1767 Edinburgh was building a whole New Town beyond the drained Nor Loch. Iron works did not generate much demand for coal before 1760, for they were based on the use of charcoal as fuel. During periods of high iron prices entrepreneurs had been tempted into the Highlands even in the seventeenth century in search of the timber which produced pig iron in furnaces and wrought iron out of pig iron in forges. In the eighteenth century English businessmen moved into the Highlands making deals with Highland landowners like Macdonell of Invergarry to gain the right to exploit timber reserves. After a lean time in the 1730s, when iron prices fell, there was more expansion and by 1750 several furnaces existed in the Highlands at sites like Invergarry in Inverness-shire and Taynuilt and Furnace in Argyllshire where Highland wood smelted English ore imported by water.

The modern pattern of iron production in Scotland was only beginning to emerge in 1759 when Roebuck and Garbett of the Prestonpans vitriol works combined with William Cadell, a merchant and laird from Cockenzie on the Firth of Forth, to set up an ironworks on the river Carron near Falkirk. There coke was used to produce iron in a large integrated business combining mining, smelting and forging. It was a significant development, but for a long time a wholly a-typical one. Indeed it is possible to argue that the landlord was most dominant in the coal-mining industry in Scotland in the period before it entered its most rapid phase of expansion. Noble houses like the Erskines of Mar at Alloa, or the Earls of Elgin at Dunfermline did indeed pioneer many developments. The Earl of Mar who was involved in the '15 was extremely interested in his mines and developed a water-powered drainage system for them on the grand scale. Even in exile his restless mind fathered the Alloa glass industry. Much later the Earls of Elgin in the 1760s built the coastal village of Charlestown where a great bank of lime kilns burned coal from their own mines brought to Charlestown along an extensive system of mineral railways utilised by horse-drawn waggons. Yet there were a number of built-in restrictions to the dynamism of the noble coal proprietors. First, the profitability of coalmines before 1780 appears to have fluctuated a great deal even for a favourably-placed mine like that of Sheriffhall in Midlothian, owned and operated by the Duke of Buccleuch, and near the Edinburgh market. The Rothes mines in Fife were not, overall, very profitable. Secondly, and not unconnected with the first point, is the fact that the servile status of colliers made them an expensive if skilled hereditary work-force, little worried by blackleg labour when they chose to be militant. Only in 1775 did the process which abolished this particular scandal and bottleneck in the labour supply begin.

The Scottish economy grew before 1780 by the combined enterprise of lairds, merchants, and the state. Of the three, the merchants, who of course overlapped with the lairds, were perhaps the most crucial entrepreneurial group, because they were the pivotal one. The nobility and gentry played an active role, though their biggest contribution was often negative or indirect. They did not veto development, because it brought them money and their rent pressure on their tenants helped mobilise the tenants for rural industry. The state was perhaps the least significant partner, because, as so often is the case in a market economy, state intervention was frequently a misguided and counter-productive waste of the tax-payers' money. However, the Old Colonial System did inject a great deal of liquidity into the economy of part of western Scotland around Glasgow, while the Board of Trustees, for all their relative failure with fishing projects, did assist significantly the already lusty growth of the Lowland linen trade.

Growth derived from the exploitation of low-cost, low-overhead trades which were favourably placed to compete in the discipline of the market. Low wages and ruthless geographical specialisation were essential parts of the pattern. One example of the last point is the Scots paper industry. It made a very shaky, state-sponsored start in the seventeenth century. By 1780 it was a vigorous industry capable of looking after itself, but it was also very concentrated. Edinburgh, with its commerce, banking, law courts, university, publishing and massive domestic demand for paper, was much the best market in Scotland. Consequently paper excised at Haddington and Edinburgh accounted for over 66 per cent of the total for Scotland in the period 1764–1800, with a peak of 77 per cent in 1772. Without the growth which occurred before 1780, there would have been no acceleration in growth in the late eighteenth century but the fact remains that neither the state nor the Improvers were as crucial to pre-1780 growth as is often supposed. The mainspring of that growth was an intelligent if often instinctive exploitation of low costs in certain products in the context of a free and substantial market.

5

The Triumph of Commercialisation
and Industry
1780–1840

In 1780 Scotland was still an agrarian, pre-industrial society, even
though its economy contained very vigorous commercial and industrial
sectors. The economic climate had changed dramatically since 1707, but
the texture of life for most people was much as it had been in 1727 or
1700. By 1840 matters were different. Urbanisation and the development of steam-powered manufacture and transportation, not to mention
drastic re-organisation of agriculture, had turned Scotland into an
industrial society based on market economics. It will be argued that
major change, far from being concentrated within a few years, was usually spread over substantial periods of time and varied in chronology and
type from region to region, despite the integrative effects of transport
developments. Nothing is more dangerous than overall generalisation
based on a single atypical region such as Clydeside. Nor must it be forgotten that for large areas of Scotland, notably the Highlands, the opportunities offered by the development of an industrial society within the
same state were on balance probably negative. Market pressures could
and did narrow the range of options available to Highland society.

It has become fashionable amongst historians of the process of industrialisation to adopt a vocabulary and frame of reference which derives
from the persuasive writings of the American scholar W. W. Rostow, and
more particularly from his seminal work on *Stages of Economic Growth*.
Rostow analyses the first industrial revolution, which he believes to be
the one which occurred in England in the course of the eighteenth century, and likens it to an aeroplane taking off. Once in motion, the aeroplane moves along the runway for some time building up speed. Then

comes a short sharp and dramatic acceleration which is the essential prelude to 'take-off'. In the same way, Rostow sees the pre-industrial economy, after a lengthy preparation of gradual change, suddenly making a decisive quantitative leap into 'self-sustained growth', a condition in which change and industrial growth become the normal condition of society. For Rostow the crucial period in English economic history came with the dramatic upsurges of industrial production and overseas trade which occurred in the 1780s and 1790s. As Scotland was linked with England in one fiscal unit after 1707 and undoubtedly experienced an industrial revolution of decisive dimensions, it is tempting to look for a similar process and period of take-off. Whether such an exercise is wise is, however, debatable. It commits the historian to searching for something more akin to an event than a process. Here it will be argued that the twin forces of commercialisation and industrialisation which transformed pre-industrial Scotland into a nineteenth-century industrial nation were essentially cumulative in character. If the decades between 1780 and 1840 are peculiarly significant in this context it is because a long-standing process of quantitative change in the distribution of economic effort in Scotland reached proportions which transformed that change into a qualitative one. More crudely: Scotland became, irreversibly, a different kind of society.

The most impressive single piece of evidence for the fundamental change coming over Scottish society is the history of Scottish population. Dr Alexander Webster in 1755 put the population of Scotland at over 1,265,000. This figure probably represented the beginning of a process of continuous population growth, for there is reason to suspect that it was probably a little higher than the population sustained by Scotland before the great famine of the late seventeenth century. Be that as it may, the next reliable figure, given by the 1801 census, gives a population of 1,608,000. This means that retained population had grown by over a quarter in 50 years, or, to put it another way, that there had been a retained population growth rate of 0.6 per cent per annum since 1755. In itself there is nothing very remarkable in such a figure. The population of most pre-industrial agricultural societies is characterised by a normal growth rate of 0.5 to 1 per cent per annum. However, these societies are also characterised by a highly-fluctuating death-rate, and periodic subsistence crises tend to eliminate the effects of surges of population growth in good times, or at least to severely moderate their long-term significance. What was unprecedented about late eighteenth-century Scottish population growth was that it continued into the nineteenth century at an even faster pace. The census of 1811 put the population at 1,806,000 and in 1821 the figure was 2,092,000. Between 1801 and 1811 population thus grew at 1.2 per cent per annum and between 1811 and 1821 by 1.6 per cent per annum, the largest figure for such an increase over a decade in Scottish history. By 1831 the population of Scotland was 2,364,000 and the 1841 figure of 2,620,000 registered the fact that total retained population had more than doubled in less than a century.

This remarkable overall growth was accompanied by two significant phenomena. First, there was a substantial increase in urbanisation. In 1750 there had been four towns in Scotland of over 10,000 inhabitants and they contained together only 9 per cent of the population. By 1820 a quarter of the population lived in 13 such towns, and probably one Scot in three lived in some sort of town. It is easy enough to argue that most Scots were still country dwellers in 1820, and that the social and economic structure of Scotland still did not diverge too widely from that of certain Western European countries like France or Holland. Such an argument is misleading because it ignores the very sharp discontinuity from the contemporary European norm represented by the massive and sustained increase in population and by the swift growth of urban units which had ceased to be simply the most sophisticated social organs of a still fundamentally rural society. In 1811 18.5 per cent of Scottish people lived in the eight largest towns, and two of these, Edinburgh and Glasgow, had for the first time exceeded 100,000. By 1841 a quarter of the Scottish population lived in the same eight largest towns and 16 per cent of Scottish population was concentrated in two urban complexes. Glasgow, with over a quarter of a million inhabitants, accounted for 10 per cent of the national population, while Edinburgh and Leith together contained another 6 per cent. An irreversible urban revolution was in progress.

Secondly, and to a large extent as a result of this process of urbanisation, there was an extensive change in the balance of population as between the different regions of Scotland. In 1755 over half the population lived north of the Tay–Clyde line, but by 1820 this proportion was down to two-fifths and more than half the population was crowded into the Central Lowlands which had in earlier times contained only a little over a third of the population. To some extent this rapid divergence between regions reflected different experiences of emigration and immigration. For example, the Highlands had experienced significant emigration overseas by the end of the eighteenth century—most of it to North America. Heavy emigration seems to have begun after the end of the Seven Years War in 1762 when soldiers from disbanded Highland regiments settled on the North American seaboard as far apart as Prince Edward Island and the Carolinas and by the glowing accounts they sent home helped 'pull' more Highland families across the Atlantic. In the 1770s a social crisis affecting the tacksmen in certain parts of the Highlands helped to reinforce this flow. In order to increase their rent rolls some Highland landlords began to squeeze out the tacksmen on the grounds that they were parasitic middlemen exploiting both landlord and tenant. Instead of meeting demands for vastly increased rents many substantial tacksmen sold up, persuaded their sub-tenants to come with them, and set out for the New World. There their conservatism stood them in bad stead at the time of the American Revolution, for most were Loyalists who fought for the British and many emigrated northwards to Canada after the Americans emerged with their independence confirmed by the Treaty of Versailles of 1783. It so happened that bad harvests in 1782 and 1783 in the Highlands coincided with renewed interest in emigration, much of which was directed towards Canada. The exact size of Highland emigration overseas between 1763 and 1803 is a matter . of dispute. The contemporary observer J. Knox suggested that at least 30,000 emigrated from the Highlands between 1763 and 1775. A slightly later writer, John Walker, estimated that only 5,800 or so souls left the Highlands between 1771 and 1794, while a modern historian reckoned that between 1782 and 1803 at least 12,000 emigrated from the Highlands, and possibly many more. It seems doubtful whether the total was such as to be really significant except in two senses. First, it contained a disproportionate number of tacksmen—the social leaders of Highland society. Secondly, it does underline the point that so far from attracting immigrants, like the contemporary Scottish Lowlands, the Highlands were exporting people.

Most of the people who left the Highlands in the late eighteenth and early nineteenth centuries went to the Lowlands. This becomes clear if an examination is made of the regional variations in population trend which can be found within the Highlands. In general terms the century between 1750 and 1850 was one of increasing population in the Highlands. Population in all four major Highland counties increased significantly, though the process faltered in Argyll after 1831, in Inverness after 1841, and in Sutherland between 1831 and 1841. After 1850 the story was very different. Even in the period of population growth the increases achieved were low compared with some Lowland counties, for no Highland county registered a population growth of over 20 per cent between 1755 and the 1790s. However, closer examination shows that in terms of population development the Highlands fell into two distinct regions, neither of which corresponded with formal county boundaries. In the south and east, in an area covering the southerly parts of the county of Argyll together with most of the Grampian Highlands and associated areas south of the Great Glen as well as the Highland areas to the east of the watershed north of Inverness, there was only a modest overall increase in population. As against this, the rest of the Highland area, comprising mainly the seaboard from Morvern in the north of Argyll to Cape·Wrath in the extreme north-west, as well as the more northerly islands, experienced an overall population growth of the order of 34 per cent. In this latter zone 32 out of 43 parishes experienced an increase of over 25 per cent, whereas in the other zone 41 out of 68 parishes experienced no increase at all. These regional differences were even sharper in the period 1801-41. The area of rapid growth was smaller, starting somewhere on the western seaboard of Inverness-shire and running north. Here population increased by 53 per cent in four decades, whereas in the rest of the Highlands the overall increase was something like 7 per cent.

At least until the second decade of the nineteenth century, virtually all Highland landlords were opposed to emigration from their estates on both social and economic grounds. Yet it is clear that these regional variations must hinge on differential net emigration, which can hardly be explained in terms of different estate-management policies. The explanation does in fact seem to lie primarily in the wide geographical spread of the Highlands and in the different degrees of nearness to urban centres in the Lowlands which were capable of attracting industrial labour. The great bulk of Highland emigrants moved towards the industrial areas in the western Lowlands which lay at the south-west end of the Highland Line. Thus the four industrial counties in that area—Lanark, Renfrew, Dumbarton and Ayr—drew 58 per cent of all Highland emigration, while the addition of the county of Edinburgh (modern Midlothian) would raise the percentage to 69. Clearly it was increasingly to the big cities in these counties, and especially Edinburgh, Glasgow, and Paisley that the emigrants were drawn. Many people from the north-western parts of the Highlands did reach Glasgow, but the distances involved seem to have ensured that the volume of emigration was in relative terms far less significant than the flow from Argyll, nearly 90 per cent of which moved into nearby Glasgow.

The Scottish Lowlands, as distinct from the Highlands which were declining in importance and the Southern Uplands which stabilised with about 11 per cent of the population between 1755 and 1821, were thus the demographically dynamic part of Scotland. In 1841 40 per cent of the population of Lanarkshire, including Glasgow, were incomers, and this figure compared with 29 per cent for Renfrewshire, 19 per cent for Ayrshire and 50 per cent for Dumbartonshire. The latter figure was abnormally high because of the long-standing role of Dumbartonshire as a transit zone between the Highlands and the expanding industries of Clydeside. A certain proportion of these incomers were migrants from Ireland. This was a natural development in view of the long history of population exchange across the narrow waters separating the south-west of Scotland from Ulster. In the seventeenth century, particularly around the 1690s, there had been a substantial flow of Scots into the counties of Antrim and Down. The eighteenth century saw the emergence, both in north-east Ulster and in Lowland Scotland, of a thriving linen industry which encouraged movement by skilled craftsmen, such as weavers. The Clyde and Ayrshire ports drove an active trade with most of the eastern seaboard of Ireland and, with the growth of population in Ireland and of industry and demand for such seasonal labourers as harvesters in Scotland, it was natural that both seasonal and permanent migration from Ireland should become a common pattern. Its impact was disproportionately significant in the Glasgow area, falling away in scale and significance further east and north. In 1831 Glasgow had a population of 202,426 composed of 353 'foreigners', 2,919 English, 35,554 Irish and 163,000 Scots. This proportion of Irish vastly exceeded the percentage of Irish in the Scottish population in 1841, when the figure was five per cent, representing 126,000 residents of Scotland who were Irish-born. The sheer industrial vitality of Clydeside held a large proportion of Highland and Irish immigration, feeding these predominantly poor people into the bottom end of its active labour market. In 1840 Dr Cowan reported that less than a quarter of the patients in Glasgow Royal Infirmary were natives of the city and that only 15 per cent of those admitted into the Albion Street Fever Hospital, at a time when fever was rampant, were native Glaswegians. Thirty per cent of these unfortunates came from Ireland and 40 per cent from the Highlands and rural areas of Lowland Scotland.

However, it is important to remember that until 1825 the expansion of Edinburgh had been in some ways more conspicuous and more influential than that of Glasgow. In the first quarter of the nineteenth century Edinburgh's population almost doubled, rising from 80,000 to over 150,000. Edinburgh was the centre of extensive regional development. Its lawyers and bankers serviced the grain and stock farming of the Lothian plain, as well as the sheep farming of the Lothian uplands. A ring of subsidiary industrial sites surrounded the city from the coal-mining, paper-making, and textile manufacturing in the valley of the Lothian Esk to the coal, salt, rope and sail making with which the smaller harbours of the Lothian coast supplemented their fishing activities. Quarrying and dairy farming were two other fields in which the demands of the city stimulated extensive development in its immediate hinterland. Edinburgh itself was the social, legal, medical and ecclesiastical centre of Scotland. Its own industries tended to be organised in smallish units and were rather old-fashioned, but there were plenty of them. Such craftsmen as skilled masons, cabinet-makers, jewellers and needle-workers abounded. Edinburgh breweries were deservedly famous. The great firm of William Younger, for example, started in Leith in 1749. In 1778 one of the founder's sons had set up his own brewery within the historic precincts of the Abbey of Holyroodhouse. By the early years of the next century Younger ale-carts were travelling as far as Glasgow and Dumbarton, while more and more Younger ale was being shipped from Leith to London. By 1840 it could be said with justice that Younger Edinburgh ale was being sold from Australia to Canada, the United States, and Latin America.

The fame of Edinburgh as a seat of literature plus the enterprise of its publishers, the excellence of its printers and its relatively low overall costs, made it a great printing centre, drawing its paper supplies from its own neighbourhood. On top of all this the port of Leith had a range of industries based partly on the building, repairing and provisioning of ships and partly on its remarkable facilities for the import and storage of bulk raw materials. Sugar-refining, soap-boiling and glass-blowing were examples of the latter. The very smallness of many firms and the absence of great manufacturing industries with generations in front of them before they reached their peak seems to have rendered the 1825 slump particularly damaging in Edinburgh. Even so, Edinburgh remained a great city and a seat of a disproportionately large middle class with formidable purchasing power.

Aberdeen remained the site of quite exceptionally strong industrial growth throughout the first four decades of the nineteenth century. Its oldest industrial tradition of any great size had lain in the field of woollens. This was essentially a rural and domestic craft but it was organised and financed by Aberdeen merchants. In 1770 there were no fewer than 22 Aberdeen merchants buying in wool from the south in order to distribute it to thousands of women in the landward parts of the North-East, mainly to be turned into stockings and gloves. By 1790 carding engines and spinning jennies were heralding the arrival of factory production. In 1798 Alexander Hadden and Sons, an old-established merchant house, built a steam-powered mill in the Green in Aberdeen—the first of many such enterprises. Nor was Aberdeen in any way backward in the field of linen manufacture. The firm of Leys, Masson and Company was the biggest Aberdeen linen business. The main building at its Granholm mill had seven stories and the complex included a foundry and bleachworks. In the early nineteenth century, when Dundee was said to produce about 5,000 spindles of flax yarn per week, Granholm's 240 spinning frames were producing 10,000 to 12,000 spindles a week. By 1882 Dundee had nine times as great an output of linen as Aberdeen, but as late as 1850 the four surviving Aberdeen linen mills could still produce nearly one ninth of Scotland's linen production.

There was even a smaller but significant cotton manufacture in Aberdeen, while the town's paper industry, which began in 1696, had a continuous history of expansion after 1751. By 1850 Stoneywood mill alone employed 1,000 hands and was using 2,500 tons of rags for special writing papers annually. Nor was this anything like the end of the list of major industrial developments. By 1840 the town had a chemical industry. The combworks established by John Stewart in 1830 with 40 employees was by 1854 turning out 9 million combs annually. Food processing and other industries flourished around an expanding and improved harbour with a substantial local fleet of ships and a famous shipbuilding tradition. In 1839 Alexander Hall and Company produced the first Aberdeen clipper, the *Scottish Maid*. By the 1840s Aberdeen clippers were fighting the famous breed of Yankee clippers for supremacy in the last great age of long-distance sailing-ships. Finally, it is impossible to omit perhaps the most characteristic of all Aberdeen industries—granite quarrying and polishing. By the late eighteenth century the London market for sets and paving stones alone was providing employment for 600 Aberdeen quarriers. In 1817 no less than 22,167 tons of stone valued at £23,275 was sent from Aberdeen to London. About the same time Aberdeen itself, which had a long tradition of using freestone rather than granite for its prestige buildings, made the transition to granite, becoming in due course 'the Granite City'. Granite polishing by hand had been established in Aberdeen before 1770, but this particular activity received a tremendous stimulus around 1830 when Alexander Macdonald devised steam-powered machinery for turning and polishing granite. What in the last analysis broke the impetus of Aberdeen's industrial expansion was the great commercial slump which followed the collapse of a wave of speculation stimulated initially by railway developments. In 1847 nearly 7 per cent of U.K. national income was invested in railways. A bank crisis pricked the bubble of speculation and bad harvests in the two previous years helped to hold demand down on a scale sufficient to create serious depression. An Aberdeen bank failed. The Aberdeen linen industry never really recovered, and Aberdeen, though it soon recovered a solid prosperity, was never again the seat of such industrial dynamism.

Examples could be multiplied to the effect that in the late eighteenth century and in the first few decades of the nineteenth century, rapid industrialisation was geographically widespread in the Lowlands. It is true that in absolute terms Clydeside was growing economically at a faster rate than any other Lowland region, partly because it started from a lower base than most others, but the exceptional ascendancy of Clydeside in manufacturing industry was a phenomenon of the second half of the nineteenth century. In the late eighteenth century towns which in the Victorian era had effectively dropped out of the industrial race might be experiencing a major industrial boom. Perth is an excellent example. In 1796 linen was the staple manufacture of that town. There were 1,500 looms at work in Perth and its suburbs, producing an estimated £100,000 sterling of product annually, mostly in the shape of linen goods, but with some cotton. On top of this £120,000 of linens woven in the surrounding countryside were annually purchased by dealers on the Perth market. Water power was the key to much of Perth's prosperity for the rivers Tay and Almond near Perth offered many sites where it was possible relatively easily to divert a powerful flow of water for industrial purposes. There were many bleachfields around Perth and several sites were adapted towards the end of the eighteenth century for water-powered spinning. Of these the most famous was the cotton mill and factory village of Stanley. Perth itself sustained many other industries ranging from a leather trade which in the 1790s was shipping £8,000 of boots and shoes to the London market annually, to linseed oil crushing plant, to paper mills and an astonishingly precocious publishing industry. At its height under the leadership of the Morison family in the late eighteenth century, Perth publishing rivalled with that of Edinburgh and Glasgow in scope and scale.

The labour force needed to man Perth's expanding industries was continually recruited from the surrounding countryside. The Reverend James Scott, minister of the East Church said in his contribution to the *Old Statistical Account* that:

> the great resort of the poor, from all parts of the country is to Perth. Some of them make a shift, perhaps for 3 years, to maintain themselves, and then when they fall into distress, or when their cart horses die by which they gained their daily bread, they apply to the public for relief.

Here we see in microcosm the close relationship between rural change and urban growth. The estates around Perth in the eighteenth century were so stable that wealthy Perth merchants had difficulty in acquiring landed property in the area, yet it is equally clear that there was a steady flow of population from the countryside into the town. Such was the industrial vitality of Perth that it absorbed these immigrants in a process of growth which in turn generated demand for foodstuffs on a scale which encouraged further commercialisation and social change in the hinterland. The great bulk of the immigrants into most expanding nineteenth-century Scots towns came from Lowland rural parishes. Here Glasgow is not an exception. In 1861 15.69 per cent of its population came from Ireland but 30.04 per cent of its population came from other parts of Scotland excluding Glasgow itself and the county of Lanark in which it is situated. Admittedly Glasgow was a mecca for Highlanders, but as the adjacent county was invariably a substantial source of immigrants, it is clear that even here Lowland Scots must have been the biggest single immigrant group. At the other end of the scale in 1861 stood Aberdeen where 76.48 per cent of the population was born in Aberdeen or Aberdeenshire, 19.31 per cent in other Scottish counties, 2.18 per cent in England and Wales, and a mere 1.25 per cent in Ireland.

The relationship between population and economic growth is infinitely complex. Because any given stimulus may produce a feedback effect it is almost impossible to separate cause and effect. If, however, attention is focused on the relationship between the countryside and urban industrial areas in Scotland between 1780 and 1840, one crude descriptive generalisation may be defended with some confidence. It is that the countryside was better at breeding and raising people than the towns, and that the towns, especially the big ones, were so unhealthy that without a constant flow of immigrants from the countryside they would have had difficulty in maintaining their existing work forces, let alone providing continually expanding work forces to cope with sustained economic expansion. In Glasgow mortality from all causes was 31.8 per thousand of the population in 1783 and still 27.6 per thousand in 1861. In between these two dates there were sharp fluctuations. A figure as low as 17.1 per thousand was recorded in 1801 but in other years, usually when epidemics were rampant, the figure could be nearly twice as high. Some idea of the causes of death can be derived from an examination of the 1,508 persons who died in the City parish of Glasgow in 1791, a year of high mortality. Of the 1,508, 403 were recorded as dying of smallpox, 274 of consumption, 151 of diseases of old age, 102 of fever, and 101 of 'bowel hives'. No less than 694 of the 1,508 deaths were of children under two years of age and 63 per cent of all deaths were those of children under ten years of age. Until 1850 or so the deaths of children under the age of ten accounted for more than half the annual deaths in Glasgow and even in 1861 the figure for such child deaths was 42 per cent.

Dundee, with its rapidly-growing linen industry, was another example of the casualty rate exacted by such progress. Epidemics were a recurrent phenomenon there. In the years 1833–39 there were 12,000 cases of 'fever' in Dundee and its crude mortality rate was 1 in 32 annually as compared with 1 in 45 for Scotland and 1 in 48 for England and Wales. We know a good deal about the social price of progress in early nineteenth-century Dundee because of the pamphlets written by the Reverend George Lewis, minister of the recently-created parish of St David's, which was an overwhelmingly working-class area. Lewis records bad, overcrowded housing; largely non-existent sanitation; low wages; and heavy drinking. He reckoned that nearly every sixth family in a parish with a population of 9,000 had lost its father, yet the poor relief of the district was centralised in the general kirk session of the town and it admitted only 161 individuals to the poor roll as permanent dependents. Those in St David's were receiving the princely sum of 1s. 0d. to 1s. 6d. per week as their share of the town's welfare. Given circumstances such as these, high mortality was quite inevitable.

To explain the underlying upward trend in the population of Scotland as a whole is not easy. Historical demographers have long debated both the timing and the principal causes of the striking natural increase in the retained population of Great Britain which undoubtedly occurred in the second half of the eighteenth century and continued into the nineteenth. Interestingly, the weight of current opinion seems to be slightly more in favour of an emphasis on decreased mortality than on increased fertility, and also inclined to argue that the crucial upward leap in the rate of retained natural increase came later rather than sooner, perhaps only in the last quarter of the century. Be that as it may, the process of growth was clearly multi-factorial in inspiration so it is possible to list the more important factors which probably lay behind Scottish population growth in this period, even if weighing their relative significance against one another is never likely to be a wholly satisfactory business.

Taking factors which affected mortality rates first, mention must be made of inoculation against smallpox, the most lethal of all the diseases attacking young children. Its record in the larger towns is well known, for it to some extent filled a gap left by the unexplained disappearance of bubonic plague, a great killer in the seventeenth century, and by the relative decline in virulence of typhus. However, it could be deadly in the countryside and in small towns like Kilmarnock, where smallpox was responsible for one in six of all deaths between 1728 and 1764. Inoculation was a process involving giving a child a mild controlled dose of the disease in isolation from others in order to bestow lifelong immunity. By the 1760s it was quite common in Scotland, but with strange regional variations in incidence. In the Northern Isles, the Highlands and the south-western portion of the country comprising Galloway and Dumfries, it was common by the 1790s and was regarded, rightly, as saving thousands of lives. Inoculation had penetrated parts of the eastern Lowlands, notably rural Fife, but in most of the Lowlands and especially in the big industrial cities like Dundee and Glasgow there was a seemingly invincible prejudice against it. The difference in response may well hinge on the fact that in rural areas smallpox was much more an adult disease liable to kill the breadwinner in the family, whereas in towns it tended to massacre children. In striking contrast to this opposition to inoculation, there was a speedy and near-universal reception of Jenner's admittedly less risky technique of vaccination after about 1800. In Glasgow between 1793 and 1802 36 per cent of all deaths in children under the age of ten was due to smallpox. Between 1803 and 1812, when vaccination had become common, the figure dropped to 9 per cent. It is true that in the cities other diseases ranging from measles, which is a very serious disease in adults, to tuberculosis were on the increase especially amongst young adults, while smallpox in children waned. Nevertheless inoculation and vaccination between them clearly made a major contribution to population growth, especially in rural areas, or to be more precise to the survival of a larger percentage of any age cohort, especially that part of it born in rural areas.

The impact of the potato in Scotland in the eighteenth century was probably more significant as a cause of retained population growth than all the activities of the medical profession, ranging from the work of well-paid town physicians, to the writing of popular guides to self-treatment, to the establishment of infirmaries in virtually every major Scottish burgh and several minor ones. The basic explanation for the limited impact of the already distinguished Scottish medical profession in Scotland itself lay in the cost of its services. Even when an infirmary was set up with the poor very much in mind, it usually lacked both staff and accommodation really to tackle existing problems. Dundee Infirmary is a typical case. One of its leading promoters, the Reverend Robert Small, DD, published a sermon on 'The Importance of the Poor' in 1794, and the infirmary project built on and absorbed the work of a pre-existing Dispensary Committee which was much concerned with visiting the sick poor. Opened in 1798 in a handsome new building, Dundee Infirmary in its first annual period from 4 June 1798 to 10 June 1799 treated 45 in-patients and 734 out-patients. The population of the town at this time was about 27,000. By comparison the humble tattie (*anglice* potato) made an impact, directly or indirectly, on the lives of a very large section of the Scottish nation.

Its initial impact was very much a phenomenon of the second half the eighteenth century. It was cultivated in the Outer Hebrides from the early 1740s, and spread over the rest of the Highlands and Lowlands in the next few decades, being common from Sutherland to Lothian by the 1760s. Like cattle, it could be raised on ground unsuitable for grain crops. It did not respond to climatic variation in the same way as grain, so usually did not fail in years of grain deficiency. Above all, it could support a family on much less ground than was needed for cereals. Potatoes not only helped feed families, but also provided them with a cash crop, directly or indirectly. Thus around Renfrew in the 1790s potatoes were produced, sometimes as much as 72 bolls from an acre, and sold readily to the rapidly-expanding population of Paisley. At the beginning of the nineteenth century the county of Dumfries was reckoned to be selling £50,000 of pork per annum. Hams were sold for the London market and flitches for Newcastle shipping and for consumption in the coal-mining districts of the north-east of England. All this hinged on an abundance of potatoes, which were the staple diet of the pigs. Elsewhere, and especially in the Highlands, the growing of potatoes freed land for cash crops such as barley which could be malted and turned into the liquid gold of whisky. One must not exaggerate the impact of the potato: it represented a substantial but 'once for all' gain in the capacity of Scottish agriculture. It was probably fully integrated into the system by the early nineteenth century and subsequent over-reliance upon it, especially on unsuitable ground in the Highlands, merely brought out its self-limiting capacity in the shape of potato disease.

Finally there can be little doubt that population increase was at least partly the result of a lower age of marriage amongst women, a consequent increase in the length of their fecund interval, and an increase in the number of births, or to put it another way, in shorter intervals between births for the average woman. In industrial or industrialising societies, before the spread of relatively safe and effective contraceptive devices in the twentieth century, the age of marriage and frequency of births does seem to have been closely related to living standards and job opportunities. Thus the most effective mass contraceptive of the seventeenth and eighteenth centuries was simply famine. Even those who survived it did so partly by a natural reduction in all non-essential bodily capacities, including the capacity to reproduce. Virtually all pre-industrial societies have elaborate forms of social control designed to restrict access to land, the normal means of sustaining a family, and thereby to keep up the average age of marriage. The spread of industry in eighteenth-century Scotland was bound to affect marriage and fertility patterns, if only because industrial development was so widespread.

It has already been shown that much of the labour which sustained the early expansion of the Scottish linen industry was rural labour. Mechanisation did not at first alter the rural emphasis of industry, for the prime mover of early mechanisation, other than muscle power, was water power. The first textile process to be mechanised was that of lint or flax dressing. Lint or scutch mills were usually single-storey stone buildings housing a series of vertically-mounted four-bladed rotors. Flax was thrust into the blades through openings in protective shutters known as stocks. By 1772 there were 252 lint mills in Scotland. Ten years later the number was 371, a figure which was not to change until after 1815. In 1790 there were five lint mills in Little Dunkeld in Perthshire each with big flax-storage sheds attached. Remains of these mills can be found all over the rural Lowlands from Ayrshire to Aberdeenshire. Though they never displaced hand-scutching, these mills were the forerunners of more substantial water-powered industrialism. The first mill using water-power to spin linen yarn in Scotland was set up at Brigton in Angus by William Douglas, who used capital put up by Dundee merchants to convert a corn mill to use machinery leased from the English holders of the patents, Kendrew and Porthouse of Darlington. This mill commenced operations in 1787–88. In 1789 James Ivory, a Dundee mathematician, became manager of a new company which built a much larger mill to replace the original. Though never very successful, this enterprise was following an established tradition in seeking a rural site, for the great new water-powered cotton-spinning works of the western parts of Scotland were nearly all in rural sites.

The first big water-powered spinning mill was opened in 1779 in the small town of Rothesay in Bute. Other early cotton mills included one at Neilston using the water of the River Levern. It was to this parish that Sir John Sinclair, the inspirer of the *Old Statistical Account* of Scotland, led a delegation of French businessmen just before the outbreak of war with Revolutionary France, in order to show them an example of industrial development in a rural context. Other cotton mills using water-power occasioned the creation of new factory villages at Catrine in Ayrshire, Stanley in Perthshire, and most notably at New Lanark where the attraction was the power of the Corra Linn Falls on the Clyde. These are all famous names, but all over Scotland in the late eighteenth or early nineteenth century meal mills were being converted into spinning mills. This was not just true of significant rivers like the Eden in north Fife, but also of their lesser tributaries such as the Ceres Burn. Bleachfields made such heavy demands on space (for laying out cloth in the day before chemical bleaching) and water that they were usually situated well out of towns, and there were many rivers like the River Leven in Fife where a comparatively short stretch of river could display a mixture of bleachfields, paper mills and meal mills. Eventually the coal-fired steam engine hastened the concentration of manufacturing activity in a smaller number of urban sites, but water power fought a lengthy rearguard action in the nineteenth century. Just as the sailing ship reached its height of functional perfection in its lengthy struggle with the steamer, so the water wheel was much improved after the initial spread of the steam engine.

The process whereby rural industry with its water-power basis became progressively less viable is a much neglected one. Here it suffices to point out that for the average Lowland countryman industry in the period 1780–1840 was a far from remote phenomenon. It penetrated the cottar's home in the shape of hand spinning and weaving. It blossomed on most sites suitable for the exploitation of water power. It assumed many forms, though all of them could use the services of the skilled wrights who had originally devoted their talents to building and servicing the rural meal mills of Scotland. Rural populations moving into the expanding towns were not necessarily passing from a 'pre-industrial' to an 'industrial' environment. They were often looking for work of a kind with which they were not unfamiliar. More generally, it can be argued that in this period, when human and animal muscle, wind, and water were still the principal keys to economic advance, the attempt to separate rural and urban developments as distinct categories of analysis is a mistake. The whole extraordinary process of expansion and change, with its accompanying massive movements of population, was essentially one, as the interlocking and complimentary nature of population developments in town and country show. That said, it is essential now to analyse, in more detail and in turn, the dynamics of industrial and agricultural change.

Industrial development

Much the most spectacular development in the last 20 years of the eighteenth century in Scotland was the rapid growth of the cotton industry, especially in the area around Glasgow. The background from which this new industry sprang is often misunderstood, as indeed is the significance of the industry itself. It is therefore best to treat of these matters, starting with the background, which is often represented as the desperate search for investment outlets by the tobacco firms of Glasgow which were left stranded by the total cessation of their business in the American colonies after the outbreak of war in 1776. In fact the first development of the Scottish cotton industry occurred at a much earlier stage in connection with the fine linen and silk industries. Scottish merchants imported, almost entirely from the West Indies, 466,589 lb. of cotton wool in 1770, and it is known that by the 1750s both Glasgow and Paisley had a tradition of combining cotton yarn with linen yarn in the weaving of fustian. Nor can it now be argued that a decisive flow of investment capital left the tobacco trade for cotton shortly after 1776. The 1770 figure for imports of cotton wool into Scotland was not exceeded until 1785. There is no denying that the wealth generated by the big tobacco firms did help to broaden and expand industrial activity in Scotland and it played a key role in supplying funds for the development of the Glasgow banks. More generally, early banking tended to flourish most easily in the context of a substantial entrepot economy, where the need for credit for the basic overseas trade was balanced by massive payments by European customers like the French and the Dutch. However, it is clear that there was no noticeably greater volume of investment by the tobacco firms in industry after 1776 than there had been before. Because they expected the British government to respond efficiently and promptly to the American crisis, most of the Glasgow tobacco firms counted, quite reasonably, on the quick suppression of the 1776 rebels, with the result that they left uncollected a great many of the debts owed to them through the hundred or so stores they operated in Maryland and Virginia. The Cunninghame group of companies, for example, claimed after the war that they were owed outstanding debts to the tune of £135,000, and although this was exceptional, the period around 1780 when cotton soared in significance was not a good one for tobacco fortunes.

On the other hand, a glance at the fortunes of the two outports of Glasgow shows that the crisis in the North American colonies did not bring universal gloom in its wake. Tobacco came to Port Glasgow and Greenock and between 1772 and 1785 their joint customs revenue fell by over a half. In fact Port Glasgow, which specialised in tobacco, carried most of this fall with a 77 per cent decline in its customs revenue. Greenock, which had a strong West Indian connection, as well as more general trade, experienced only a 15 per cent overall fall. It was the combination of the West India trade with the legacy of the fine linen industry which made the transition to cotton feasible. The war if anything helped, for it tended to raise wages and demand at a time when cotton was in real terms becoming cheaper, flax more expensive, and silk more expensive still. Glasgow West India merchants were anxious to market more and more cotton, partly because West Indian planters tied supplies of such lucrative commodities as sugar and rum to a willingness to absorb more cotton. Then again, the fact that the fine linen areas of Lancashire had effected this transition to cotton a few years ahead of the Glasgow–Paisley area meant that the Scots could draw on the experience and technology of the English industry without having to pay the inevitable development costs shouldered by any pioneering industry. One example of this is the immense increase in supplies of yarn made possible by the use of the spinning device known as Crompton's mule, which was itself the product of considerable development, combining the best features of Hargreaves' spinning jenny and Arkwright's water frame. It placed a high premium on the skills of the fine weavers of the Glasgow–Paisley area.

As the pioneers of the early Scottish cotton industry were usually leading figures in the linen trade of Glasgow and its surrounding district, it is not surprising that the bleachfields and dyeworks set up by the linen trade proved also to be a major convenience to the emerging cotton trade. From an early stage, cotton tended to produce quite large factory complexes. This is not to say that the cotton industry was entirely concentrated in such factories. On the contrary, it had a substantial domestic component even on the spinning side. Arkwright's water frame, which was the basic machine used in some of the earliest spinning mills, span a strong yarn suitable for warps, which due to their length need to be capable of standing stress during the weaving process. Wefts were finer and often produced on jennies, which could be domestic machines. The mule failed to sweep away jennies and water frames partly because it was dependent on them for rovings or cotton prepared for finer spinning. It was as late as 1830 that a wholly satisfactory wholly power-operated mule came on the market and at the Committee on Manufactures, Commerce and Shipping (a government body) in 1833 Kirkham Finlay, one of the outstanding Glasgow businessmen of his day, said that the self-acting mule was just coming into use in Scotland. Hand-loom weavers were, of course, very numerous indeed in the cotton industry. Mechanisation using water power was very difficult to apply to the much more delicate and complex process of weaving. The flying shuttle, which became common in Scotland after 1770, doubled a weaver's output but even so mechanisation produced such an abundance of cheap yarns that weaving became a bottleneck in the production process and therefore well paid.

Around 1795 it was estimated that there were 39,000 cotton handloom weavers, nearly all full-time workers, supported by at least 13,000 women and girls in their families who helped them with the complex process of dressing the loom or setting it up for the weaving process. Weaving was a comparatively easy trade to master, even in its finer variations, and after 1800 the spread of the Jacquard loom in linen weaving actually introduced a very precocious form of automatic programming into certain kinds of fine weaving. Between 1785 and 1800 cotton weavers earned from 30s. to 40s. per week for a four to five day week, and lived comfortably. By 1838 when the Assistant Handloom Commissioners made their enquiries there were 51,060 looms in the Lowlands and with the exception of 2,400 linen and woollen looms they were all cotton looms, 90 per cent of them being in the employ of Glasgow or Paisley manufacturers. By this time, however, handloom weavers had indeed fallen on evil days. Their wages ranged from 4s. to 8s. a week. Partly this was because of an excessive influx of labour into the trade, which was bound to depress wages. Partly it was due to the catastrophic failure of a premature strike in 1812, by means of which the weavers had hoped to enforce regulations restricting access to the trade and also enforcing a minimum scale of prices for cloth. It was also partly due to the gradual introduction of power weaving. Tolerably efficient power-driven looms had been developed in England by 1807. By 1813 there were 1,500 of them at work in Scotland. In 1820 the figure was 2,000. By 1829 it was 10,000 most of which were working on calicoes (white cottons) and fustians in and around Glasgow. In 1831 there were 15,127 belonging to Glasgow firms and by 1845 that figure had risen to 17,620, representing 79 per cent of all such looms in Scotland.

Obviously, the latter figure reflected the impact of steam power, for one result of a widespread adoption of the steam engine as the main prime-mover was a strengthening of the tendency for manufacturing industry to concentrate in the larger towns. However, the cotton industry had developed substantial concentrations of fixed investment long before steam was its main source of power. In 1812 Sir John Sinclair estimated that the industry employed 151,300 people (many in their own homes), produced goods worth £6.2 million, and included 120 spinning mills which alone were worth £1.4 million. By 1840 or so there were some 190 mills but the adult labour force was much lower at just over 100,000 altogether in spinning and weaving. Partnerships were the normal form of enterprise in cotton spinning. During the boom years 1788–92 landowners and farmers undoubtedly participated in fair numbers in the setting up of cotton mills, though often the role of the great landowner was that of a sleeping partner willing to lease land and water rights to the company. The Earl of Bute simply leased land for the Rothesay mills. The Duke of Atholl's relationship with the Stanley Mill was no more dynamic in reality. Lord Justice-Clerk Braxfield, who feued the site of the New Lanark Mills to David Dale, was a laird and lawyer, never an active businessman interested in manufacturing. On the other hand, lairds who came from existing or recent merchant backgrounds tended to be more directly involved in the enterprise. Examples here include Claud Alexander who co-operated with David Dale at Catrine; William McDowall of Garthland who worked with George Houston and Robert Burns at Lochwinnoch; Robert Dunmore of Ballikinrain with the Buchanan brothers at Balfron, and many others. Active merchants, and especially West Indian merchants were very prominent in partnerships formed to build and run cotton mills. Thus James Finlay and Company, the largest cotton firm in Scotland after 1801, was supported by several West Indian firms who held substantial amounts of the company's shares. Robert Owen, the son-in-law and successor of David Dale at New Lanark, had West India merchants as his principal partners between 1810 and 1824. Perhaps the most valuable service such merchants performed for the cotton industry was to provide it with cordial contacts with the Scottish banks.

Precise statistics of the cotton industry are lacking. Often only indirect evidence or estimates are available. Thus it has been estimated that the capital invested in the industry may have expanded from an aggregate of some £650,000 in 1790 to not far short of £4.5 million by 1840. By the latter date the period of most rapid growth was over. Between 1775 and 1812 imports of raw cotton into the Clyde went up from 137,160 lb. to 11,114,640 lb. By 1820 the United States of America were much the most important single source of this raw material, and the Scottish industry was beginning to face competition from cotton industries in several European countries. Indeed in his *Report To The County Of Lanark* of 1821 Robert Owen regarded it as a commonplace 'that under the present system no more hands can be employed advantageously in agriculture or manufactures; and that both interests are on the eve of bankruptcy'. In fact what was happening was that the vulnerability of the new industry to cyclical slumps was being demonstrated. Its growth continued, even though after the 1820s the tendency of the cotton industry to expand outside its original western stronghold ceased. Inevitably manufacturers squealed as profit margins were squeezed. In such lines as water-powered spinning in the late eighteenth century they had clearly been abnormally high. What was most important, in the long run, about a development which was originally more concentrated around Paisley than Glasgow and which after 1825 was again largely concentrated around the Paisley–Glasgow area, was the leap in the scale of industrial organisation and concentration which it brought. That was the true significance of the giant water wheels of Catrine or the mills, tenements, and educational institute of New Lanark.

To talk about an industrial 'take-off' in the Scotland of the 1780s is thus to generalise from the experience of one rather regional industry, albeit a big one. The linen industry showed a pattern of much more gradual growth, but it did continue to grow despite the fact that cotton grew largely at the expense of the fine linen manufacture of Lanarkshire, Renfrewshire, and Ayrshire. The mechanisation of even the spinning side of the linen trade was a slow business because there is a gum in flax fibres which made them difficult to adapt to mechanical spinning. Hand spinners could moisten their flax continuously and stop to sort out tangles. Machines tended to jam or to break the fibre. Eventually John Kay of Lancashire solved the problem by inventing wet spinning in 1825, but before that date there was already a great deal of mechanical spinning in the eastern linen area of Scotland. After the pioneering experiments in water-powered spinning at Brigton in Angus and at Inverbervie in Kincardineshire, many meal mills were converted for spinning linen yarn. The main demand was for coarse linens for sacking, sails, tarpaulins and cloths, waggon covers and tents. If cotton was a cheaper substitute for fustians, silks, and Indian fabrics, and was geared to expanding individual consumer demand at home and abroad; coarse linens were closely linked to the expansion of international trade. The very coarseness of the goods being made in eastern Scotland, always excepting Dunfermline, facilitated such mechanisation as was possible. There was a Boulton and Watt 'sun and planet' type engine of 20 horse power operating in a Dundee spinning mill in 1799. By 1847 the 36 spinning mills in Dundee disposed of steam power to the amount of 1,242 horse power to drive 71,670 spindles. There was a great surge in the rate of installation of steam engines in the early 1820s and though it was quite common for small engines to be installed in rural mills, there is no doubt that the steam engine hastened the doom of rural industry.

There were two principal reasons for this. First, the steam engine freed towns from the limitations imposed by their natural endowment with potential water-power sites. There were many such good sites in and around Perth, but Dundee was a notably waterless town which needed another prime-mover before it could develop and exploit industrial units big enough to enjoy substantial economies of scale. Secondly, in areas which did not contain active coalfields coal was not usually difficult to obtain, nor particularly dear provided the consumer was sited in a significant port. On the other hand, due to the costs of landward carriage, the price of coal was much higher inland. Curiously enough, although James Watt, a Glasgow instrument mechanic working in Glasgow university, made a decisive contribution to the development of the steam engine, the main result of his career, at least until his patents expired in 1800, was to tie the most progressive of Scottish manufacturers to a Birmingham works for the supply of their engines. Working on a defective model of a Newcomen engine (widely used in English collieries) in 1763–4, Watt seems to have grasped that its efficiency could be massively enhanced by building a separate condenser. Years of experiment ensued, with encouragement from his old employer, Professor Joseph Black. Black at one stage introduced Watt to the English industrialist John Roebuck who needed more efficient pumps for his coalmines near Bo'ness and was willing to finance Watt's experiments. However, in 1773 Roebuck went bankrupt, like many industrial pioneers, and Watt migrated south into eventual partnership with the Birmingham industrialist Matthew Boulton, of the Soho works. A series of further improvements such as rotary motion and a steam throttle operated by a centrifugal governor made Boulton and Watt engines incomparably more efficient than their clumsy rivals and the despatch of small numbers of Boulton and Watt engines to Scottish textile mills in the 1780s and 1790s was highly significant. Perhaps more significant was the way in which Scotland rapidly became capable of producing the most efficient modern steam engines after 1800. The foundries of Glasgow and its surrounding region virtually all produced engines, but so did engineering works in all major Scottish cities. In Arbroath, for example, the Boulton and Watt engine in the Brothock linen works was soon matched by an engine from Carmichael of Dundee.

As with the cotton industry, we lack precise statistics for the growth of the linen trade in Scotland. We do know that around 1820 total annual imports of flax and hemp into Scotland were of the order of 300,000 cwt. and that by 1850 Dundee, the biggest single importer, was importing about 500,000 cwt. annually. It is undoubtedly true that technical problems in applying steam power to linen weaving were one of the factors which ensured that the expansion of the industry in the early nineteenth century lacked the explosive quality characteristic of cotton. In 1821 an attempt to weave linen by machinery was made in Kirkcaldy. History is silent as to what happened, probably with good reason. In 1824–5 a new attempt was made by the London speculator and banker John Maberley, who had bought the Broadford linen factory in Aberdeen in 1811. Maberley installed, with success, 200 power looms in his Aberdeen factory, becoming in the process an acknowledged expert on mechanisation in the linen trade, consulted as such by the government in 1825. By 1832 he was bankrupt, though he had sold off his factories before the final crash. In Dundee in 1833 it could be said that power looms were just not worth the trouble of working them, and it was only in 1836 that Baxter Brothers and Company of Dundee finally built and operated the first powerloom factory in the town. Baxters had abandoned an earlier experiment with power weaving in 1828. Like cotton, linen was subject to cyclical slumps, complicated by a reliance on the Baltic for raw material which led to industrial disruption as the result of war in the first decade of the nineteenth century. The 1825 slump produced staggeringly high mortality amongst linen firms, and the early 1840s were not notably prosperous. To find bursts of sustained growth and investment comparable to those of the cotton industry in the 1780s we have to look to the 1850s and 1860s in the linen areas.

The Scottish woollen industry has its own distinctive history in the period between 1780 and 1840, though it resembles cotton and linen in that the foundations of the modern industry were laid in this period through a combination of mechanisation and relocation, or rather shifting of regional emphasis. Production in such old strongholds of the Scottish woollen trade as Stirling, Haddington and Musselburgh fell away to nothing. Only Aberdeen retained its reputation as the capital of a regional woollen industry and a big exporter of woollens, especially hosiery. The bias of the Aberdeen industry remained very much in favour of the finer end of the trade and in 1814 the Board of Trustees, which bestowed attention on wool as well as linen, claimed that very fine woollen cloth was made in Aberdeen 'equal in quality to any of the kind manufactured in Britain'. By about this time over 7,000 hands were said to be employed in the hosiery and fine woollen cloth industry in and around Aberdeen. The most striking example of expansion and vigour in the Scottish woollen industry in this period lay at the opposite end of Scotland in the Borders and more particularly in the small towns in the valley of the Tweed and its tributaries. The explanation for this phenomenon is complex. Partly it was due to abundant native supplies of wool on neighbouring pastures; supplies which improved in quality as Cheviot sheep, with finer wool, tended to replace Blackface sheep, at least on lower pastures. Then the area had abundant water supplies for power, scouring, and dyeing. Its labour force was not large but re-organisation of agriculture with consolidation of farms did lead to a steady drift to the towns. At the same time other developments made it possible to achieve higher productivity in the woollen manufacture with a given set of resources. The decline of the linen industry around Melrose released workers and looms for wool. More important was investment in power-driven teasing, carding, and spinning machinery which survived the transition from water to steam in reasonable competitive shape, despite the remoteness of coalmines and the poor quality of local roads. The key to the vitality of Border woollens was market opportunity. Yorkshire woollens, the main rival, tended to be fine and relatively expensive, leaving a real gap in the area of coarser woollens; a gap which the Scottish Borders filled.

The Border woollen industry then grew and adapted, mainly in the light of developments in Yorkshire, but always achieving the essential aim of cutting unit costs. Its capital requirements were comparatively modest and could usually be met within the industry by the dyer-fullers who controlled the network of production and sales which lay on either side of their own central function. Around 1829 the industry was clearly approaching a turning point which was marked by a large number of bankruptcies. Fashion was changing. Demand was for a lighter, more colourful product which would involve importing finer wool. Foreign wool for flannel manufacture was used in Hawick for the first time as late as 1826 and a few Galashiels firms were following suit, though consumption of imported wool in Galashiels in the 1820s was only about 5 per cent of total consumption. To the enduring benefit of the industry, the period after 1830 was marked by the successful transition to fine tweeds as its staple and very fashionable product. As with linen, power weaving came late, in this case around 1850, due to technical snags. Here is a history of steady change. If there is 'take-off' it is after 1830.

In many ways the history of the Scottish chemical industries in this period is closely linked to the history of Scottish textiles. The oldest of Scottish chemical manufactures was that of salt. It was very much an offshoot of coalmining but between 1780 and 1840 it was virtually wiped out. English capital did try to enter the trade in the late eighteenth century when Dr Francis Swediaut established Port Seton salt works near Prestonpans in East Lothian in 1784, investing over £1,500 before he was bankrupted by a dispute with his mason. Like the collier, the salter was emancipated after 1779 and this was followed by a substantial increase in production. Between 1787 and 1792 the output of salt at Prestonpans and neighbourhood alone increased to about 84,000 bushels per annum. The repeal of the salt duty effectively in 1825 was followed by an invasion of Scotland by cheaper English salt produced from rock-salt deposits and brine springs. This competition gradually destroyed first many of the smaller Scottish salt pans and then from the 1830s most of the bigger ones including old works like that established by Robert Cunninghame at Saltcoats in Ayrshire in 1686.

In an economy which needed a steadily-increasing labour force, such a decline in an old industry was no disaster. It freed resources and men for more profitable work for which Scotland was better-endowed. Fortunately one such field lay in the production of chemicals for the textile industry and especially for its vital bleaching stage. Originally bleaching was effected entirely by organic substances. First a mild alkali was needed, and this would be an extract of wood ash or kelp (seaweed ashes). Next an acid was required; until 1750 usually sour milk. The alkali removed oil and dirt while the acid removed earthy stains which prevented even dyeing. By the 1740s, however, sulphuric acid was being imported from Holland, and in 1749 the first Scottish chemical factory of a modern kind was set up at Prestonpans by the partnership of John Roebuck and Samuel Garbett, in order to manufacture vitriol or sulphuric acid. The land on which the works was built was owned by William Cadell and in 1784 this was the largest acid works in Britain, with a big export trade to the Continent. Interestingly, by the 1790s the principal partner in the Prestonpans Vitriol Company was Henry Glassford of Dougalston, heir to the fortune established by John Glassford, one of the biggest of the Glasgow tobacco merchants. The great advantage of sulphuric acid lay in its speed of action. What required five days with sour milk could be achieved in five hours with vitriol. In addition chemical bleaching eliminated the need to lay out cloth, releasing significant stretches of grassland.

One reason why Scotland was so forward in matters chemical was undoubtedly its admirable tradition of medical education. A medical degree was the only university qualification likely to contain a significant element of chemical education, and Scots medicals had the happy habit of studying on the Continent, and more particularly in the United Netherlands, after taking courses at their native institutions. Thus the university of Leiden, where many Scots studied and taught, was one of several Dutch institutions through which the advanced science of the period reached Scotland, and was there further developed. Thus Professor Francis Home, of the chair of *materia medica* in the University of Edinburgh did research for the Board of Trustees on bleaching, as did Professors William Cullen and Joseph Black of the University of Glasgow. How far Home's work in demonstrating the efficiency of sulphuric acid as a bleaching agent may be regarded as a cause of the 'chemical revolution' in Scotland may be debated. Vitriol was already being imported from Holland and England. On the other hand John Roebuck, though an Englishman, had studied chemistry at Edinburgh and Leiden, and there is no doubt that the situation in Scotland was very favourable for the rapid spread of chemical bleaching. Its virtues were rapidly recognised and there was no shortage of men with enough chemical knowledge to set up and run chemical works.

At a time when links with textile-finishing were strong, Glasgow was a natural focus for chemical manufacture and by the 1820s the Port Dundas area of the city had six or seven works producing sulphuric acid. However, vitriol was by no means the only inorganic bleaching agent in use by 1800. Chlorine had been discovered by the Swedish chemist Scheele in 1776 and in 1787 Professor Patrick Copeland of Marischal College Aberdeen and the Duke of Gordon were shown in the course of a Continental tour, by Professor de Saussure of Geneva, how chlorine could be used as a bleaching agent. Copeland demonstrated this to Aberdeen textile manufacturers on his return, with the result that by July 1787 chlorine bleaching was in use in the works of Gordon, Barron and Company, a cotton company. In gaseous or liquor form chlorine was difficult to handle, so it was a significant moment when in 1799 Charles Tennant patented the production of a dry bleaching powder (actually invented by Charles Macintosh). This powder was the basis of the early growth of the St Rollox Chemical Works in Springburn, Glasgow. In 1798 Tennant established the works. In 1799–1800 it produced 52 tons of bleaching powder. In 1825 the figure was 9,251 tons. One by-product of bleaching powder production was sodium sulphate, a substance usable in the production of industrial alkali vital for not only bleaching, but also the production of soap and glass. With the removal of a crippling excise of £30 per ton in 1815 the use of sodium sulphate for alkali production vastly increased, thereby sealing the doom of the Highland kelp industry, whose high costs had already greatly stimulated chemical alkali production. St Rollox was in the 1830s and 1840s reputedly the biggest chemical works in the world, making bleaching powder, soda, soap and a range of sulphites and sulphates. In 18l41–2 the firm advertised its greatness by building 'Tennant's Stalk', a chimney 455½ feet tall. It was, sadly, demolished in 1922 but it ranks with similar symptoms of lum-mania like 'Cox's Stack' in Dundee, which still proudly lances the skyline as a remainder of slightly later prosperity.

Individuals could do very well for themselves if they had the knowledge and capital to invest in Scottish chemical manufacture in the late eighteenth century. James Hutton (1726–97) was an Edinburgh man who studied medicine at Edinburgh, Paris, and Leiden. He is best known as the father of the modern conception of the theory of the Earth. Yet this great geologist owed his fruitful and learned leisure to a partnership in a chemical works producing industrial alkali in the shape of sal ammoniac. As the pace of technical change sharpened, the lifespan of any given industrial chemical process was liable to shorten. Thus the Leblanc process for soda manufacture (invented in 1787) reached Scotland only in 1818 when St Rollox started to use it. By 1830 St Rollox was producing 10,000 tons of alkali a year by the process, which was in use in four other Glasgow alkali works. Yet by 1870 the process was obsolete in the face of competition from the Solway process, already at work in England. Nevertheless, chemicals in the period 1780–1840 derived a capacity for steady expansion from their close association with textiles.

The production of mordants and dyestuffs is the last striking example of this. Mordants were essential to help fix the colours in dyeing. The principal mordants were alum and copperas (ferrous sulphate). A Liverpool firm had started the first Scottish copperas plant at Hurlet near Paisley in 1753. The plant was still flourishing under the Lightbody family in the 1790s, and a relative by marriage established the Bo'ness Copperas works around 1808. Another copperas works was established in 1807 at Househill near Hurlet by Charles Macintosh, Tennant's partner at St Rollox and a very great chemical entrepreneur in his own right. Macintosh exploited the local aluminous shales which formed ferrous sulphate and aluminium sulphate when heated. Then, when the copperas had been extracted alum crystals could be produced by adding potassium sulphate to the residue. A huge expansion in demand helped make Macintosh's Hurlet works the biggest in Britain and justified him in starting another plant at Lennoxtown which by 1835 was producing 2,000 tons of alum each year. Macintosh was also active in manufacturing other mordants such as acetates and chromates. In 1786 he introduced into Scotland Dutch techniques for producing lead acetate or sugar of lead. After 1793 he also made iron and aluminium acetate. The processes required a substantial supply of acetic acid (originally in the shape of sour beer) which was produced from malt and barley or by the destructive distillation of wood. The latter process gave pyroligneous acid plus many other products.

Altogether, it was a prodigious record of innovation, but Charles Macintosh did have the enormous advantage of being born into the chemical industry as the son of George Macintosh. The latter was the fourth son of a Highland tacksman. George Macintosh made his way into the tannery business in Glasgow before he seized an opportunity to provide decisive financial backing for the manufacture of cudbear. This curiously-named product was a vegetable dye extracted from a seaside lichen by a process including the maceration of the lichen in ammonia. Cuthbert Gordon (the eponymous inventor of cudbear), his uncle, and the Alexander brothers of Edinburgh had been trying, with inadequate resources, to manufacture cudbear in Leith. George Macintosh organised a wealthy Glasgow co-partner to back the venture, and in 1777 moved the factory from Leith to a site on the eastern side of Glasgow where behind a ten foot wall he built himself a mansion called Dunchattan and a chemical works where a largely Highland and predominantly Gaelic-speaking workforce was an essential part of his security precautions. Cudbear could only be applied to silk or wool. The art of producing the much-prized adrianople or turkey red colour in cotton goods was the next challenge which George Macintosh tackled, in this case with the assistance of a French dyer Monsieur Papillon. In 1785 Macintosh, in conjunction with his friend the textile manufacturer and banker David Dale, opened at Barrowfield the first works in Britain capable of producing the turkey red dye. Known locally as 'Dale's Red' the dye had a long and successful run. The Barrowfield works were sold in 1805 to Henry Monteith of Carstairs under whom it maintained its high reputation in the world of calico printing. The only other dyestuff made in Scotland on any scale was Prussian blue, first made in Edinburgh in

1785 by an English company, and later one of the substances manufactured by Charles Macintosh.

Dyestuffs were manufactured elsewhere in Scotland; under the aegis of the Pullar family in Perth, for example, but Glasgow remained the main centre of chemical activity. This was even true of such relatively widespread enterprises as the distillation of coal for tar. The pioneer here was Archibald Cochrane, Lord Dundonald, who erected tar kilns at Culross on the northern shore of the Forth in 1781. Heavy tar protected ships and roofs; a lighter tar was used to varnish ropes; and ammonia liquor and coke were by-products. Coal gas was another and Dundonald demonstrated its potential as an illuminant before his personal foibles led to bankruptcy. By the 1790s the Muirkirk Iron Company was lighting its workshops with gas and in the early nineteenth century Glasgow and Edinburgh had gas lighting before Manchester, Liverpool, or Dublin. By the 1820s and 1830s relatively remote places in Scotland were being lit by gas. At first the tar and ammonia produced by gas works went to waste. Then the Glasgow Gas Company, whose first superintendant was J. B. Neilson (the inventor of hot-blast for iron furnaces), started selling its by-products to Charles Macintosh. The latter used the ammonia in cudbear manufacture and distilled the tar to produce pitch. In producing pitch Macintosh also produced coaltar naphtha which was a solvent of india rubber and the basis of the water-proofing process which added the word macintosh to the English language. Altogether, the swift rise of the Scottish chemical industry between 1780 and 1840 underlined the way in which the industrialisation of the country was being effected primarily by a closely-connected, textile-centred group of industries.

The Scottish iron industry did not display a dynamism comparable to that of cotton or chemicals in the late eighteenth century, though it did expand substantially between 1780 and 1805. Thereafter stagnation set in and persisted until the middle of the 1820s. The foundation of Carron Company in 1759 was related to the stimulus provided by the ongoing Seven Years War, and it is certainly true that there was a long pause before the foundation of the second significant Scottish ironworks at Wilsontown (1779–81), during the American War of Independence. Four other Lanarkshire ironworks were founded by 1801: Clyde (1786), Omoa or Cleland (1787), Calder (1800), and Shotts (1801). In Ayrshire works were established at Muirkirk (1787) and Glenbuck (1795), while Clackmannan had the Devon ironworks (1792), and Fife the Balgonie or

Markinch works (1801). Significantly four of these later works were established during the Revolutionary and Napoleonic Wars which broke out in 1793. It is nevertheless clear that normal market forces are the key to this pattern of intermittent development and stagnation. The use of Baltic bar-iron had a long history in Scotland, and the furnaces set up before 1755 in the Highlands to take advantage of Highland timber resources never seriously threatened to replace imported bar-iron by pig-iron produced from cheap Highland charcoal and imported English ore. On the contrary, Scottish demand for pig remained so low that the Highland furnaces had to sell to England, incurring in reverse the high transport costs they had to face for their ore. Apart from Furnace and Bonawe these Highland establishments had a brief history. Heavy capitalisation and advanced organisation enabled Carron Company to survive on the basis of the coke-smelting technique which was the answer to rising charcoal costs. Carron specialised in fine casting and in the famous carronade, a short quick-firing gun of limited range but substantial calibre which was primarily designed for mounting in merchant shipping. A privateer had to come in close for his prey, and like all predators simply could not afford to be severely mauled for the sake of one kill. Though Carron did supply Scottish markets, it always sold much of its output outside Scotland.

The new ironworks which were founded after 1778 reflected more favourable conditions. There was a great expansion in the demand for iron goods within Scotland as the result of industrial growth, urban development, and agricultural change. Nails, pots and pans, ploughs and harrows were only a few of a myriad of iron goods which could be sold to a rising domestic, and profitable foreign market. Their sheer variety made it possible for comparatively small ironworks and independent craftsmen to dominate the trade. Extensive mineral prospecting revealed several fortunate conjunctions of fuel and raw material. Technical improvements such as steam blowing engines and new ways of converting pig-iron into bar-iron helped to make sites previously deemed impractical a feasible proposition for iron working. At the same time, it is clear that many of the new ironworks suffered from chronic under-capitalisation. Credit was extended by banks to a couple of them on a long-term basis and like the linen merchants the iron founders expected the merchant to whom they consigned their shipment of goods to issue a bill of exchange on delivery and in advance of retail sales. It is still clear that many iron firms went bankrupt in the period before 1830 because they could not secure sufficient capital resources to cope with routine difficulties, and this shortage of capital, with the inevitable consequent stagnation in capacity which marked the 1820s, reflected the limited potential for profitable expansion which was characteristic of the industry. Indeed, it is possible to argue that only transport charges protected Scottish iron producers from irresistible competition from Welsh iron, which was cheaper. English and Scottish iron seem to have been roughly competitive in price with one another.

The crucial breakthrough to cheaper Scots pig-iron required the combination of two discoveries. One was made comparatively early when David Mushet, co-founder of the Calder ironworks with William Dixon, owner of the Govan Colliery, discovered black-band ironstone. Scotland possessed massive reserves of this particular ore. The parish of Old Monkland, for example, contained a great deal of it. At first it was only used at the Calder Works and then only when mixed with richer ores. Not until 1825 did the Monkland Company use it alone with only the addition of limestone flux. It was, however, the combination of black-band ironstone with James Beaumont Neilson's invention of hot blast which massively reduced the costs, particularly the hitherto high fuel costs of Scottish iron. Neilson had been an enginewright at a colliery at Govan, but it was as manager of the Glasgow Gas Company—a post he held from 1817 to 1847—that he conducted the experiments which led to his taking out a patent in October 1828 for the pre-heating of furnace blast. There was still a major technical problem in that the hot blast tended to melt the tuyere or orifice through which it penetrated into the blast furnace. Only in 1834 did the manager of the Blair Iron Works patent a water-cooled tuyere which solved this problem.

Even before this it was clear that the heated blast was astonishingly more efficient than the cold. The first works where hot blast was applied was the Clyde Iron Works where the proprietor, Colin Dunlop, had a stake in Neilson's patent. By heating the furnace blast before entry to 300 degrees Fahrenheit the amount of coal needed to produce a ton of iron was reduced by two and a half tons. In 1831 when Dixon, the owner of the Calder Works, suggested substituting raw coal for the coke in the blast furnace and heating the blast to 600 degrees, the result was a tripling in the amount of iron which could be produced for a given quantity of coal. In a sense the new era in Scottish iron started with the founding of the Gartsherrie Works by William Baird in 1828. Yet while hot blast remained experimental there was a lull and it was not really until after 1835 that there was a boom in the Scottish iron trade. That boom and its repercussions were so fundamental to Scottish economic development in the period 1835 to 1870 that they are best treated as the basis of the next era of development. Between 1780 and 1835 iron made a modest contribution to overall growth.

The Scottish coal industry had a rather curious history in the decades after 1780. Coal prices rose steeply, to the extreme distress of consumers who sought about for culprits to blame for the problem. Steam power in the shape usually of Newcomen engines was essential for the deeper pits of the late eighteenth century and it was argued that the engines ate up profits. This is clearly nonsense for many pits could not have existed without their engines and provided they were run on a big enough scale to absorb overheads, steam power should have increased rather than lowered their profitability. On the other hand, wages in mines did undoubtedly rise sharply until about 1810. Between 1715 and 1785 rates of pay for hewers roughly doubled and then between 1785 and 1808 they more than doubled again. Much of this increase was due to shortage of labour in a very labour-intensive industry. The servile status of colliers undoubtedly made it difficult to increase the labour supply, thus placing the very unservile serfs in Scottish coalmines in a very strong bargaining position. Emancipation was embarked upon late and falteringly. By 1800 effective legislation to this end was a fact but it had comparatively little impact on wages for a couple of decades, when a flow of cheap Highland and above all Irish labour helped to solve the recruitment crisis and simultaneously strengthen the hand of the employer in wage negotiation. However, it would be wrong to blame all the increase in coal prices between 1780 and 1810 on labour costs. All prices rose within the British economy in the period 1792–1813. One price index shows an increase of over 100 per cent in domestic prices between 1792 and 1812–3.

What seems to lie behind the undoubted escalation in real coal prices in Scotland is a breakdown in balance between supply and demand. Demand was rising. Increasing population plus accelerating urbanisation meant that the urban market for coal for both domestic and industrial use was very buoyant. Edinburgh and Leith, for example, simply outgrew the scale of production possible in the Midlothian coalfield where many mines were run on very conservative lines, working difficult edge seams with female bearers and horse drainage. The deficiency was made up either by importing English coal, or, much more frequently, by importing coal from Fife and Clackmannan by ship across the Forth. This goes far to explain the precocious transport developments which marked several mining areas on the northern shore of the Forth. Waggonways on which horses could pull coal trucks were often used to link mines to tidewater. The idea that the Fordell waggonway was opened as early as 1752 is misguided. It did not exist in the early 1760s and most documented early waggonways in this area appear to have started in the second half of the 1760s. By 1791 Sir John Henderson of Fordell was spending £440 per annum on his wooden waggonway (the rails were relaid in iron only in the 1830s). The sixth and seventh Earls of Elgin created extensive waggonways to serve their coal, salt, and lime interests, all of which were geared to their own mineral harbour at Charlestown. In the late eighteenth century the seventh Earl of Wemyss built a waggonway connecting Wemyss mines with Methil harbour. About 1781–3 the Halbeath Collieries were connected with Inverkeithing by a timber track. In Clackmannan the Erskines of Mar opened the Alloa waggonway in 1768, extended it in 1771, and relaid it with iron plates over the wooden rails in 1785. The cost of the original track was about 10s. a yard or £880 per mile. Each horse could pull 4½ tons of coal in three waggons, and the increase in output and sales appears to have repaid the investment in the waggonway very rapidly. Interestingly, a waggonway linked the Devon Ironworks and its associated mines with Clackmannan Pier.

It seems that the domestic market was much the most important one for late eighteenth-century Scots coalmines. They did not fare well in competition with English collieries in foreign markets and until 1793 they were actually burdened with a coastwise duty on shipments to the northern parts of Scotland at a time when coal from northern English mines was not so burdened. Thus the stimulus of the Edinburgh–Leith market goes far to explain the Fife waggonways and coal harbours. In the western parts of Scotland several of the waggonways built in Ayrshire between 1770 and 1815 were designed to link landward collieries to ports like Irvine which, in addition to coastal shipments, sent coal in quantity to Ireland. In general, however, 25 miles was a long land carriage for Scots coal before 1820 and this alone helps to explain the rising prices in a city like Glasgow where coal nearly doubled in price between 1790 and 1799, rising from 5s. 10d. to 10s. 10d. a ton. It is not surprising that the Monkland Canal which was opened in 1790 was specifically designed to bring coal from the parishes of Old and New Monkland into Glasgow.

The ironworks of Scotland consumed formidable quantities of coal. It was said at the time, no doubt inaccurately, that one of the new iron-works of the post-1780 generation consumed as much coal as a city. In practice these works often followed the example of Carron and were run as vertically integrated enterprises with their own coalmines as part of the complex. Indeed in the case of establishments like the Muirkirk Ironworks the industrial establishment was set up in an extensive moor-land parish on the borders of Ayrshire and Lanarkshire, remote from urban, let alone industrial activity but endowed with minerals such as limestone, ironstone, and the vital 'Nine-foot' coal seam. The latter was abundant enough to supply both the ironworks and the British Tar Company. Transporting of coal was a short-haul businesss, nor can it be seriously argued that Muirkirk Ironworks helped to raise the price of coal in Glasgow. There was plenty of coal-consuming industry in places like Glasgow and Paisley by 1815. The steam engine was becoming ubi-quitous and all chemical works, dyeworks, and bleachfields tended to consume considerable quantities of coal.

Some indication of the growth of the Scottish coal industry between 1821 and 1828 may be derived from an examination of the figures for shipment of coal from Scottish ports. In that period shipments increased by 27.45 per cent, but it is clear that nearly all of this increase was destined for home consumption, for of the 454,999 tons of coal shipped from Scottish ports in 1828 only 34,760 tons were sent to for-eign markets. The fact seems to be that the Scottish coal industry was an essential adjunct to the general expansion of the Scottish economy in the late eighteenth and early nineteenth century, but it did not ade-quately reflect the general rate of expansion, let alone provide an inde-pendent stimulus for growth. Witness the way in which coal prices tended to rise at a rate in excess of the quite high general increase in prices. Only after 1830 can it be said that a series of bottlenecks ranging from the labour shortage, which was solved by an influx of cheap dis-placed labour; to the landward transport problem, which led to the creation of a network of essentially mineral railways in Lanarkshire and Ayrshire between 1830 and 1845, were broken. After that coal had a dynamic comparable to and of course intimately linked with iron in the Scottish economy of the high Victorian era.

Agricultural Developments

The way in which labour flows from rural to urban areas was an essential part of and precondition for the expanding labour-hungry economy of Scotland between 1780 and 1835 has already been demonstrated. It remains to see exactly what was happening in the rural areas themselves, and as there is a very sharp difference between the detailed experiences of the Highlands, and those of the Lowlands, it is best to deal with them separately. This is not to argue that such a division is wholly justified or wholly coherent. The Highlands themselves can be shown to contain very different regional patterns of development in this period. Many of the economic forces lying behind agricultural change were the same in the Highlands and the Lowlands. Wherever roughly comparable geology and topography can be found, similar responses to similar pressures can usually be identified. Nevertheless it does seem that there was such a dramatic difference between the dubious vitality and viability of Highland rural society and that of its Lowland counterpart at this time that separate treatment is justified. We start with the quantitatively more important Lowlands.

The Lowlands

It has already been argued that the Improvers of the period before 1780 were primarily important as setters of an example and founders of a tradition. They were living in a rural economy which was labour-intensive by modern standards. The social structure was an exploitative one, but exploitation was increasingly carried out through the mechanism of the market, and unless the market was buoyant there was, in the long run, little point in screwing up direct demands on tenants, who would simply be unable to meet them. On the other hand, it is clear that the nobles and lairds of Scotland were increasingly disposed to exact much higher rents from their tenants in order to meet their own vastly enhanced idea of what constituted a scale of expenditure consonant with their dignity. Their assimilation into the life-style of the much wealthier English aristocracy was very advanced by the late eighteenth century. The patronage machines which were an essential part of the quasi-autonomous satrapacy which the first and second Viscounts Melville ran in Scotland could only hasten this process by giving Scots access to many civil, military, naval and colonial positions. This was a great age of building in Scotland, much of it of a prestige nature. Country houses were built or rebuilt in a range of styles, at first predominantly classical in a tradition which culminated in such princely structures as Hopetoun House, West Lothian, the product of two generations of work by the brilliant Adam family. Later came the cult of the picturesque early exemplified in Roger Morris's design for Inverary Castle, the seat of the Dukes of Argyll which was built between 1745 and 1761, and reaching its apogee in Robert Adam's castellated masterpieces at Mellerstain, Culzean, Oxenfoorde, Seton and Pitfour. There was plenty of prestige building in towns, notably in the New Town of Edinburgh whose general plan was laid down by James Craig in 1767. All this cost money much of which had to be extracted from tenant farmers.

Paradoxically, it seems to be the case that rent increases were possible on many estates long before any extensive changes in farming organisation or techniques. This was because the expansion of rural textile industries enabled tenants to meet enhanced rent demands from non-agricultural activities. There were, however, limits to the exploitation of this situation, if only because the rural industry was past its apogee by about 1780. Other possibilities allowing of higher rents with little basic change included increased commercialisation, such as distinguished the rise of the black cattle trade. However, as we have seen, that phenomenon hinged on specific market advantages for a couple of regions in a particular product. Sustained rent increases throughout the Lowlands could not be obtained without a willingness to invest on the part of the landlord and that in turn depended on a reasonable certainty of increasing prices for increasing quantities of produce. It was the absence of these favourable market conditions which had penalised so many early Improvers. Yet increasingly from 1770 onwards there was an uneven but persistent upward trend in agricultural prices. Partly this was due to general growth in demand for food and raw materials. Grain export died away. Grain imports became common. The Corn Laws whereby the British legislature discriminated against imports of grain had to be suspended annually throughout the 1760s and were revised in a liberal direction in 1773. When war broke out with Revolutionary France in 1793 it provoked more than two decades of government-sponsored inflation, with an inevitable upward trend in agricultural prices, a trend reinforced by the accelerating pace of industrialisation and urbanisation. Here was a context within which the ideas of the Improvers could be profitably applied on a large scale.

From about 1770 academic commentators like Adam Smith began to remark that enclosed land produced higher rents than unenclosed land, and though like all generalisations this one can be faulted in detail, it appears to correspond with the view of most contemporary landlords. They, after all, employed the surveyors who were essential to efficient reorganisation, and there were many more surveyors working in Scotland in 1780 than in 1715. The main forms of change may be summarised as:

(1)   enclosing, consolidating and enlarging farms;
(2)   abolition of co-tenancies and feudal servitudes to make way for individual leases;
(3)   reduction or elimination of cottagers;
(4)   adoption of a three-course rotation of crops with liming a regular procedure;
(5)   rebuilding of steadings, farmhouses and cottages;
(6)   increase and enlarging of country houses with expansion of policies;
(7)   reclamation of moor and bog; and
(8)   improvement of stock and implements.

Obviously no area experienced all these changes simultaneously. Both cartographically and in terms of systematic contemporary narrative accounts, the process of change is well-documented. We can therefore distinguish with some accuracy the differential impact of Improvement in different regions in the late eighteenth and early nineteenth centuries. In the van were counties like West Lothian where conditions were abnormally favourable to change. Thus it was owned by thirty or forty substantial landlords, was well-favoured country, and was near the big Edinburgh–Leith market. Even so about a sixth of the county was still unenclosed in 1805. The rest was dominated by big farms with a lot of specialised cattle farming aimed at the production of meat, hides and dairy products for the Edinburgh market. Elsewhere in the county mixed farming was the norm. The Glasgow market exerted the same stimulus to change as the Edinburgh market and Lanarkshire was noted for widespread planting of potatoes and turnips. There was a steady market for potatoes in Glasgow while turnips provided winter feed for cattle and sheep. A variety of crop rotations were in use in Lanarkshire and liming was very common. Along Clydeside orchards and dairy farms were clearly geared to the Glasgow market. Stirlingshire, two thirds of which was enclosed by 1805, reflected similar pressures with its large farms (some cattle farms were of the order of 1,000 acres) and extensive cultivation of potatoes for the Glasgow market. Ayrshire was often regarded as rather backward, and it is true that the upland parishes of its southern areas were quite unenclosed as late as 1793, with arable land scattered in small packets, but wherever it was profitable to Improve the Ayrshire plain, this process was marked from about 1760–70. Artificial grasslands had been pioneered on the Loudon estates in Ayrshire in about 1735 but it was not until 1760 or so that in conjunction with heavy liming such grasslands became common and capable of sustaining improved breeds of cattle. An illustration of the process and enforcement of change can be found in the career of a Mr Fairlie who had seen advanced farming in the Lothians and who became manager of the Eglinton estates around 1770. He introduced a new type of lease into Ayrshire whereby the tenant might not plough more than a third to a quarter of his land in any one year, and no land was to be cultivated for more than three years in succession. Combined with enclosure these leases effectively destroyed the 'infield-outfield' system and ensured rotation of crops.

It must be emphasised that agricultural change was an uneven and inherently limited exercise in this period. In the small county of Kinross, which is surrounded by hills and lies on the western boundary of Fife, enclosure had not progressed very far by the 1790s, nor had many aspects of Improvement commanded widespread support. The explanation seems to be that a very high percentage of Kinross farmers owned their own feus. Without a superior hounding them, they could and did adopt new methods selectively and at a pace consonant with their own limited resources. Turnips and sown grasses, for example, were just becoming normal in Kinross in the 1790s. The long-term result, it is sobering to reflect, was a pattern of husbandry in late-Victorian Kinross which was recognised as on a par with the most advanced agriculture of its day. Fife itself had a highly commercialised agriculture dominated by mixed farming but containing areas of specialisation such as extensive dairying, often carried on in association with breweries and distilleries for the sake of their spent grain refuse. Yet only a third or so of Fife was enclosed and run-rig was still to be found within its enclosed areas. The explanation here is quite simple: much of Fife was still moor, loch and bog, because drainage techniques were not sufficiently advanced to reclaim it. This fact is the key to much of the limitation on otherwise desirable change in Lowland Scotland in the late eighteenth and early nineteenth centuries. Cheap, efficient tile drainage was not available. Improvement could therefore often most profitably take the form of an intensification of pre-existing patterns. Thus in Angus the extensive estates of the Airlie family in the 1790s were innocent of that basic tool of Improvement, the lengthy and conditional lease. Rents were moderate. Customary security of tenure was high. Turnips were being grown on a large scale for winter feed for stock, and it does seem that this, combined with a more aggressive commercialisation of the business of buying in Highland cattle for fattening, ensured rising incomes from the cattle farming which had long been the principal source of cash for the agriculture of Strathmore.

This is not to deny that quite remarkable feats of land reclamation could be achieved, under exceptional circumstances, in late eighteenth century Scotland. Perhaps the most outstanding was the 'floating' away of several thousand acres of bog in the upper reaches of the Forth. These bogs had been a major feature of Scottish topography for centuries, making Stirling the key to a very narrow strip of land which linked the north and south of Scotland together. Prominent in this enterprise, as proprietor through marriage of the Blair Drummond estate, was that fine flower of the Scottish Enlightenment and Lord of Session, Lord Kames. Kames wrote on feudal law, history, trade, philosophy, drains, poetry and sub-soil. His land-reclamation hinged on the availability of running water into which the bog was systematically thrown by tenants who were granted very favourable leases. Obviously, this was a raised bog covering quite reasonable soil, and so placed that it could be floated into the Forth. Highlanders were imported in fair numbers as 'bog-tenants'. Even progressive agriculture in this period tended to be labour-intensive. In a region like Orkney extensive re-organisation of a run-rig and smallholding-dominated countryside came very late indeed. The owner of the earldom estate led the way in granting leases and enforcing detailed 'Regulations' which, among other points, enforced a rotation of crops. However, virtually no reorganisation occurred before 1815, and the series of processes known as 'plankings' (i.e. dividing the land into fields) only started in the 1830s. Nevertheless Orkney, apart from an active kelp trade, a significant provisioning trade for ships, and a large proportion of local manpower in the merchant marine, also developed a substantial agricultural surplus in the late eighteenth century. Between 1770 and 1790 exports of agricultural products from Orkney doubled in value. It is therefore not at all surprising to find that by 1830 there were still extensive areas in the Lowlands where what are often regarded as essential features of Improvement had simply not been adopted. In general, however, it is clear that nearly every Lowland region's agriculture experienced change between 1780 and 1840, ranging from an intensification of well-established trades, such as that in black cattle, to a total re-organisation. When the English journalist and politician William Cobbett (1763–1835) toured Scotland in 1832 and described the great farms of Berwickshire and the Lothians as outdoor factories producing corn and beef with the aid of landless labourers and steam power, he was describing one extreme in a range of responses to the stimulus of unprecedented market opportunities.

The fate of the Highlands

It is deeply instructive to compare the history of the rural economy of the Highlands with that of the Lowlands between 1780 and 1840 because they are both responding to roughly the same set of influences and the divergence between the experience of the two different areas can be used to cast a good deal of light on the fundamental limits of what was economically possible for each. First, then, it is necessary to look at the impact of Improvement on the Highlands. Impact there was bound to be, for the bulk of the Highland nobility and gentry were well-educated men who shared the polite culture of the Scotland of the Enlightenment. Above all they shared the unshakeable dislike of all articulate eighteenth-century Scots for any form of land tenure other than the individual tenancy held from a single and permanent landlord. The old semi-communal groupings of Highland farmers living in townships; clusters of houses, with their associated lands lying open with arable in alternate ridges, seemed an affront in an age of reason and industrialisation. From the 1770s the assault on run-rig began, though it must be recalled that reorganisation applied only to arable. The grazings remained common and at first quite unfenced.

Predictably, the Dukes of Argyll, chiefs of Clan Campbell and political magnates at Westminster, were the catalysts speeding change in the Highlands by introducing it early to their vast estates in the south-west parts. In 1776 the Duke of Argyll ordered that the farms of Tiree be consolidated. By 1800 most of the Campbell empire from mainland Argyll to the islands had been affected by this process. Where the Duke of Argyll went the second great Campbell chief, the Earl of Breadalbane, ever jealous of his paramount chief, was likely to follow and by the 1780s similar measures were being taken on the Breadalbane properties. One result of all this was an extension of systematic surveying from the Lowlands eventually into the far north of the much more difficult Highland terrain. Lochtayside, a Breadalbane territory, was duly surveyed and its farms consolidated, though the consolidation came as late as 1797. In 1800 Skye, the Long Island of Lewis and Harris, and most of Wester Ross were relatively unaffected. By 1820 run-rig had crumbled even there and the 30 years to 1850 saw the destruction of the pockets of run-rig which had survived the first wave of re-organisation throughout the Highlands. Inevitably, the deliberate destruction of subtenure, which was a central feature of landlord policy during this re-organisation, tended to diminish the numbers and reduce the power of the once influential class of tacksmen whose military functions were now superfluous and whose rents were deemed inadequate. By 1850 all land was let in working units (some still very small) and there was no room for the tacksman as a pure middleman in land. In the 1770s, at a crucial stage in the formation of policy on many Highland estates, tacksmen had been particularly unpopular because of their real or alleged connection with emigration to America. Black cattle prices experienced a secular decline at this period; there was dearth in some areas; arrears of rent were common, and Highland proprietors were anxious to keep population on their estates in the hope that hands would be available for kelp burning, fishing, and a re-organised agriculture. Proprietors were liable to blame tacksmen for either organising and financing emigration or alternatively for oppressing their subtenants and driving them thereby into emigrating. Many tacksmen survived in the Highlands of 1850, but not as tacksmen, rather did they become capitalist tenant farmers, often with a big stake in sheep-grazing.

Undoubtedly the most dramatic single development in Highland farming between 1760 and 1850 was the enormous increase in the importance of sheep. In 1760 cattle were the only bulk agricultural export from the Highlands. Less than a century later sheep and wool were leaving the Highlands on a scale which made them comparable in value to the flow of cattle, which had not diminished significantly in size. Sheep farming, however, usually involved large new-style farms, new varieties of stock from further south in the shape of Linton or Cheviot sheep, and often new men. Since both marketing and transport had to be organised for sheep, which did not have the drove roads or trysts of the black cattle trade, only large units carrying 2,000 sheep or more gave a big enough return to justify the investment and trouble. Where the existing arable was not already inadequate for the population, or where there was some prospect of urban and industrial development, the change to sheep farming did not necessarily involve heavy loss to the tenants. Thus the south-west of the Highlands, and particularly the mainland and island parts of the Campbell empire tended to pass through the transition without excessive trauma, at least before 1815. Elsewhere it was a very different story, for the new sheep could only have been absorbed in smaller units if the Highland farms had been extensively modernised before they came. In practice there was a fatal lag and the destruction of run-rig was too often the destruction of traditional Highland society for the benefit of sheep.

Yet there were reasons why run-rig was still so common in the Highlands in 1780 that the High Society defined a small farm in 1790 as one occupied by at least four tenants. In that year Mackenzie of Applecross referred to run-rig as 'Republican Farming' at a time when 'republican' was a dirty word. He was fair neither to Revolutionary France, nor to traditional Highland farming, neither of which were as incompatible with increased incomes for his own class as he seems to have imagined. It was possible to extract a much bigger marketable surplus from many parts of the Highlands by partial change within the framework of the traditional agriculture. The parish of Kenmore, around Loch Tay was still in the 1790s operating on the old basis of infield, outfield and common grazing. There were no leases. The minister, a man of progressive views, regarded the situation as stagnant. He was wrong. The hill grazing carried nearly 11,500 of the new black-faced sheep, as well as over 3,000 black cattle and many garrons or Highland ponies. A changed pattern of stock had increased the marketable surplus in an age of rising wool, mutton and beef prices. The adoption of potatoes in the infield had a similar effect, for they not only increased the yield of subsistence commodities, but also freed arable for cash crops like barley. In the nearby parish of Weem regional specialisation had been carried to the point of abolishing garrons from the common grazings in favour of black-faced sheep. Draught horses were imported from Argyllshire and the Lowlands when necessary.

Yet there were limits to what could be done within the traditional social framework, even in the more favoured parts of the Highlands and under the most conscientious and well-meaning of landlords such as the 5th Duke of Argyll. That nobleman inherited the Argyll estates in 1770 at their widest extent and ruled them through regional chamberlains or baillies. It was a time of increasing population on his lands. Between 1779 and 1792 there was a rise of 20 per cent in population over the whole estate. Some islands displayed even sharper population growth. Tirce had some 1,500 souls in 1750, nearly 2,000 by 1776, about 2,500 in 1792, 3,200 in 1808 and 4,453 by the official census of 1831. Yet the Duke of Argyll was hostile to emigration, reluctant to evict, and determined to stimulate industry and fishing on a sufficient scale to provide a living for more people. Especially around Inveraray, the clan capital, and Campbeltown, ambitious schemes were launched, but they went against the trend of the times, which was one of concentration of industry in Lowland centres. The upshot was an excessive reliance on the wartime boom in kelp prices. In 1770–1 Tirce paid a rent of £852 mainly from barley and whisky sales. By 1805–6 the island paid £2,606, largely out of kelp sales.

The Duke of Argyll's gross revenue from his Argyll lands rose in the thirty years after 1770 from £10,284 to around £25,000, but this was an age of inflation. His rent increases were moderate and his need for money great. Generous to a fault to his relatives and dependants, he had to keep up an expensive London establishment, as well as pay for very expensive developments at Inveraray, where the ducal house had moved the burgh from the neighbourhood of its new castle and recreated it as a neo-classical work of art a short distance away. To boot a disastrous fire required very costly rebuilding of the Duke's other seat at Rosneath in Dunbartonshire. The collapse of kelp prices after 1815 was inevitable, in the short run because of the inflow of cheaper but similar organic-based alkali from the Mediterranean, and in the longer run because of the rise of even cheaper industrial alkali from the chemical industry. Unfortunately, virtually all the other staple products of Highland agriculture experienced a similar collapse. Kelp prices fell from £20 per ton in 1810 to £3 in 1834. Black cattle prices in the mid 1820s were a mere half of what they had been in 1818. Freedom of passage along the old drove routes was increasingly challenged by the new proprietorial spirit in agriculture while freedom of grazing was restricted. With increasing centralisation of production, the value of yarn and cloth produced by scattered rural part-time workers fell steadily.

Arguably large parts of the Highlands were already only marginally viable in the 1770s. Thomas Pennant pointed out at that time that despite the widespread adoption of the potato, many Highland regions had to import meal in increasing quantities as their population grew. In poor years (with bad crops or low cattle prices) such communities came close to the very margin of survival. Something had to be done, and the tragedy of the Highlands is not so much that they were subjected to drastic change in the early nineteenth century but that that change failed to produce a stable and dignified human community. The best-documented of all the attempts to restructure the Highland economy is the extraordinary story of the Sutherland estates. Though well worth studying, it must be emphasised that they were atypical. George Granville Leveson-Gower (1758–1833), Lord Trentham, Earl Gower, and (in 1803) first Marquis of Stafford, was created first Duke of Sutherland in the year of his death as a belated salute to his marriage in 1785 to Elizabeth, Countess of Sutherland and Baroness of Strathnaver (1765–1838), only surviving child of William Gordon, seventeenth Earl of Sutherland. The Countess owned roughly two thirds of the County of Sutherland, a vast and remote estate of between 800,000 and a million acres. By her marriage this property was united with a vast landed and industrial fortune from the Midlands of England. It was rumoured that the Sutherland estates were in financial difficulty before 1785, but after that date they were actually extended by purchase from neighbouring lairds like Mackenzie of Assynt who was ruined by the fall in kelp prices, on which his rents were heavily dependent. After these purchases, many of which were in the 1820s, the Sutherland estate reached the staggering dimensions of 1¼ million acres. Between 1812 and 1815 the power of the Sutherland dynasty was mediated largely through their 'Metternich' or man of business *par excellence* James Loch, an Edinburgh lawyer, economist and estate manager. Through his mind the wealth of industrial England and the ideas of the Scottish Englightenment were brought to bear on Sutherland. Though aware of the need to make allowances for human nature and ingrained custom, Loch was more concerned with the need for improvement of and progress on the Highland properties.

As early as the 1830s Loch's record was fiercely denounced by the Swiss economist Sismondi, but it can be argued that Loch, a liberal rationalist and paternalistic planner in an age addicted to *laissez-faire*, was motivated throughout by high ideals. Basically he proposed to revitalise the Sutherland economy by turning the interior over to its optimal use in terms of revenue-producing activity—Cheviot sheep farming in large farms. Displaced tenants were not to be driven abroad. On the contrary they were to be resettled on the coast, some in new consolidated farms, some in industrial settlements such as Helmsdale. All were to have new cottages and new jobs such as arable farming, coal-mining at Brora, textile work, and above all herring fishing. The process of transition was known as the Sutherland clearances, and even at the time they caused a violent debate which has not stilled itself yet. For technical reasons, the more dramatic measures could not be taken much before 1806 and by 1809 the Countess of Sutherland was much under the influence of two Morayshire capitalists, William Young and Patrick Sellar. At first these men merely confirmed the optimism in the Sutherland dynasty about the potential for development in the coastal areas. After all, similar plans had worked in Moray. Later William Young became the estate factor and Sellar an extensive sheep farmer, clearing reluctant tenants from such areas as Strathnaver with a ruthlessness which has surrounded his name with obloquy. He and his colleagues pointed to the simple fact that, under the old system, there had been repeated dearths. Far better to move population to a life of industry and progress.

The damning comment on the whole enterprise was made by a local minister as early as 1818 and was underlined by the events of the 1840s: people still starved after passing through the traumas inflicted on them by Sutherland estate policy. Sutherland was not Morayshire. Expensive as the attempted rationalisation of the economy was, there was never enough capital to establish really viable coastal farms, let alone an adequately-equipped herring fishery in the face of stern competition from established North-East fishermen. Industry proved lame. Worst of all, the general collapse in prices extended to wool after 1820. In the decade 1820–30 wool prices were on average only half what they had been in the decade before 1820. The tragedy is that the house of Sutherland effectively subsidised its estates while making its principal northern seat, Dunrobin Castle, a symbol of tyranny.

Too much has probably been made of the case of the Sutherland estates. They were very unusual in their size and especially after 1816, when the system of financial control was tightened, the Scottish property was treated as part of an integrated complex of assets whose revenue-producing heart lay in England. The few surviving great traditional dynasties such as those of Sutherland, Breadalbane, and Argyll were themselves by 1850 exceptions in a Highlands where the turnover in the ownership of land was very rapid. The south and west of the Highlands had been deeply affected by economic change in the Lowlands and had tended to assimilate increasingly to the dynamic possessive individualism of the Lowland culture. Highland Perthshire suffered from depopulation in its side glens such as Glen Fincastle, but nearby towns such as Pitlochry grew while tourism, forestry, distilling, and railways all had a vigorous future ahead of them. In Argyll Campbeltown and Inveraray were joined by the new urban phenomenon of Oban, built on land belonging to the Duke of Argyll and Mr Campbell of Combie. Situated between the Caledonian and Crinnan Canals, it was hailed as 'the Charing Cross of the Hebrides'. On the western seaboard north of Fort William and in the islands north of Mull a very different society was developing with most of its population crowded on smallholdings known as crofts (though there was also a substantial landless or cottar population, especially in the islands). Inland, despite frequently drastic reorganisation, it had not proved possible to establish consistently profitable large-scale farming. The human population was excessively dependent on the potato. Rising expenditure and falling wool prices had already ruined many old landed families.

In short, in the north-west of the Highlands a precarious society was approaching the cataclysm of the Great Famine and the long-term spread of those remarkable treeless, wet man-produced deserts known as deer forests. The industrial revolution in the Lowlands created differential regional opportunities for rural Scotland, but for a very large part of the Gaelic-speaking Highlands those opportunities were probably negative. In other words the existing situation became intolerable, especially to landowners fully assimilated to the expectations of the British aristocracy, but no stable, profitable alternative order consonant with the human dignity of most Highlanders could be found. The bankrupt laird and the 'cleared' tenant became typical figures. Full assimilation with English industrial and commercial values, plus the suppression of violence, were deemed a blessing in the Lowlands. In the Highlands the story was very different, but *de facto* autonomy had been irredeemably thrown away by the folly of the 1745 rising, so no social or political buffer stood between the Gael and the irresistible market pressures which ravaged his society.

Communications

When in June 1816 James Loch penned a critique of William Young's policies as factor of the Sutherland estate in Scotland, he suggested that there was a need for an urgent shift in the direction of expenditure. In particular Loch felt that there should be less emphasis on expensive land policies, more on 'the great sinews of improvement' and more specifically on roads and bridges. Whatever one thinks of Loch's judgement in a Highland context, this does give one a good idea of the significance attached to improvements in communications by the intelligent and enlightened elite of early nineteenth-century Scotland. The grave analytical problem for a modern historian is the difficulty of separating cause and effect in this field. Improvements in transport were both a consequence and a cause of general economic development. Indeed, very often cause and effect are so intertwined that there is no point in even trying to distinguish them sharply from one another.

However, it can be held that, at least initially, extensive and permanent improvements in the communication network in Scotland could only occur after general economic activity had reached a certain level of intensity. Roads are the classic example. The statute labour system was notoriously ineffective. The alternative of turnpiking, with conversion of statute labour obligations into money payments, was dependent on the prospect of a sufficient volume of traffic to reimburse, directly or indirectly, the trustees of the turnpike for the money they sank into improving the road. Ayrshire is a good example of a county very heavily dependent on roads, for even its biggest rivers are too small, shallow and rapid to allow of navigation. In 1767 a turnpike trust for the county was established as a result of a petition by the Commissioners of Supply and Justices of the Peace of Ayrshire for an enabling act of parliament. Ayrshire's landowners taxed themselves to pay the cost of the necessary legislation. Once this was obtained, a trust was established and at its first meeting it considered a proposal for an eight-mile stretch of roadway between the industrial town of Kilmarnock and the port of Irvine. Responsibility for other roads was usually delegated to local committees, but the county trust kept a sharp eye on construction details and fees. When a proposed turnpike was to pass through several counties it was normal for negotiations to occur between the heritors or landed proprietors of the relevant counties. Thus in 1788 a proposal for a road from Glasgow to Dumfries and Carlisle involved consultation between the county authorities of Lanark, Ayrshire, and Dumfries, as well as with the Muirkirk Ironworks, which had an interest in a road from its works to Glasgow. Lairds tended to dominate the turnpike movement, partly for such simple reasons as their ownership of the relevant land and their control of county government. It is, however, clear that landowners expected to derive substantial benefit from improved communications, mainly in the form of enhanced land values and rents.

That there was an element of contagious optimism in the boom in turnpikes, especially after 1780, is not to be denied. Sir John Sinclair of Ulbster reckoned that turnpike roads cost on average some £5,300 per mile, and that in the 20 years before 1814 £2 to £3 million sterling had been invested in roads. Sinclair believed that over 3,000 miles of road had been built since 1750, most of it since 1780. Yet by 1821 the financial state of most Scottish turnpikes was deplorable, as an official report in that year underlined. Income was usually barely enough to cover upkeep and interest charges. It proved impossible in most cases to repay the large debts contracted when construction costs proved, as they always did, higher than those estimated. Of course, this does not mean that every participant in a turnpike trust lost money. In Aberdeenshire the Inverurie turnpike is one of the few known to have yielded a reasonable return on capital invested, but many turnpike trustees, indeed most of them, probably saw this particular investment as one of a bundle of investments which had to be taken together to assess overall gain or loss. Roads articulated the economic system. James Skene of Rubislaw, for example, was an Aberdeen businessman-laird who was also an Edinburgh lawyer. His investment in turnpike trusts in and around Aberdeen must be seen in the light of his calculations about the likely effect of new or improved roads on his land values and rents, and on the markets and prices for the stone from his big quarries. Rightly or wrongly, he must have reckoned the roads were worth their price.

Not all major investments in communications in Scotland in this period were an economic proposition, even in this indirect sense. The extreme example is provided by canal development. Geographically most of Scotland was wildly unsuitable for canals, but there had been a boom in canal construction in England in the 1760s and 1770s following the immense success of the Duke of Bridgewater's (mainly coal-carrying) canal from Worsley to Manchester, which had been opened in 1761, and it was very likely that the idea would catch on in Scotland. Indeed, the idea of linking the North Sea and the Atlantic by means of a canal across the narrow isthmus between the Firths of Forth and Clyde was so obvious that its history goes back to the seventeenth century and Daniel Defoe strongly advocated it in his *Tour* (1724–6). Its commencement was delayed by disputes between advocates of a route via

Loch Lomond; advocates of a ship canal from the Forth to a point on the Clyde north of Glasgow; and the Glasgow interest which would have preferred a barge canal to Glasgow. Eventually the Loch Lomond route was dismissed and a compromise proposal for a 7-foot waterway from Forth to Clyde, with a branch of similar depth to Glasgow, was accepted. Its construction was a lengthy business, plagued by financial crises. Work began in 1768. By 1775 the canal had reached from the Forth to Stockingfield, a place three miles from Glasgow. Here expenditure finally exceeded authorised capital and funds ran out. Glasgow merchants financed a branch to Glasgow which left them satisfied, with a route to the North Sea, but no Firth-to-Firth communication. It was at this point that John Knox, a Scot who made his fortune in England before becoming a publicist for economic development, especially fisheries, in Scotland, stepped into the scene. In a book published in 1783 he urged the completion of the Forth–Clyde Canal as well as the construction of two other canals. Both were eventually built for Knox recommended the canal from Inverness to Fort William eventually known as the Caledonian Canal, and the canal across the top of the Mull of Kintyre which was called the Crinan Canal when completed. In 1784 the British government advanced £50,000 to the Forth–Clyde project to restart work. Even so, it was 1790 before the first vessel actually passed from the Forth to the Clyde by canal. Thereafter modest prosperity set in greatly aided by the construction of two short connecting canals. The first of these was the 12-mile Monkland Canal linking the richest mineral area of Lanarkshire with Glasgow. The gestation of the Monkland Canal was almost as lengthy as that of the Forth–Clyde. Started in 1770, completed only in 1792, and paying no dividend before 1807, the Monkland Canal eventually proved very profitable. The other connection was a cut from Falkirk to Edinburgh which linked the nation's capital to its most valuable canal complex. By the second decade of the nineteenth century it was clear that the size of merchant ships had increased to the point of making the more ambitious hopes for the Forth–Clyde Canal anachronistic.

The other canals recommended by Knox proved much less defensible. The Caledonian Canal, passing down the Great Glen via a series of lochs was planned by Thomas Telford, greatest of Scots civil engineers, and approved by the state in 1802, with estimates of seven years and £350,000 for the building period and cost. In fact it had already cost over a million when it was opened in an unfinished state in 1822. In size it was fit only for fishing boats and its construction was of the poorest. In 1839 it was estimated that only 2½ per cent of the shipping rounding the northern mainland of Scotland was passing the canal. Justified originally partly on strategic grounds, it was virtually a complete waste of public money, so more was poured in to reconstruct it and it reopened in 1847, a white elephant in the age of steam. The Crinan Canal, which issued its prospectus in 1792 and obtained its enabling legislation in 1793, was heavily supported by the great Campbell peers such as the Duke of Argyll, his heir Lord Lorne, the Marquis of Breadalbane, and Lord John Campbell. It openly emphasised the indirect benefits of investment in the project, which it was hoped would link western seaboard estates and the Hebrides more directly with the Glasgow market. A manly emphasis on the virtues of self-help rapidly collapsed in the face of difficulties and soaring costs. Even though Rennie, the engineer, revised his original estimate of £63,628 to £107,512, and subscriptions raised £98,000, it proved essential to borrow £25,000 from the Barons of the Exchequer to open an unfinished and inadequate canal with a depth of only 10 feet in 1801. Thereafter it never paid its way and was transferred to the state by a complex process lasting from 1817 to 1848. The remaining Scottish canal was in Aberdeenshire. It ran eighteen miles from Aberdeen Harbour to Port Elphinstone which is just south of the burgh of Inverurie. Its aim appears to have been to lower the cost of importing fuel and manure, and thus assist agricultural improvements while facilitating the export of timber and stone. Opened in 1805, it was of the modest depth of 3 feet and only 17 feet wide. Bought by a railway company in 1845 it was converted into a railway line by 1854, ending an unexciting life with an unusual distinction. Other Scottish canal projects remained abortive, though the St Fergus and River Ugie Canal near Peterhead had a few miles of bed dug before it died. The final comment lies with the parish minister in the *Old Statistical Account* who discussed the much canvassed and surveyed Strathmore Canal. The divine pointed out that it was unlikely that the traffic revenue on a canal linking Perth to Strathmore would ever give a tolerable return on the sums needed to build the canal.

There is no comparison between the never-never world of most Scottish canals and the crucially important sphere of harbour improvement. This was a bottleneck which had to be broken if the industrial development of Scotland was not to be checked. Low overheads had been one of the outstanding characteristics of most of the expanding sectors of the Scottish economy in the earlier part of the eighteenth century. The facts that most parts of the Lowlands were relatively close to navigable water; that ships, especially coasting ships, were quite small; and that elaborate harbour works were not necessary to cope with the bulk of shipping using Scottish ports, all contributed to the dynamism of the eighteenth-century economy. By 1800, however, the improvement of at least the major Scottish harbours had become a necessity. Both the volume of trade and the size of merchant ships were increasing. Turnpike roads were economic for bulk commodities only for short and medium hauls. Water was still the only economic way of moving large weights long distances. Before 1755 only vessels of 20 to 30 tons could come up the Clyde as far as Glasgow. By the 1780s, as the result of an ingenious, simple, and relatively inexpensive engineering operation, nearly 7 feet of water enabled ships of up to 100 tons to reach Glasgow. Nevertheless, this excluded the larger ships trading to England and Ireland, let alone the trans-Atlantic vessels. These had to use the outports like Port Glasgow and Greenock. Between 1799 and 1807 two outstanding civil engineers, John Rennie and Thomas Telford, confirmed the wisdom of the established policy of restricting the Clyde by jetties, thus ensuring a deeper scour as the same volume of water forced its way through a smaller space. In 1809 a third River Improvement Act set up the Trustees of the Clyde Navigation and pursued the policy of turning the Clyde into a ship canal. By 1824 steam dredgers were at work and in 1828 700,000 tons of shipping used Glasgow harbour, two-thirds of this being coastal steam tonnage which was relatively unaffected by tide and current. By 1836 as the result of 60 years' work and an expenditure of £1.5 million, ships of up to 400 tons could reach Glasgow.

On the east coast the story was similar. John Smeaton, who had been a consultant engineer on the Forth–Clyde canal and who designed a vital new bridge over the Tay at Perth which opened in 1772, also supervised the first significant harbour improvement in the Forth at Eyemouth. Ironically the future lay elsewhere. At the east end of the Forth–Clyde canal the wholly artificial new harbour of Grangemouth grew rapidly, partly at the expense of nearby Bo'ness, itself once Glasgow's gateway to the North Sea. Leith, totally controlled by Edinburgh, had to look to its laurels. In 1799 John Rennie recommended massive pier and dock construction to Edinburgh Town Council. By 1817 Edinburgh had spent over £300,000 on Leith docks and was heavily in debt to the government and tempted to milk the commerce of Leith to stave off ruin. The result was a major row and the vesting of Leith harbour in 1826 in a body of commissioners, evenly balanced between Leith and Edinburgh to the point of deadlock. In 1833 Edinburgh went bankrupt. By 1838 a Leith Dock Commission with a substantial government-nominated element controlled the most important single harbour complex on the east coast. Harbour improvement was necessarily financed by borrowing based on calculations of increased tonnage. It was fear that the unreformed municipality of Dundee would use the increased revenue to service its own debts which made the merchants of Dundee wrest control of their harbour out of the hands of Provost Riddoch and his cronies. In 1825 the first wet dock opened. By 1830 the Dundee Harbour Trust was established in perpetuity, and in 1834 another wet dock, named after Earl Grey, the premier who carried the Reform Act of 1832, was opened. Similar patterns of improvement occurred at smaller ports like Arbroath, and at large ones like Aberdeen. Very often Smeaton, Telford, or Rennie were the consultant engineers and the setting up of a body of Harbour Commissioners was standard practice. In Aberdeen in 1810 the Commissioners were the Town Council and Magistrates wearing different hats, but an act of 1829 introduced other interests. The immense importance of buoyant future trade for these enterprises is underlined by the experience of the Perth harbour authorities who embarked on an ambitious scheme of river and harbour improvement just when the railways drastically reduced coastal traffic in harbours like Perth. The result, by mid-century was a bankrupt harbour, quite incapable of servicing its debts.

At least the process of bankruptcy was available to put an end to enterprises which had palpably ceased to justify further financing. One of the snags about state finance was that it tended, as in the case of the Scottish canals, to enable projects which failed to produce adequate results within a reasonable time to consume funds which might more usefully have been employed elsewhere. The Commissioners for Highland roads and bridges are arguably another example of the difficulties and dangers of large-scale state intervention in transport problems in the early nineteenth century. Military roads in the Highlands had ceased to be built by 1775, and by 1800 land communications in the Highlands consisted of 800 miles of road, much of it ill-constructed, all of it poorly maintained. In 1803 a Commission was set up by parliament with responsibility for bringing Highland roads up to Lowland standards, building new roads and bridges in the Highlands, and for cooperating with local landowners for these purposes. The great Thomas Telford, who was already consultant to the British Fisheries Society for their proposed harbour at Wick, became permanent consulting engineer to the Commission. The Commission was prepared to pay half the cost of schemes it approved, leaving the other half to the gentry of the relevant area. Under this system the modern road pattern of the Highlands was established, not least by some remarkable and strategic bridges such as Craigellachie Bridge over the Spey and Bonar Bridge over the upper part of the Dornoch Firth. Nearly 900 miles of road were constructed by the Commission between 1803 and 1821 and over 300 miles of existing roads were improved. Whether the results justified the original programme may be doubted, for the main aims of government in setting up the Commission had been to check emigration, and to encourage the development of trade and industry in the Highlands. Neither objective can be said to have been attained. Indeed it can be argued that by the late eighteenth century many people were incapable of distinguishing between what a road system could and could not do. One worthy clergyman in the 1790s was convinced that the town of Huntly in Aberdeenshire would develop into 'the Paisley of the north' provided it was given a good road system 'which was the foundation of the prosperity of the south country'. At a certain point in economic development adequate roads were indeed important, but they could not create industry or prosperity.

It is therefore interesting to note that the most dramatic single innovation in communications in this era—the coming of the railways—was the result of a gradual development of pre-existing systems and owed nothing to state funds. The £1.5 million spent on Highland roads and bridges and on the Caledonian Canal by the state in the first quarter of the nineteenth century naturally attracted much more public attention than the elaboration of the mineral waggonway systems serving the needs of coal and quarry masters near navigable water, but the latter carried the seeds of a transport revolution. Beginning as an accessory to coal pits and developing into an adjunct to canal systems, the railway ended as a mighty force in its own right. Waggonways had, of course, existed for so long that the battle of Prestonpans, where Bonnie Prince Charlie's army routed the unfortunate General Cope at the start of the '45, was fought near and partly over the rails of a horse-operated waggonway. By 1800 ideas about extending the scope of such systems were widespread and were partly implemented in waggonways like the one built by the Duke of Portland between Kilmarnock and Troon and opened in 1812. Designed primarily to convey the ducal coal to the coast, and costing £50,000, the waggonway carried a great deal of the general trade of that part of Ayrshire including timber, grain, salts, and lime as well as coal, not to mention a fair number of passengers.

The application of steam power to such railways in the form of a locomotive was merely a question of time and Scotland's first modern railway of this kind, the Monkland and Kirkintilloch Railway, opened to traffic in October 1826, a year after the Stockton and Darlington in England. Originally operated by horses, the Monkland and Kirkintilloch made provision in its enabling legislation for locomotive working and by 1832 most of the work was being done by two locomotives. An even more intriguing example of the transition period in railways was the Dundee and Newtyle, an 11 mile line started in 1826 and opened in 1832 with the idea of linking Dundee, over the Sidlaw Hills, with the vale of Strathmore. Its extraordinary direct assault on severe gradients required the use of stationary engines to pull its originally horse-drawn waggons and coaches up three steep inclines. To steam and horse-power must be added the sail which was later hoisted on the northern end of the line when the wind was favourable. Even so, the Dundee and Newtyle was not an economic proposition like the mineral-based Monkland and Kirkintilloch. Agricultural Strathmore never generated adequate return traffic to compensate for, above all, the cost of the winding engines. It is therefore understandable that further developments in locomotive working were most rapid in the west. Two branch lines, the Ballochney Railway, and the Slamannan Railway connected the Monkland and Kirkintilloch with further mineral areas, and like the parent line were essentially designed to supplement the Forth and Clyde Canal system.

In 1831, however, the Glasgow and Garnkirk railway was opened, and it was different, for it was a locomotive-operated railway built in open rivalry to the Monkland Canal. It rapidly cut the cost of transporting coal to Glasgow from Monkland from 3s. 6d. to 1s. 3d. per ton. Within five years its annual tonnage of minerals was 140,000 and its annual number of passengers 145,000. Further extension of the Lanarkshire railway system followed rapidly. There was enough traffic here to justify something like a modern railway system at a time when the Edinburgh and Dalkeith Railway, opened in 1831, was using horses supplemented by a stationary engine and employing an operating technique more reminiscent of the stage coach era than of things to come. Thus coal, more than anything else, was the commodity which sustained the development of Scottish railway systems before 1840. All the successful and progressive lines were coal-carrying. It was a new era when in 1841 the Glasgow, Paisley and Greenock line opened, followed in 1842 by the first trunk-line in Scotland, the line between Glasgow and Edinburgh.

In general the history of communications in Scotland between 1780 and 1840 or so reinforces the view that this decisive era of industrial development and agricultural change was a market-orientated one. Whenever political pressure was used to produce or sustain investment unrelated to market opportunities (whether directly or, as with many roads, indirectly) the result tended to be disappointing or even barren. The concept of 'take-off' in the 1780s is a dubious one, the product of an artificial aggregation of regional histories still very different in the nature and time scale of their economic development and therefore best disaggregated for separate study. However, by 1840 we are on the verge of a 'Railway Mania' heralding a new, if still only partial, unifying force. Scotland was now irreversibly committed to a pattern of steadily accelerating urbanisation, industrialisation, and technical change. In world terms she had become a very unusual society, for she was a full partner in the first big industrial state. It was a far cry even from 1780, when Scotland was simply a progressive, but not at all abnormal, segment of north Atlantic society.

6

The Building of a Mature Industrial Economy 1840–1914

Between 1840 and 1914 post-Union Scotland scaled the heights of relative economic success. It became the seat of one of the most advanced and prosperous industrial economies of the period. Not all of Scotland shared this experience. On the contrary, Gaelic-speaking Scotland suffered economic crisis, mass depopulation and cultural collapse. It will be shown that Lowland Scotland, which was in contemporary terms a very successful industrial economy, paid a heavy price, in terms of deprivation, suffering, and social tension, for its achievements. Furthermore, by the early twentieth century the heavy-industry-dominated economy of the Lowlands was caught in a circular pattern of development which made it increasingly vulnerable in a world where more and more countries were passing through the experience of primary industrialisation and emerging as rivals in world markets. Market economics, the supreme engine of change in modern Scottish history, eventually lost the power to produce that change, but all this lay far ahead in 1840.

By the fourth decade of the nineteenth century the face of the predominantly rural pre-industrial Scotland of the mid-eighteenth century had been changed beyond recognition. In the Highlands there had been extensive population movement and drastic reorganisation and innovation in land use. Lowland Scotland had not experienced the widespread social dislocation and population loss which characterised large parts of the Highlands but it had experienced change of a very extensive and at times traumatic nature, both in a rural and in an urban context. Many Scottish thinkers of the late eighteenth and early nineteenth century seemed to contemporaries to contemplate this triumph of industrial

156

and commercial values with something like unholy glee. Adam Smith, for example, did realise that there were problems of alienation and atomisation in the emergence of an urban, industrial society but *The Wealth of Nations*, which he published in 1776, was effectively a formidable sermon on behalf of minimally-regulated market economics, Smith was clear that growth was a good thing and was best achieved by the individual pursuit of maximum economic reward, which could be transmuted by an Invisible Hand into the General Good. David Hume, the philosopher, wrote extensively on politics and economics and he was clear that the beneficial automatism of free trade economics would ensure that Scotland caught up with the richer English economy. Indeed, Hume was very worried that 'fanaticism' might lead the Scots to interfere with these beneficent market forces. Nothing of the kind happened, and it can be argued that by the time of the year of parliamentary reform (or more accurately franchise reform), 1832, the Scots in the Lowlands at any rate, had created a society which was economically as advanced as industrial England and was politically and socially rapidly assimilating to it.

Of all the great names of the Scottish Enlightenment perhaps only Adam Ferguson, professor of moral philosophy in the University of Edinburgh and author of an *Essay on the History of Civil Society* published in 1767, can be said to have laid strong emphasis on the price of progress as the eighteenth century understood progress. Ferguson, however, was the exception which proves the rule, being a Gaelic-speaker from the parish of Logierait in Perthshire and a former chaplain to the Black Watch. It was natural for him to emphasise the threat to the sense of community implicit in commercial values. The main emphasis of Scottish economic thought lay elsewhere. Classical economics, to which Scots like Sir James Stewart and Adam Smith made fundamental contributions, was developed with increased intellectual rigour by men like the Englishman David Ricardo whose ideas were in turn popularised and publicised by writers like the Scot J. R. McCulloch. The latter was a Whig in politics and it was through such Edinburgh Whig publications as the *Edinburgh Review* and the *Scotsman* that he made his name in the 1820s. In 1827 he called for a campaign to instruct the working classes in the economic principles which 'must determine their condition in life'. What those principles were may be guessed from the wish of William Cobbett, the English radical Tory, expressed at about the same time, that he live to see the day when 'Scottish political economy is blown to the devil and the

Edinburgh Review and Adam Smith along with it'. Francis Jeffrey, Editor of the *Edinburgh Review* was an advocate of the introduction of political economy into the courses taught in Mechanics' Institutes, specifically to guide working men away from the dangers of trade unions and strikes. There does in fact seem to have been a serious effort to do this in the many Schools of Art, Watt Institutes and Mechanics Institutes which were set up in Scotland in substantial numbers between the 1820s and 1846, when a fierce secular depression in the economy killed or permanently crippled quite a few of them. That there was also opposition to this particular form of brain-washing is hardly surprising, for the message was the bleak one that life was governed by inexorable laws of market economics, not susceptible to alteration by mere human volition, and that self-improvement as a means to promotion into the entrepreneur class was the true, indeed the only, way for the aspiring working man. This message permeated the pages of the very successful *Chambers Edinburgh Journal* founded by William Chambers in 1832, as well as the pages of the manual of political economy for schools which Chambers published in 1852.

The same message rang from pulpits, notably that of Thomas Chalmers, a St Andrews graduate who became the incumbent of the Tron Kirk of Glasgow in 1815. He was a convinced believer in the idea that economic matters were best left to the providential interplay of unshackled economic forces. He was also deeply concerned about the poverty and social dislocation which he saw in the overcrowded slums of Scotland's industrial cities. His solution to this pauperism was self-help within the Christian framework of a revitalised parish and he tried in St John's parish in Glasgow to demonstrate the validity of his, in the last analysis, impractical and anachronistic theories. Chalmers was a leading figure in the Free Kirk established in 1843 after the Great Disruption in the Established Kirk. Essentially an assertion of the rights of the City of God against English Erastianism, the Free Kirk was also, through its eldership, a vehicle for the advancement and self-expression of rising and aggressive sections of Scotland's Victorian middle class. It became an important part of the Whig-Liberal ascendancy in Scottish life and great and good men associated with it, such as the geologist and journalist Hugh Miller were liable to preach lay sermons of a kind similar to those of Chalmers, Chambers, or McCulloch. Hugh Miller's great classic *The Old Red Sandstone* starts with a strong appeal to working men to abandon the radical cause of Chartism, an agitation for drastic political change which was being undermined in 1841–2 (Miller's book was published in 1841) by unemployment and food shortage on so grave a scale as to break the spirit of the proletariat. Instead Miller held out the prospect of self-help by intellectual self-improvement, and one must never forget that Miller started life as a working mason.

In practice neither Chartism nor trade unions offered much of a challenge to a vigorous capitalist economy run by an aggressively self-confident middle class with a monopoly of the effective media of communication from pulpit to press. The 300 delegates, representing 50,000 weavers in Scotland and Ulster, who assembled in Glasgow in 1834 to demand minimum rates for handloom weavers represented a doomed interest. The Association of Operative Cotton Spinners of Glasgow which called a strike against a reduction in wages in 1837 was broken by a combination of the arrest of five of its leaders and exhaustion of funds. The Association survived as a mere shadow of itself. Workers' organisations tended to be stabler in skilled crafts, but even here a Carpenters' Union in the Glasgow area, dating from the early 1830s, collapsed after a bitter winter strike in 1837–8. Its books were burned. The masons were more fortunate, despite the vociferous hostility towards their union displayed by the most remarkable of all Scots masons, Hugh Miller. The United Operative Masons of Scotland Society was founded in 1831. Its organisation was not very strong but during a strike in 1835 for an increase of summer wages to 3s. a day it survived a legal battle. Several of its members were acquitted of charges of intimidation while the legality of the Society as a workers' combination was upheld by Sheriff Alison, a Tory and a historian with working-class sympathies which were shared by his brother the philanthropist W. P. Alison. During the desperate crisis of 1846–7 workers' organisation (in the shape of the Northern District of the National Typographical Association) even collapsed in the printing trade.

Unions naturally revived and re-emerged with better times, but usually in highly chastened form. Perhaps the most significant event in what has been called 'the mid-century revival' of unionism in Scotland was the formation in 1855 of the United Coal and Iron Miners' Association of Scotland. It was a federation of local societies and its small central executive was dominated by its secretary Alexander Macdonald. This able man despaired of the strike weapon, preferring the road of negotiation and public agitation to secure widespread support for the abolition of abuses which could reasonably be presented as moral evils. After 1874 he sat in Parliament as a Liberal MP for an English constituency. There was more fire in the bellies of the local associations such as the Fife and Kinross Miners who in 1870 were first to extract an agreed eight-hour day from local employers. The building trades were generally endowed with some sort of effective union organisation by the 1860s, with the masons leading the way and securing by 1866 a virtually universal nine hour day in Scotland for masons. By way of contrast, it proved difficult to organise workers in the new heavy industries which were dispro-portionately concentrated on the Clyde, partly because of the militantly anti-union attitude of the Clyde Shipbuilders and Engineers Associ-ation, an employers' combination formed in 1866. Even so, it was here that the Amalgamated Society of Engineers (ASE) gave Scotland a first display of a highly organised union with an efficient central executive seated furth of Scotland. The ASE was a classic example of the so-called 'New Model' English trade unions, with their emphasis on organisation, financial soundness, and prudence rather than pugnacity. Its mixed suc-cess in obtaining an agreed 51-hour week may be measured by the fact that there existed in Glasgow in the engineering trades around 1880 a 51 Hours Recovery League. The admission of the urban working class to the franchise in 1867 was in the long run a very significant signpost on the road to a less docile labour force. Nevertheless, it can be argued that well after that date there was very little in the way of militant organised working class pressure to challenge the management of the Scottish economy by a Whig-Liberal Establishment, which contained aris-tocratic elements, but which was ultimately based on a triumphant urban bourgeoisie.

Protest by the lower orders in the countryside was even rarer than working class resistance in the towns. That is not to say that it was com-pletely absent. The Highland clearances gave rise to intermittent phy-sical resistance by those threatened with eviction, and to a great deal of passive resistance. The people of Kildonan in February 1813 chased the valuers sent by the Countess of Sutherland off their threatened holdings. When the factor was able to call in troops from Fort George and Inver-ness the resistance in Kildonan collapsed, even before the slow-moving soldiery reached the area. In March 1820 there was a pitched battle on another part of the Sutherland estate between a sheriff, a posse of con-stables and armed militia, and hundreds of infuriated people threatened with clearance. This was at Culrain, but even there the threat of large-scale military intervention shocked the population into acquiescence.

Highland resistance was, however, sporadic. It lacked leadership. Significantly, women played a very large part in Highland disturbances. In 1841 at Durness women drove off the sheriff's officers. At Sollas in 1849 the officers were confronted and abused by women. Women led the battle at Glencalvie in 1843, and many women were severely injured by attacking constables at Greenyards in 1854. It was the same tale at Knockan and Elphin in 1852 and at Coigach and Ullapool in 1853. Women were prominent in the 'Battle of the Braes' in Skye in 1882, when at last protest began to produce political results, but in many respects that battle was very similar to the battles of the 1840s and 1850s and the different results were the result of changes in public opinion outwith the Highlands. It can be argued that before 1882 it was the passive resistance of whole populations which deprived the Sutherland dynasty and, on the periphery of their empire at least, the Dukes of Argyll, of the chance of success in their plans for an economic transformation of parts of the Highlands.

In the Lowlands, by way of contrast, landlords seemed to secure the best of several possible worlds. They restructured rural society with a high hand, but with a safety valve in the shape of expanding industrial towns which not only ate the produce of their lands but also absorbed surplus rural population on a grand scale. In all fairness it must be said that a great many landowners built and developed villages on their estates in the hope that such villages, both as markets and as places of employment would absorb superfluous rural population and thereby limit emigration. Of course, the landlord also expected to reap direct and indirect gain from such villages, in the shape of enhanced rent rolls. The concept was fairly common amongst the aristocracy of the British Isles in the eighteenth century. When, for example, Lord Gardenstone published a *Letter to the People of Laurencekirk* in 1780, on the occasion of the raising of the status of this planned village to that of a burgh of barony, he attached to his publication 'an Abridgement of two letters published by Sir Richard Cox, containing an Account of the establishment and progress of industry in his village near Corke [sic] in Ireland'. It has been estimated that between 1745 and 1845 over 150 planned villages were started in Scotland, excluding coalmining and urban development. The sponsors ranged from Sir John Sinclair of Ulbster and the Duke of Sutherland in the north, to the Duke of Argyll at Inverary, to a host of gentry and businessmen in the Lowlands.

Regional studies make it clear that 150 is a gross underestimate for the number of villages in rural Scotland either planned or reconstructed in this period. In Morayshire, for example, outside the royal burghs of Elgin and Forres every nucleated settlement except the former ports of Garmouth and Findhorn originated as a planned village. Since 1900 no new nucleations have been built in Morayshire other than ones adjoining distilleries or Kinloss airfield. In many counties in addition to Morayshire, villages planned in the century after 1750 remain the dominant type of nucleated rural settlement. Though many of these planned villages failed to meet the expectations of their founders, it is clear that landlords continued to think of them as a worthwhile enterprise up to about 1850 when the concentration of industry in towns and the reduction in the significance of rural markets due to vastly improved transportation rendered the original concept of the planned village obsolete. Thereafter they continued to be created but as little more than feuing plans for speculative housing designed to meet an existing nearby known demand. By about 1880 the tradition of establishing planned villages was dead. The stagnation of rents and agricultural prices in the so-called 'Great Depression', and the introduction of Estate Duty in 1894, as well as changing patterns of industrial location finally destroyed the enthusiasm of Scottish landlords for this sort of investment. It is nevertheless important to recognise that even today the shape of nucleated rural settlement in Scotland reflects the will of a landlord class which retained all its economic power after being compelled to share political power with the middle classes.

Indeed the landlords appear to have contrived to secure a very advantageous arrangement with respect to the pressing problem of poor relief in an economy marked by extensive pauperisation. To grasp how advantageous their position was it is necessary to look at the arrangement for poor relief in the burghs. Poor relief was based on sixteenth- and seventeenth-century statutes which remained fundamental in this field until 1845. The care of the aged and impotent poor was entrusted to heritors and kirk sessions in every parish. Legal assessments for support of the poor might be imposed, but were not obligatory. Settlement in a given parish was a relatively uncontentious matter involving three years' continuous residence. There was no legal provision for the removal of a person likely to become chargeable. In burghs, where the failure of the medieval kirk to provide a proper parochial system had often led to the creation of a single very large (and later often divided) burghal kirk, the authority of the session was reinforced by that of the magistrates in matters relating to poor relief. The bias of the burghal establishments was emphatically towards avoiding stenting and towards reliance on church collections and other forms of voluntary charity for the relief of those in need. In practice, with the massive flow of immigrants into the towns to take up lowly jobs in expanding industries, this approach had become obsolete. Aberdeen had consolidated its voluntary charities into a United Fund in 1768. The fund was managed by the magistrates and town council, the kirk session of St Nicholas and the managers of St Paul's. In accordance with a well-established convention that dissenting bodies make at least some effort to look after their own poor, dissenting congregations from the Roman Catholic to the Methodists made contributions to the United Fund. Nevertheless, by 1838 it had proved essential to impose a compulsory poor rate on owners and occupiers and when in 1839 a committee of the town council of Aberdeen published a report on the assessment and management of contributions for poor relief in burghal parishes in Scotland it was able to point out that nearly all the principal burghs had compulsory assessment on the basis of 'Ownership and Occupancy'.

In the countryside a much less widespread use was made of assessment or stenting. Heritors were very often Episcopalian in religion and absentee, often in England. By a series of legal decisions in the mid eighteenth century a group of such lairds with what can not unfairly be described as the active collusion of the Court of Session had asserted their ultimate financial control over the management of poor-relief funds by the kirk sessions. This was the essential background to the hammering out of a singularly ungenerous set of norms for the administration of poor relief in Scotland; norms which by the early nineteenth century were known, farcically enough, as 'the Old Scots Poor Law'. These norms included no relief except to the permanently disabled; very little use of compulsory stenting or assessment; and no contribution whatever by non-resident heritors unless they were compulsorily assessed. The upshot was a system which could be so run as to ensure that the poor were largely supported by the poor, usually to the accompaniment of smug reflections from their betters about the virtues of independence and thrift. Though it is easy to find specific examples of compulsory assessment and of poor relief granted to able-bodied labourers, the general trend of the system, especially in the countryside, was notably meaner than similar provision in England and contemporaries were clear that the lack of adequate relief in rural areas was a powerful 'push' factor in moving poor people into the more generous towns.

There was mounting criticism of the system by the 1830s. In 1840 Dr W. P. Alison published a pamphlet entitled *Observations on the Management of the Poor in Scotland*, in which he denounced the inadequacy and inhumanity of the existing pattern. He asserted that Scotland spent but 1s. 3d. a head of her population annually on poor relief, while for Holland the corresponding sum was 4s. 4d., for Hamburg 4s. 0d., and for France no less than 10s. 0d. The Great Disruption of 1843, by splitting the national kirk, dealt a death-blow to the ecclesiastical basis of the poor relief arrangements and by 1845 legislation established a new statutory system headed by a Board of Supervision in Edinburgh. Under that Board were parochial boards for every burghal parish, rural parish, or combination of rural parishes (the Board of Supervision encouraged rural parishes to combine if the union enabled them more adequately to cope with the problem of the poor). Each parochial board consisted of nominees of the heritors or, where appropriate, magistrates; nominees of the kirk session; and usually a majority of managers elected by property owners in the parish at large. Inspectors of the Poor were created for every parochial unit. Inevitably, the result was a sharp increase in expenditure, which rose from just under £260,000 in the year ending February 1844 to nearly £550,000 in the year ending May 1848. Yet the system was still very far from adequate. It avowedly tried to preserve as much as could be preserved of the pre-1845 arrangements and principles. The able-bodied unemployed, despite the prevalence of cyclical slumps in an industrial economy, were denied any right to relief. W. P. Alison had as early as 1844, by which time he had become Professor of the Practice of Medicine at Edinburgh, expressed the view that the proposed new legislation was likely to be grossly inadequate. A modern historian has described the 1845 statute as appallingly drafted and frequently nonsensical. It is true that under it the number of parishes assessed rose from 420 in 1846 to 840 by 1894 (Scotland has between 900 and 1,000 parishes), but this did not in itself solve the problem of destitution. Even prosperity as the Victorians understood it could only ameliorate it.

In a deep sense, critics like W. P. Alison were out of time with the society they lived in. Victorian Scotland rose to industrial greatness on market economics; a hierarchical social structure, albeit a fluid and flexible one; and a great deal of sheer ruthlessness on the part of its ruling élites. Their achievement was to keep control of a society continually experiencing traumatic economic and social change. They were ruthless with any section of the current élite which refused to accept the often brutal rules of the game of survival. The chiefs of the Robertsons, the Clan Donnachaidh, evicted nobody after being restored to their ancestral estates in 1784 (the properties had been forfeited for notorious Jacobitism). The result of this heroic refusal to come to terms with commercialism, a refusal which represented the views of most of the Robertson gentry, was ruin. By 1854 Struan, the principal seat of the chiefs had to be sold. The last Rannoch properties went in the 1920s. The gentry fell with the chiefly house, Robertson of Auchleeks alone excepted. This was a tragedy oft repeated amongst the older noble families of the Highlands. Pseudo-feudal enthusiasms were toys for the very rich, or psychological indulgences for the kirks or studies of the middle classes. On the margins of survival, it was a very unsentimental world. Patrick Brewster, minister of the second charge of Paisley Abbey and an active 'moral-force' Chartist, accused the wealthier classes of his own day of being 'unchristianised' in so far as they refused to regard society as a whole as a field for the exercise of Christian compassion. Brewster hurled in the face of an early Victorian bourgeoisie the very different social vision of John Knox and the Fathers of the Scottish Reformation, as well as the organic view of society explicit in the writings of the Covenanters of the Scottish revolution of the seventeenth century. By and large Brewster's views made as few converts as one might expect.

They were almost certainly incompatible with the scope and speed of industrial development in Scotland before the later Victorian period. A large, cheap, expendable migrant labour force tends to be a common feature of societies experiencing very rapid industrial expansion. Even in the second half of the twentieth century France used, in every sense of the word, the Moroccan and Algerian immigrants packed into the bidonvilles or shanty towns on the edge of her industrial cities. Brazil's explosive growth in the 1970s utilised a pool of marginal labour, much of it immigrant rural poor from the north-west of the country, shockingly housed in clapboard hovels on the edge of the big conurbations. These are modern examples. Brewster's Scotland was experiencing something which may be described as primary industrialisation. The surge of urban and industrial development which occurred in certain parts of Western Europe in the sixteenth century seems to have been accompanied by extensive pauperisation. The far more decisive process of industrialisation which occurred in Great Britain in the eighteenth and nineteenth centuries seems, at least in its crucial earlier phases, to have needed a large pool of reasonably docile and relatively cheap labour. Historians can and do argue learnedly about working-class living standards in the early nineteenth century. No generalisations hold up well for long periods or large areas, but it may be significant that recent analysis of the cost of living in early nineteenth-century Glasgow seems to show that between 1810 and 1831 the real wages of the more highly paid craftsman showed only a very modest increase indeed, while there was little or no improvement in the lot of the unskilled labourer or the hand-loom weaver. With the 'hungry forties' ahead, this is not a particularly cheerful picture, and it is certainly clear that, despite the very real gains made by sections of the working class in the later nineteenth century, the Glasgow unskilled labour market was considered to be grossly over-supplied with marginal labour at the end of the century. At an earlier period a steady flow of cheap labour was essential: decent working-class housing a luxury which would have depressed profit margins and slowed growth. After analysing industrial and agricultural growth in the heyday of Scotland's classic nineteenth-century economy, it is therefore wholly appropriate to conclude by considering the price of such progress.

Industrial development

The single most dramatic development across the face of virtually all Lowland Scotland, and later and to a lesser extent in the Highlands, was probably the creation of a railway system. Not only did it unify the Scottish economy in an unprecedented fashion but it also linked that economy with England for the first time by land with fast, efficient and reliable transport. The locomotive and inter-city lines were therefore crucial determining factors in the growth of the Scottish Victorian economy and it was natural that the Edinburgh and Glasgow Railway should show the way and, especially on its financial side, set important precedents for future Scottish railway development. The 45 miles between Glasgow and Edinburgh posed few serious engineering difficulties, and the commerce between the two cities, much of which was being carried by the Forth and Clyde and Union Canals, was great and likely to grow. Edinburgh and Leith had a population of 162,383 in 1831. The figure for Glasgow was 193,548 and by 1891 Glasgow had reached 638,198, Edinburgh–Leith 322,353.

The proposed railway obtained its enabling legislation in 1838 specifying a route which followed the line of the pre-existing canals. The line was managed by Scots, for of the 11 original directors only two were Englishmen. However the finance for its construction appears to have been overwhelmingly English. The *Railway Times* said that 90 per cent of the shareholders lived in England, with a heavy concentration in the Lancashire area. Engineered as a high-speed trunk line, the efficiency of the Edinburgh and Glasgow was marred by the need to tunnel on a steep gradient under the Forth and Clyde Canal to reach its Glasgow terminus at Queen Street. Thus was created the costly and time-wasting Cowlairs Incline, which had to be worked with a stationary engine and cable. The total cost of the line was approximately £1,200,000 and it opened on 2 February 1842. From the start, the growth of passenger traffic exceeded the expectations of the directors. They had calculated on carrying 340,000 passengers a year when fully established. By the year ending 31 July 1846 the figure was already over a million, giving receipts in excess of £100,000. The river canal system lost nearly all its passenger traffic as well as a large slice of its goods traffic, though it did retain a substantial mineral traffic. The railway was therefore more successful than most people had expected, but it was soon plunged into the extraordinary power-politics of railway rivalry, for the Caledonian Railway, incorporated in 1845, built a line from Carlisle to Glasgow which was opened in 1848. Despite bitter opposition from their Lancashire shareholders, who could see no point in buying out a beaten rival, the Edinburgh and Glasgow directorate bought the Union Canal in 1849 for £209,000 for fear that it might fall into the hands of the Caledonian.

By then Scotland had passed through the maelstrom of the Railway Mania which engulfed Scotland in the summer of 1845 and burst like the bubble it was in the spring of 1846. While it lasted the pace of railway projection and speculation in the stock of projected railways simply beggared description. On one page of one issue of the *Glasgow Argus* 13 new railway companies were announced. They covered all parts of the Lowlands and did not neglect parts of the Southern Uplands. Fortunately, no permanent damage appears to have been done by this wave of speculation, for Scottish railways resumed a fairly sensible pattern of development after it was over. An 1841 Royal Commission on Anglo-Scottish railway routes had taken two years to pontificate to the effect that only one Anglo-Scottish route would be necessary and that would be provided by a chain of railways coming up through Crewe, Lancaster and Carlisle, and thence by Annandale to Glasgow. However John Learmonth, chairman of the Edinburgh and Glasgow Railway, emerged in 1842 as the guiding spirit of a new proposed railway, to be called the North British. This line was originally scheduled to run from Edinburgh to Dunbar but even the charismatic Learmonth could not persuade enough Scots to hazard their capital in it. On advice from George Hudson, the English railway promoter and speculator who came to grief in the slump of 1846, the North British announced that it would drive its line as far as Berwick where it would meet English lines stretching towards the Border and thus form part of a great international trunk line. Subscriptions thereafter became brisk and by 1849 there were 927 Scottish shareholders with 23,904 shares and 3,163 English shareholders with 77,937 shares. The 3 to 1 preponderance of English shareholders was highly significant, as was the heavy preponderance of north of England shareholders in the English group. But for them, there would have been no ceremonial opening of the Edinburgh to Berwick line in June 1846.

The railway boom is rightly regarded as the catalyst which produced for the first time in England a national capital market in which the provincial middle classes actively participated. Despite the use of debentures and preference shares, the bulk of railway capital was invested in ordinary stock facing all the hazards of the market. With an unincorporated company and unlimited liability in event of failure, these could be grave under English law. The process of amending English company law to allow easy incorporation and limited liability was only extended formally to Scotland by the Joint Stock Companies Act of 1856. This was largely because the Scots legal tradition already allowed to any formal business partnership a legal personality which could sue or be sued; transferability of shares; and to a lesser extent limited liability. Incorporation itself was much easier in Scotland than in England. The assimilation of the company law of the two countries, very much on English lines despite the undoubted merits of the Scottish tradition, was an important index of mounting English domination of the Scottish economy. Trunk-railways were perhaps the first decisive step in this process, for here was a vital development which simply could not have been initiated when it was without massive inputs of English capital.

Not that the great Scottish railway companies failed to develop distinctive personalities. The reverse was the case, and the rivalry between the North British and the Caledonian in particular seemed at times to leave all commercial good sense behind. Having started as rivals on Anglo-Scottish routes, the two companies battled against one another to secure continuous northern routes by the only possible process—progressive take-over of other companies. The original trunk line pattern stopped at the Forth–Clyde line, but in 1848 the Scottish Central Railway was opened, giving access to Perth while the Scottish Midland carried the railway up Strathmore to Forfar and the North-Eastern Railway completed the route to Aberdeen. The Caledonian aspired to have a continuous line from Carlisle to Aberdeen, while the North British was anxious to gain access to Glasgow, the Clyde and the Lanarkshire coalfield. After decades of manoeuvre and negotiation in the style and manner of hostile sovereign powers, both the North British and the Caledonian moved into an era of major amalgamations in 1865. In that year the North British absorbed the Edinburgh and Glasgow Railway and the Monkland Railway. On the same day the Scottish Central Railway became part of the Caledonian, which went on in due course to absorb the Scottish Midland and the North Eastern in order to reach Aberdeen. There the large southern companies were on the verge of what was arguably the most formidable of all railways, the Great North of Scotland Railway. Bristling with fight and notoriously cantankerous, as befitted a fine flower of the North-East, the 'Great North' was originally designed to link Aberdeen with Inverness. Unfortunately building progress was slow and by the time Keith was reached, the extension between Keith and Inverness had become a separate railway, the Inverness and Aberdeen Junction Railway, which subsequently, to the extreme fury and chagrin of the 'Great North', became part of the Highland Railway.

To some extent railway companies' feuds stimulated technical progress and the extension of services. Even the incredible behaviour of the Great North of Scotland Railway, which included express prices for funereally-paced trains and a deliberately provocative approach to connections with other lines, can be shown to have had some good effects. The 'Great North' for some time controlled the only through route to Inverness. Its technique of starting its connecting trains off just as hurrying passengers from other lines puffed towards its station ensured that a direct connection between Perth and Inverness through the Highlands was built earlier than might otherwise have been the case. By the late 1880s the 'Great North' had 'resolutely set itself to live down the reputation acquired by long and patient continuance in ill-doing'. 1888 saw the start of the Race to the North, a rivalry between the east and west coast routes from London to Scotland which bred on the east coast the superb tradition of the Flying Scotsman. That great train reached its peak in the late 1920s after legislation of 1923 had amalgamated all east coast British lines into the London and North Eastern Railway and Sir Nigel Gresley, the Chief Mechanical Engineer of the new company, produced his magnificent three-cylinder Pacific type express locomotives. Nevertheless, the tradition of excellence can be traced back to the rivalries of the later nineteenth century.

Those rivalries were by no means always beneficial in their effects. A classic example here is the bridging of the Tay. As early as 1850 the Edinburgh, Perth and Dundee Railway had introduced a special ferry on the Forth which provided the first roll-on, roll-off train ferry service in the world. This vessel had been designed by Thomas Bouch, manager and resident engineer of the company. A smaller version of the Forth ferry was soon crossing the Tay. In 1862 the North British, under the ebullient chairmanship of Richard Hodgson, absorbed the Edinburgh, Perth and Dundee, but found its new conquest, renamed the Northern Section, difficult to run. The only effective way of grafting it into the main North British empire and also offering another challenge to the Caledonian's northern ambitions, was to bridge both firths. Astonishingly, by 1878 a slender malleable-iron lattice-girder bridge mounted on high brick columns spanned the two miles of the Tay between Wormit and Dundee. Designed by Thomas Bouch, now a consulting civil engineer, it had a series of very high girders in its middle to allow for ships moving to and from Perth. It also embodied a whole range of weaknesses both in workmanship and in design which ensured that its central portion fell down, taking a passenger train with it, on 28 December 1879. Apart from the tragic loss of life, the disaster had mixed consequences. On the debit side, it provoked from William McGonagal, the Dundee bard, a poem of immortal badness. On the credit side, it stopped dead the building of a bridge across the Forth designed by the now Sir Thomas Bouch. The pugnacity of the North British under the chairmanship of John Stirling of Kippendavie would certainly have authorised the completion of this bridge, as yet another blow at the hated Caledonian. Equally certainly the bridge would then have fallen down, even more promptly than the one over the Tay. Not much wonder that the Forth rail bridge designed by John Fowler and Benjamin Baker which opened in 1890 was a massive iron cantilever structure allowing a colossal safety margin. The specialist engineering firm which executed the bulk of the work, Messrs. Arrol of Glasgow, were also responsible for the more solid and sober Tay rail bridge designed by W. H. Barlow and opened in 1886 at a cost of £650,000 (compared with £350,000 for the first bridge).

By the end of the nineteenth century company rivalries were producing railway lines of very dubious economic value. The West Highland Railway is a case in point. It was heavily backed by the North British, which proposed to run it. To the North British this line was an opportunity to break out from its furthest outpost on the Clyde, Craigendoran west of Dumbarton, and plunge north into the Highlands with a view to reaching out for the trade of the western seaboard north of Oban (already annexed by the Caledonian), and possibly for that of the Great Glen. To reach either objective it was necessary for the West Highland to drive a very long line north from the Clyde to the vicinity of Fort William. The route chosen was scenic and in winter almost unbelievably bleak. It passed through territory where population was scarce. Indeed the railway station erected in the middle of Rannoch Moor was widely considered to be, in winter, the most isolated and god-forsaken outpost in the railway world, with the possible exception of some of the remoter halts in Siberia. The West Highland did eventually reach Mallaig by an extension, thus reaching a strategic point on the western seaboard, but it never approached Inverness nearer than Fort Augustus, due to the stout and sustained opposition of the Highland Railway. Needless to say, the West Highland lost money, though the Treasury, which had given it a guarantee for political reasons never had to pay it more than £4,000 a year. When the West Highland was authorised in 1889 the crofting areas on the west coast of the Highlands were in high ferment due to the 'Crofters' War'. Between 1901 and 1914 the line made a trading loss of £72,672 10s. 3d. while the Treasury contribution amounted to £36,672 19s. 11d. When the North British absorbed the West Highland in 1908 the 142 miles of track and accessories represented an investment of £2,370,000.

There were in fact far more impractical railways, of which one example will suffice. The Invergarry and Fort Augustus Railway at the southern end of the Great Glen has been described as an incredibly ill-conceived venture, and a classic example of a railway which should never have been built. Sponsored by Lord Burton and a small group of friends, it was lavishly over-built for a Highland terrain which for a radius of 50 miles around Fort Augustus was 99 per cent deer forest and 1 per cent arable. Latterly the North British bid £22,500 for this £344,000 line, and was refused on the grounds that the line should be able to sell itself for more as scrap. Legal objections to the latter gambit helped to give the North British control of the line by 1914. However, it can be convincingly argued that wherever population and economic activity were adequate to sustain a railway system, the results of its construction included overall multiple gains for the Scottish economy. Perishable goods reached wider markets. Where feeder roads supplemented the railway price differentials between town and country could be much reduced, if not abolished, for low-value bulky goods. Land values rose around expanding towns as commuter services enabled people to live at much greater distances from their work. Many new jobs were created and the mobility of the general labour force enhanced. The extensive earth-moving, rock-cutting, and track-laying operations which accompanied all railway construction meant that the railways continued the tradition originally started by the canals and employed large forces of navvies, including substantial immigrant elements, overwhelmingly Irish in origin. Thus in February 1847 on the Edinburgh and Northern Railway line in Fife there were 6,245 navvies made up of 4,103 Scots, 2,110 Irish and 32 English. Many of the immigrants became a permanent addition to the Scottish labour force.

The extent to which the railways as an operating phenomenon consumed the products of other Scottish industries, or stimulated industrial development closely linked to railways, is a complex problem. A study of the relationship between the railways and the Scottish iron industry illustrates this very clearly. Even the producers of Scottish iron had no exact idea of the nature of their markets. The president of the West of Scotland Iron and Steel Institute in the 1890s admitted that he was incapable of an accurate calculation of demand outside the field of shipbuilding. There was, of course, a steady demand for metal from Scottish railways. Between 1840 and 1900 permanent-way requirements seem to have risen from 25,000 tons average per annum to over 90,000 tons per annum. Rolling-stock iron (and in 1890 the Caledonian alone owned 63,000 waggons and reckoned a further 33,000 traders' waggons used its system) experienced a similar rise in demand from an annual average of 6,000 tons in the 1850s to nearly 33,000 tons by the 1890s. Yet it can easily be shown that the bulk of iron rails used in Scotland were imported, due to weaknesses in the Scottish malleable iron industry. By the 1870s steel rails were in the ascendant but the Scots were slow to enter this field. Not until the 1880s was there a substantial Scottish steel industry. A very large percentage of the rolling-stock on Scottish lines was imported. Locomotives were a different story, for most early locomotives used on Scottish lines were built in Scotland. Even Dundee had a locomotive-building industry and at least one very great designer of locomotives, Patrick Stirling, served his apprenticeship in the Dundee Foundries, though he rose to fame as locomotive superintendent of the Glasgow and South Western Railway. The 'Great North' with characteristic perversity, was the one Scottish company which in its early days placed its locomotive orders furth of Scotland.

Though time brought its changes, Scotland remained a very great centre of locomotive manufacture well into the twentieth century. Increasingly the industry was concentrated in and around Glasgow. The Caledonian's principal locomotive shops were at St Rollox; those of the North British at Cowlairs; and between them lay Springburn with the Hyde Park Locomotive Works, probably the best known of the three. In the years before 1914 Glasgow was the biggest locomotive manufacturing centre in Europe and its overseas trade in steam locomotives was the biggest of any centre in the world. When in 1903 three big Glasgow locomotive firms united into the North British Locomotive Works, their combined capacity was roughly 800 main-line locomotives per annum. Glasgow locomotives could be found all over the British Commonwealth and Empire. They were used in large numbers on British owned railways in South America, but they were also built in significant numbers for France and even for Canada, where fierce American competition was a fact of life.

Locomotive manufacture was merely one aspect of the development of heavy metallurgical industry to the point where some historians would claim for it a hegemony in the Scottish pre-1914 economy. The basis of all this was cheap, abundant pig iron, based on the hot blast and cheap iron ore. There was in fact a disparity between the amount of pig produced by Scottish furnaces and the amount which could be utilised within the Scottish economy. As a result a great deal of iron was exported. Foundries were the main internal market for Scottish pig. They increased very rapidly in numbers, if not necessarily in size, as industrialisation accelerated and in 1846, the first year for which we have figures, were absorbing nearly 200,000 tons of pig iron. One surprising failure of the Scottish industry lay in its highly tentative approach to the problem of producing malleable iron, a product suitable for more sophisticated finishing. The essential technique for removing impurities to produce good bar iron was one of puddling and investment in facilities for this came on any scale only in the 1840s in two bursts, the second of which ended in the spectacular failure of three Scottish malleable iron works. The explanation of this failure at a time when the demand for iron rails alone was providing an unprecedented opportunity for malleable iron producers, can be explained in various ways. Due to a certain phosphoric content in Scottish ores, the resultant iron, though good for the foundry and casting as pig, tended to be brittle and unsuitable for the forge in the shape of malleable iron. Indeed, it was necessary to mix Scottish pig with other iron to obtain a suitable mix for the production of malleable iron. Then there were specific factors relating to these particular works. The decision to invest coincided with high construction costs while the production of malleable iron did not start until prices were on a downward trend. High borrowing and low returns were a fatal combination, the more so because malleable iron had been envisaged as a way of sustaining profits at a time when pig was not as profitable as it had been in the 1830s. The rise of a substantial malleable iron industry in Scotland came late. By the late 1860s the Scots mixed their own iron with English Cleveland iron in order to cope with competition from that district in the ship plate market. In 1867 Scotland imported 70,000 tons of Cleveland ore, but malleable iron accounted for a mere 142,000 tons out of a total of 1,031,000 tons of Scottish iron in that year. Nearly all Scottish malleable iron works were connected with the rise of iron shipbuilding on the Clyde, for that industry in the 1860s and 1870s absorbed up to 70 per cent of all Scottish malleable iron production.

Since, for long periods, domestic consumption did not absorb even half of Scottish production, there was a very large export trade in Scottish pig iron. In 1846 21 per cent of Scottish iron production (119,000 tons) was shipped foreign and 257,000 tons or 46 per cent went coastwise (and some of this would undoubtedly later go foreign). By the 1870s the proportions were reversed with, in a typical year, something like 30 per cent being shipped coastwise and 40 per cent foreign. Between 1848 and 1854 Scotland sent overseas more than 90 per cent of United Kingdom total exports of pig iron. Thereafter came a fall, but the figure remained in the 70s until the end of the 1870s. Thereafter, very rapid decline set in. Scotland was running out of cheap ore. Production of iron ore, which in the 1870s had run at over 3,000,000 tons per annum, was under 600,000 tons by 1913. The better kinds of coal for ironworks became scarcer and dearer just when it became necessary to import dearer Spanish ore, and the upsurge in production costs marked the end of one of the pillars of Victorian Scotland's economic prosperity—cheap pig iron.

Fortunately, just when iron was faltering, the modern Scottish steel industry was born in the second half of the nineteenth century. Before 1850 Scottish steel production was negligible. Even after 1850 the growth of production was slow. There were two sets of reasons for this. One was the still comfortable profit margins on pig iron, which discouraged most Scots ironmasters from further experiment, and ensured that the future of steel lay disproportionately with a small minority of malleable iron producers already used to processing iron beyond the pig stage. The other set of reasons was technical and closely related to the fact that Scottish ores were phosphoric and not the non-phosphoric hematite ores which were common in other centres of iron production. The two new steel manufacturing processes of the second half of the nineteenth century, the Bessemer converter and the Siemens-Martin open-hearth process, both proved difficult to establish in Scotland because they could only use low-phosphor ores, and this grave defect was only remedied by the application of the Gilchrist-Thomas process from the 1880s. Crudely put, the Bessemer process involved blowing cold air through molten cast iron in a Bessemer converter. In the course of losing most of its carbon and turning into steel, the iron in the converter became very much hotter, despite the unheated nature of the blast. Sir Henry Bessemer, who never claimed to have any great scientific knowledge of metallurgy, but who was an immensely versatile pragmatic inventor, was knighted in 1879. Yet his attempt to supervise the successful installation of his process at Dixon's ironworks at Govan was a complete failure to the point where Bessemer returned the money Dixon had payed for the licence to use Bessemer's converter patent. Unfortunately, even after the need for hematite ores was recognised, there were other technical problems involved in the use of Bessemer converters which were therefore less than satisfactory in the only Scottish works in which they were used between 1861 and 1875.

The next big technical innovation in steel manufacture was the Siemens open-hearth furnace which by a process of reversing airflows through a furnace and storing the heat of one flow in a honeycomb of firebrick to help heat the next, effected dramatic savings in fuel consumption. This process also preferred hematite ores but was more easily controlled and was suitable for the use of scrap, of which Scotland had increasing quantities. It was on the basis of open-hearth production of acid (i.e. derived from non-phosphoric ore) steel that the Scottish steel industry finally established itself. The key stimulus was undoubtedly the adoption of steel for shipbuilding. There was one significant development before then in the shape of the founding of the Steel Company of Scotland in 1872. Siemans himself was an important shareholder, and a site was obtained at Hallside near Cambuslang, south-east of Glasgow. The main drive behind the investment decision came not from the iron manufacturers but from the Tharsis Company, a copper and sulphur producing firm with vast mining interests in Spain but a base in the chemical interests of Sir Charles Tennant of St Rollox, one of the greatest of Victorian entrepreneurs. The Tharsis Company was looking for a profitable use for 'blue billy', a residue left after copper and silver had been extracted from iron pyrites. St Rollox was to provide carbonate of manganese, which it was hoped could be combined with 'blue billy' to produce mild ductile steel of a kind in increasing demand. It did not prove an economic proposition and the Steel Company of Scotland had to revert to much more orthodox methods. Securing its first Admiralty order in 1876, it passed out of a phase of poor financial results into one of increasing prosperity and by 1900 produced a million tons of steel annually.

Such a history explains why it was only after 1880 that Scottish steel firms began to emerge in any number. Scotland's small number of malleable ironmakers transferred into steel after William Beardmore converted his Parkhead Forge to steel manufacture in 1879, and David Colville installed Siemens plant at his malleable iron establishment at Dalziel in 1880. A few iron manufacturers followed suit, most significantly Merry and Cunninghame who installed both Bessemer and Siemens plant after 1884. By 1885 Scotland had ten steel firms with preponderantly open-hearth plant producing 42 per cent of all British made Siemens steel or 240,000 tons in round figures. The fact that Scottish steel was so closely linked to Clyde shipbuilding explains many otherwise puzzling features of the record. For example, by the 1880s there was available a process devised by the Welsh inventor Sidney Gilchrist Thomas (1850–5) whereby Bessemer converters were lined with dolomite limestone which reacted with any phosphoric content in ores to produce a basic slag which not only eliminated the phosphor but also could be ground up and sold as fertiliser. The Scots were slow to adopt this technique, but with good reason for in 1887 Lloyds banned the use of

Bessemer steel in shipbuilding and Scottish firms like Merry and Cunninghame, who had built Bessemer converters, faced acute financial problems.

Clearly, the history of Scottish iron and steel manufacture between 1840 and 1914 is intimately linked with the history of Scottish shipbuilding and in the field of shipbuilding the tale is one of concentration and growth to quite extraordinary heights by 1914. Originally it was a very widely dispersed industry. In the seventeenth century it had been common for Scots owners to buy ships abroad, especially in the Netherlands, but by the eighteenth and early nineteenth centuries wooden shipbuilding appears to have been carried on at every significant Lowland port. Specialist yards of some size naturally evolved in the larger ports but it was not until the mid nineteenth century that iron hulls came generally into favour. For certain types of fishing vessel and all whalers wood remained the favoured hull material for a long or indeed an indefinite period. The combination of the marine steam engine, iron hulls, and a steady upward trend in the size of merchant shipping produced two trends which shaped the future destiny of Scottish shipbuilding. The first was a tendency for the larger harbours to attract all significant shipbuilding to themselves. The first iron ship built on the Tay, for example, came from a Perth yard in 1836, but the Dundee yards rapidly became the dominant complex on the Tay as the sheer cost of modern equipment became too much for smaller centres. Even here the pull of the Clyde was felt. The firm of Alexander Stephen and Sons started shipbuilding in Aberdeen, then moved by stages southward down the coast acquiring yards in Arbroath and then in 1842 in Dundee. In 1850 the firm established a yard on the Clyde, which soon became its chief centre of activity, and by 1894 the firm's Dundee yard had been sold to the Dundee Shipbuilders' Company. From Stirling round the coast of Fife and up as far as Montrose there were still about 20 shipyards active in 1869, exclusive of small yards building only wooden fishing boats. In terms of tonnage, however, two big Dundee yards were pre-eminent in this region in the late nineteenth century. One was the Caledon Yard, founded as late as 1874 by a marine engineer called W. B. Thompson. From a ship of 174 tons in 1874 the Caledon rapidly progressed to vessels of over 3,000 tons in the 1880s. The other big Dundee yard was Gourlay's. It had originated in marine engineering activity at the Dundee Foundry, and as late as 1897 the *Encyclopedia Britannica* had used a Gourlay double-ended marine boiler to illustrate the latest developments in high-pressure steam, but all this was really ancillary to Gourlay's shipyard. In 1893 Gourlay's accounted for no less than 76 per cent of the tonnage built at Dundee. The firm was very much geared to a world market for shipping, so it was very vulnerable to secular depressions in the 1880s and 1890s. In the early 1900s technical innovation forced the firm into the bold decision to invest heavily in requipping itself. Unfortunately a very severe slump in orders in 1907-8 hit the firm when it was staggering under a burden of debt and needed all the revenue it could secure. Bankruptcy was the inevitable outcome.

The transition from wood to iron was no more clear cut than the transition from sail to steam. Many sailing ships were given composite hulls (iron-framed with wooden planking) or iron hulls, and sail achieved its supreme efficiency and beauty in competition with steam. Aberdeen shipbuilders were in fact famous for their great and beautiful clipper sailing ships which held steam at bay for decades on the longest runs. In 1845 the Aberdeen-built *Torrington* was sent to rival the fast American clippers in the Chinese opium trade. In the 1850s and 1860s Aberdeen clippers were at their peak in the China and Australian trades. For George Thompson and Company's Aberdeen White Star Line trading to Australia Hood and Company of Aberdeen built many clippers including the peerless *Thermopylae* of 947 tons. This ship could complete the Melbourne run in 60 days, and the Foochow run in 90. Her greatest run was 380 miles in a day—probably the record for all sailing ships. In a sense, such ships underlined the way in which Scotland was becoming part of a world economy centred in a North Atlantic capitalism which drew from peripheral areas what it needed by way of raw materials and luxuries and paid for them, on very favourable terms usually, with its own mass-produced manufactures. With the abolition in 1833 of the monopoly of British trade with China held by the Honourable East India Company, many Scottish firms penetrated that vast and remote market. They ranged from Jardine Matheson and Company, a very big firm whose affairs are intertwined with opium, cotton and other manufactures, to quite humble firms such as Andrew Melrose and Company of Edinburgh. The latter were wholesale tea dealers and their founder's son William Melrose spent a good number of years at Canton as a tea-buyer in the middle decades of the nineteenth century. It was for this trade that Messrs. Hall of Aberdeen built the *Sobraon*, the largest composite ship ever built, of 3,500 tons burthen with an overall length of 317 feet, an iron frame and solid teak, copper-fastened planking. Her lower masts were wrought iron, her topmasts and lower yards steel. Launched in 1866, she came near the end of an era in Aberdeen shipbuilding, for in 1867 Hall Russell and Company started building iron ships. By 1870 five Aberdeen yards employed 2,000 workmen and produced a great many steamships, quite a few of them for the Aberdeen Line of John T. Rennie and Sons trading to South Africa, but the glory had departed.

Leith never developed an impressive shipbuilding industry, though its yards could be busy enough. In 1882 they launched 16,250 tons of steamship, but many of Leith's seven yards at this period did more ship repair work than shipbuilding. It was on the Clyde that Scotland hammered out a uniquely important position for so small a nation in the world of shipbuilding. In terms of shipbuilding in wood the Clyde was a very minor river and as late as 1835 or so it was launching less than 5 per cent of Britain's annual production of new tonnage, so it will not do to argue that the subsequent greatness of the Clyde in shipbuilding rested on an accumulation of skill and experience before 1840. Rather was it the result of the exploitation of new means of propulsion and construction. Steam engines, be they Newcomen engines or the improved Watt models, were commonplace in the Lanarkshire and Ayrshire coalfields, so it was possible for Henry Bell in 1812 to assemble his epoch-making *Comet* (the second commercially successful steamship in the world) from existing shipyards, boiler works, and engineering works capable of producing a steam engine. The lead which the Clyde derived from the *Comet* was such that between 1812 and 1820 60 per cent of all British steam tonnage was launched on the Clyde. However, these ships were small. Their engines consumed enormous quantities of coal and they had very low boiler pressures (sometimes as little as 1½–2 lb. per square inch). It was the Napier family, and primarily David Napier, who combined marine engineering and shipbuilding at his Camlachie foundry and Lancefield yard, which pursued those technical improvements essential if steamships were to become efficient long-distance carriers. Just how important these technical improvements were was underlined by the rapidity with which the Clyde lost its early pre-eminence in steamship construction in the period after 1820. Between 1816 and 1836, when he moved to London, David Napier pioneered the search for fuel economy, higher boiler pressures, improved engines, and hull and propulsion systems suitable for seagoing steamships. His work was taken up by his cousin Robert Napier who succeeded him in both his yard and his foundry. The Napier yards produced a very high percentage of the names associated with the founding of major Clyde yards. They included a Denny; George and James Thomson who set up a yard at Clydebank which later became John Brown's; William Beardmore, the Elders and Charles Randolph who later combined to co-found Fairfields shipyard at Govan; and many more.

However, expertise of this kind does not adequately explain the spectacular relative growth of Clyde shipbuilding after 1840. Two technical developments were essential. One was the adoption of screw propellors instead of the paddles which were standard on early steamships. This presupposed higher pressures in marine boilers, as screws had to revolve much more rapidly than propellors. After 1840 pressures of over 40lb. per square inch became feasible and with them screw propulsion, which was rapidly adopted on the Clyde. The other development was a more economical marine engine and with the coming of the compound marine steam engine which expanded steam successively in two cylinders to make a double use of energy, massive economies were made. Charles Randolph and John Elder in the 1850s produced modified versions of this kind of engine which at last made steamships competitive on the longest ocean routes. Above all, changes in construction materials worked massively to the advantage of the Clyde. Originally iron ships were more expensive than wooden ones but by 1852 it was estimated that on the Clyde wooden hulls cost on average £14 per ton, but iron ones only £12, and iron hulls had the advantage of greater strength, lightness, and durability. Given the vigour of the Scottish iron industry, and the technical sophistication of Clyde shipbuilders unburdened by any long-standing conservative traditions, it can be seen why the Clyde between 1851 and 1870 produced the astonishing proportion of 70 per cent of all iron tonnage launched in Britain. By 1870 24,000 out of 47,500 men employed in shipbuilding in Britain were employed in Scottish yards and perhaps about 20,000 of these men were on the Clyde. Until 1914 the Clyde comfortably maintained this preeminent position. It made the transition to steel hulls without trauma and continued to lead the field in developments in propulsion. To secure higher boiler pressures (of the order of 150 lb. per square inch) A. C. Kirk of Napier's devised the triple-expansion engine in the 1870s. Nor was the Clyde content with the triple and later the quadruple expansion engine. C. A. Parsons' steam-turbine which achieved rotary motion direct from the engine was patented in 1884 and first installed on a Clyde steamer with Denny's as builder and Parsons as engineer. For maximum efficiency the turbine had to rotate faster than the propellor, and the holder of the Chair of Naval Architecture at Glasgow University claimed to be the originator of the geared-turbine marine engine, first installed at Fairfields' in 1912.

It is tempting to produce a 'leading-sector' explanation of Scottish economic development in the second half of the nineteenth century, because shipbuilding occupied such a strategic position in the Scottish economy, with strong linkages with the iron and steel and engineering industries; linkages often expressed in the form of vertical integration in industrial organisation. Another industry with strong links to the Clyde shipbuilding complex was the coal industry, but a careful examination of its history in the period after 1875 underlines the danger of such simple analytical tools, for Scottish coalmining splits into an eastern and western region after 1875 and these regions had very different experiences. In the west many coalmines were owned by iron manufacturers and suffered from two pressures. One was the general decline in Scottish pig iron production, which led to sales of mining interests by the iron industry, especially when depression was squeezing profit margins on iron. The other lay in the increasingly economical use of fuel by iron manufacturers. At its apogee the Scottish iron trade had been prodigal of cheap ore and cheap coal so there was plenty of room for approximation to best practice elsewhere as a response to more difficult times. The result of all this was a mining industry under considerable pressure which manifested itself in a bad record in industrial relations, with frequent strikes, nearly always over the stark issue of wage rates. When David Bremner wrote his classic series of articles on Scottish industries in *The Scotsman* newspaper in 1868 (subsequently reprinted in volume form in 1869 as *The Industries of Scotland*) he could remark on the very different strike records of the mining districts of the east and west of Scotland. Wages did fluctuate a great deal in the mines around Glasgow. In 1851 they were said to average 2s. 6d. a day. By 1854 the figure was 5s. 0d. but it then fell to an average of 3s. 0d. in 1858, recovering to an average of 4s. 5d. in the early 1860s, though it was reckoned that 3d. a day had to be subtracted to cover the cost to the miner of lighting his work and sharpening his tools. On the east coast, to use Bremner's words 'wages have not fluctuated so much as in other quarters'. Generalisation is difficult but in real terms they seem to have maintained a level of about 4s. 6d. a day.

Part of the explanation for this sharp regional difference undoubtedly lay in the export orientation of many eastern pits, especially those in Fife.

The Fife Coal Company, founded in 1872 by a group of Leith, Fife and Dundee capitalists, was floated during a period of buoyant prices during the economic boom which accompanied the Franco-Prussian War, but it had to start operations during an era of falling prices. Nevertheless, the company survived, extended its mineral holdings around Kelty, Leven, Hill of Beath and Methil, and went forward to prosperity and a good deal of expansion by means of amalgamation with neighbouring collieries in the early twentieth century. This particular company was well managed. It searched for new markets successfully, having agents in Denmark and Holland (it was on the Dutch Navy List), exports to the United States of America, and eventually a brisk trade with France. To boot, it was technologically progressive, installing new equipment ranging from mechanical coal-cutters to improved coal washing equipment imported from the Continent. Nor was it unique amongst Fife coal owners. Randolph Wemyss, the head of a very old family, showed great enterprise and courage in the late nineteenth century not only in developing his collieries and linking them with a light railway, but also in sponsoring massive development at his specialist coal port of Methil where the tonnage of coal shipped went up from 35,000 in 1886 to 2,823,720 by 1907.

Fife was exceptional, but it can be argued that the regional economics of eastern Scotland pursued distinctive paths in the period 1840–1914, paths which diverged very markedly from the experience of Clydeside. Aberdeen, for example, was very much the regional capital of the North-East, that dour shoulder of Scotland thrusting out into the North Sea. Though it never quite recovered the tremendous industrial vitality it displayed in the first four decades of the nineteenth century, Aberdeen enjoyed very real prosperity in the period to 1914 on the basis of several industries. Granite quarrying and polishing continued to flourish to the point where it proved necessary to supplement the quantity and restricted price range of local granites by importing black and red granite and labradorite from Scandinavia in a rough state. In 1896 £55,452 worth of worked stone was exported to America and France. In 1909 no less than 27,000 tons of Scandinavian granite were imported into Aberdeen to supplement the very substantial production of local and Peterhead granite. The paper industry of Aberdeen's Donside suburbs and Inverurie continued to use rags as its main raw material. At one stage at the end of the nineteenth century a single mill employed 400 women in its rag sorting department, but the port of Aberdeen enabled the industry to make the transition to the use of esparto grass and wood pulp, and the industry survived and prospered despite its remoteness from the principal areas of consumption (apart from Aberdeen's own printing industry). Much the most spectacular area of economic growth in late nineteenth century Aberdeen, however, was steam trawling. In the 1860s and 1870s the city had lagged behind in this field, relying on a fleet of over 100 open boats of 3½– 5 tons which fished inshore with baited lines. Then the combination of the railway, which offered speedy access to distant markets, and the technique of steam trawling, which had developed around the mouths of the Tyne and the Wear in the north of England, unleashed an unprecedented expansion in the Aberdeen fishing industry.

In 1882 the *Toiler* demonstrated the potential of steam trawling in Aberdeen Bay. By 1892 Aberdeen had 86 steam trawlers, many locally built. The number was 156 in 1902 and 230 in 1912. By 1911 Aberdeen had become the first fishing port in Scotland and the third largest in Great Britain. Its greatness was based on white fish—cod and haddock primarily—and it was well placed to exploit the increasingly important Faroese and Icelandic fisheries. As a herring port, Aberdeen had a chequered history and at the time of the introduction of the steam drifter into the herring fishery around 1889, the white fishery was making maximum demands on Aberdeen harbour space and available capital. The result was that the herring fishery by steam drifter became the speciality of Moray Firth ports like Fraserburgh, or more northerly Aberdeenshire ports like Peterhead. In both cases, the transition from many small open boats to far fewer but far costlier ships was marked by the end of the system whereby fish curers made bids at the start of a season for the whole catch of a given boat. Fish prices fluctuate, and curers were liable to go bankrupt, so a system of auctioning catches at recognised markets was both logical and progressive. This rise in the fortunes of the white and herring fisheries compensated to some extent for the progressive decline in the east coast whale fishery.

The history of that fishery is a complex one which falls into two stages. It grew originally under the impetus of a government bounty. Without that bounty it is difficult to see how the Scottish whaling fleet could have survived, for in pure business terms it simply did not pay its way between 1750 and 1780, a period during which the state paid out no less than £185,955 to Scottish whaling firms. During the half century to 1799 bounties to Scottish whaling amounted to £301,746 and the impact of such sums on such poor communities (in relative terms) as Dunbar,

Dundee and Aberdeen was considerable. State bounties were arguably self-defeating but they nursed Scottish whaling along until it entered the nineteenth century capable of operating profitably. The bounty was withdrawn in 1824 and with the return of adverse market conditions Scottish whaling withered. In 1820 Aberdeen had 20 whaling vessels: in 1838 the number was two. The same story was repeated from Peterhead to Dunbar, but from about 1860 there came a rebirth of east-coast whaling based on the use of bigger boats with steam engines supplemented by sail for the sake of range. They hunted Arctic whales, often in the Davis Straits to the west of Greenland, with oar-propelled catcher boats and hand harpoons. For a period there was a remarkable upsurge in Scottish whaling during which Dundee was for a time the leading British whaling port. By 1873, the Dundee whaling fleet comprised ten ships, all steamers with auxiliary sail, and ranging from 270 to 439 tons. They could fit in two voyages a year, hunting seals off Greenland and Newfoundland in the spring, and whales in Davis Straits in the summer. Peterhead was another leading whaling port but by the 1890s a combination of over-fishing and falling prices for whale and seal oil due to competition from mineral oil was killing the industry. By 1914 it was virtually dead. The Norwegians with factory ships, powered catchers and their new harpoon cannon had left the Scots far behind technologically. The Scots never caught up nor did they manage to break into the Antarctic whaling which was becoming the most profitable branch of whaling after the reckless over-fishing of Arctic whale stocks. The one exception to this merely proves the rule, for it is the firm of Salvesen of Leith which was itself of Norwegian origin. Its rise dated back to the 1850s when Christian Salvesen left Norway to join his brother Johann who had established a shipbroking, owning, timber and grain merchanting business in Grangemouth. The firm never lost its Scandinavian connection, so the decision to enter whaling in the late nineteenth century was taken on a scale and in a context alien to the dying traditional whaling industry of Scotland.

Curiously enough whaling in Dundee appears, in the early decades of the nineteenth century, to have played a key role in another process of industrial growth. The Honourable East India Company was notoriously anxious to develop the export of staple commodities from its Indian territories to Britain, mainly because of sustained criticism of its own financial basis. Packets of Jute, a coarse fibre from Bengal, were sent to various textile centres in Britain in the hope that the cheapness of the product might render it attractive to manufacturers. In fact its dryness and brittleness defied even the coarse linen trade of Dundee until somebody struck on the idea of 'batching' the jute, i.e. softening it by the application of a mixture of water and whale oil. Mineral oil was inevitably later substituted for whale oil but the latter had served a historic purpose by enabling a commercial relationship to grow up between the biggest centre in the east-central Scottish linen area and a province of British India. By the 1830s jute carpeting was being manufactured in and around Dundee and by the 1840s jute bagging was being used for commodities ranging from East Indian coffee to South American fertiliser in the shape of guano. It was, however, the era of the Crimean War (1854–6), with its combination of a restricted and uncertain supply of flax from Baltic Russia and unprecedented demand for coarse textiles, which gave jute its opportunity. Inevitably the war boom was followed by a secular depression heightened by adverse American tariffs. Then in 1861 the American Civil War broke out and until it ended in 1865 Dundee enjoyed fantastic prosperity, selling linen and jute goods on a vast scale to both sides in the first modern war of mass armies and industrial technology. Jute had become the leading product of Dundee and the Angus textile towns linked to Dundee.

There was a further, if smaller, war boom in 1871–2 at the time of the Franco-Prussian War. The period of expansion between 1861 and 1871 was in absolute terms the greatest ever in the history of Dundee. Population grew, mainly by migration from the Angus countryside, from 91,664 in 1861 to 119,141 in 1871. By 1872 it was being said of Dundee's flax and jute products that 40 per cent went to the United States but that the Indian and Colonial markets were also very good. There was the unavoidable post-war depression in the mid 1870s but such was the labour shortage in Dundee textiles that until 1877 it was believed that depressions and bankruptcies had never caused more than a very temporary rise in overall unemployment. As early as 1855 the Englishman George Ackland had started the Rishra Mill at Serampore north of Calcutta, producing eight tons of jute yarn a day with the help of Dundee machinery and a Dundee foreman. In theory the Indian jute industry was in a strong position to compete. It could use extremely cheap labour and it was nearer its raw material by several thousand miles than any Scottish jute manufacturer. In a sense it was ironic that the biggest jute factory in the world, with some 5,000 hands in the 1880s, was Cox Brothers' Camperdown Works in the Dundee suburb of Lochee. Yet the

Indian industry had to surmount formidable problems such as lack of skilled manpower, shortage of capital, and above all lack of experience. The early 1870s saw substantial investment in the Bengal jute industry, much of it lost in the subsequent slump, but the Dundee-sponsored Samnuggar Company proved a pioneer which spearheaded the first Indian assault on overseas markets. By 1885 Dundee had lost the market for sacking for the Californian, Australian and New Zealand grain trades to Calcutta. Between 1895 and 1909 the Indian jute industry made huge strides. In the later year its total labour force of 184,500 dwarfed the total population of Dundee.

All this still only cut away at the cheaper end of the trade. Calcutta had colossal capacity for coarse hessian sacking. Dundee also produced hessian but it increasingly concentrated on finer and more specialised lines. During the so-called Great Depression in British industry between 1873 and 1896, which even critics of the whole concept would admit was a period of relatively low profits and dividends in many industries, the balance sheets of many Scottish jute and linen firms remained remarkably healthy. Contemporaries regarded the demise of a few firms during recurring depressions simply as a weeding-out process which left the healthy firms untroubled. Dundee never ceased to be a flax town. Baxter Brothers were as famous a linen firm as Cox Brothers were a jute firm. Nowhere in the history of the pre-1914 east-central Scottish linen trade (a term used locally to embrace hemp, jute, and flax) do we find the sort of visceral crisis such as forced Courtaulds, the English silk and crape firm, to go through an agonising re-appraisal of itself and adopt an entirely new staple product in the late 1880s. The Boer War generated the usual war boom for coarse textiles. South American demand for sacking was buoyant in the early twentieth century due to sheep and grain booms in Argentina, and a revival in the American market in 1912 ushered in the last pre-war boom, which left the linen trade bigger and more heavily capitalised than ever. Only on the southern edge of Fife, in Kirkcaldy, was a significantly new product developed within the coarse textile area. This was linoleum, but its manufacture developed in the later 1870s as a logical extension of a long tradition of producing heavy floor cloth in linen. The new product was closely linked to the jute trade, which supplied the backing to the mixture of linseed and cork known as linoleum. Two very great firms—Nairns and Barry Ostlere and Shepherd—came to dominate the Kirkcaldy trade. Both were plagued by foreign tariffs to the point of establishing factories in North America and on the Continent, but both had very strong home markets and both remained solidly prosperous in the decade to 1914.

The Border woollen trade had its own distinctive experience, though here too the decade to 1914 was a satisfactory one. The period between 1830 and 1860 had seen almost continuous expansion in the sale of Border tweeds. There had been considerable investment in new mills, steam-powered weaving machinery, and after a lag, in power-driven self-activating spinning mules. The industry acquired a jaunty confidence in itself which reached a peak after the Franco-Prussian War boom, which levelled out about 1873. Almost at once the industry rang with complaints of falling sales and profits, which was perhaps to be expected in the recession following a boom. However, by 1880 it was clear that the honeymoon era in the industry was over, for a variety of causes. During the 1880s falling prices were to some extent masked by rising sales but after 1890 falling prices coincided with falling production. Between 1891 and 1901 the population of Hawick fell from 19,204 to 17,303 and that of Galashiels fell by a quarter. Partly this can be explained by the rise of protective tariffs in Europe after 1870, though it does seem that very often the growth of efficient mechanised European woollen industries behind protective tariffs created a situation in which the removal of tariffs would not have restored to the Border woollen trade its old ascendancy in export markets. The crippling tariff barrier was the American one imposed by the McKinley tariff of 1890, which effectively placed a 90 per cent duty on Scottish woollens. Before 1890 the trade of Border manufacturers with the USA was over £500,000 annually, but by 1905 this had dropped to £50,000 or so. Galashiels was particularly hard hit because it had sent three-quarters of its annual production to America before 1890 and in the early 1900s the figure was a mere twentieth. On top of this changes in fashion undoubtedly had an adverse effect on the Border industry. There was a swing towards lighter woollens in the domestic market; a swing with Yorkshire manufacturers successfully exploited with worsted goods often based on cheaper grades of wool. Those Scottish Border manufacturers who saw fit to follow them did not bring much profit to themselves and usually threatened their industry's priceless reputation for quality. Recovery was achieved, by those firms who survived the ruthless selection process imposed by the late nineteenth century depression, by maintaining standards, and by following the swing of fashion. In men's goods the move was to high quality worsted and flannel suiting, while in the ladies' wear section new light tweeds were devised. Despite set-backs in 1904–5 and 1907, prices steadily improved after 1900 and when after 1909 wool prices fell at a time of good demand for Border textiles, reasonable profitability was restored.

In a sense it was precisely the sustained success of old-established industries which posed the gravest problems for the future of the Scottish economy. There was very little industrial discontinuity in Scotland before 1914. Such dramatic changes as occurred very often occurred as early as the 1860s. The cotton industry is a case in point. Between 1840 and 1860 the Scottish cotton industry, highly concentrated in Lanarkshire and Renfrewshire, had adopted a pattern of a low-wage female labour force producing high-quality goods. Badly hit by the cotton famine during the American Civil War, the Scottish industry became increasingly inefficient and under-capitalised compared with its competitors in Lancashire or America. It was a vicious downward spiral as inability to compete made it difficult to raise capital. Significantly the specialised thread industry of Paisley survived partly at any rate because it was in relative terms very large. When the two biggest Paisley firms, Coats and Clark, amalgamated in 1896 they controlled between them a very large part of the world's thread industry. Even if a good deal of production lay abroad, the Coats empire was controlled from Glasgow, whereas amalgamation in the calico printing and some aspects of the dyeing industries, on a British basis, led to the removal of control from Scotland and the closing down of Scottish plants with a good record, as surplus to a centrally-judged requirement. A similar pattern could be observed in the chemical field where Scotland was in any case losing some of its earlier natural advantages and where the formation of the United Alkali Company was followed in the 1890s by the closing down of alkali production at some of the most famous of Scottish chemical works.

There were new industries in late Victorian Scotland, but with one exception, and that an exception with a finite life, they tended to be established by foreign entrepreneurs. The exception was the shale-oil industry established as the result of a process developed by James Young, who patented it in 1850. He first used it on a large scale at Bathgate in West Lothian, a community which soon bore the marks of his success, ranging from his own vast mansion, to a colossal bing of spent shale behind his chemical works. After his patents expired in 1864 others entered the industry, producing burning oil, naphtha, paraffin and other products. In 1877, however, natural petroleum from Pennsylvania came on to the market and cut the price by a very large margin. Increased efficiency and more emphasis on useful by-products enabled the Scottish industry to survive. Production in 1909 amounted to 2,261,086 tons worth £621,799. In the long run survival was impossible and the development of Middle Eastern oilfields with their extremely cheap oil spelled the doom of shale oil. However, the Middle East began to assume its modern position as a source of fuel oil only in the year or two before 1914. Other innovative industries proved more enduring. The Swede Alfred Nobel established a dynamite works at Ardeer in Ayrshire in 1873. It grew into a major chemical works. Americans, too, were active in Scotland. It was American capital which established the North British Rubber Company in Edinburgh in 1856 and, perhaps most significant of all, it was the American Singer Company which in the 1880s built a large factory at Clydebank for the manufacture of sewing machines. This sort of mass-produced new consumer-durable was precisely the sort of good which Scottish entrepreneurs were extremely slow to adopt as a major line for their factories. Instead, Scottish industrial effort tended to be concentrated on the production of heavy capital goods, such as ships and locomotives, or on traditional textiles like linens, high-quality tweed (much of it for export), or jute, a textile not unfairly described as the 'brown paper of commerce'.

It was not that Scotland lacked a native banking system capable of mobilising funds for new investment. Quite the reverse was the case. The Scottish banks had evolved very rapidly, indeed occasionally traumatically, between 1845 and 1878. By the latter date they had evolved a pattern for banking in Scotland which, with all its faults, was good enough to last into the 1950s. By 1836 it was clear that Scottish banking could not hope for real autonomy because the Scottish banks were ultimately dependent on London liquidity to work their distinctive system, with its economy in the use of gold and its buoyant note issue. By the time of a banking crisis in 1836 it was clear that the Bank of England, massively supported by the British government, was assuming a central role in the entire British banking system. The Bank Charter Act of 1844 could not, of course, persuade the nineteen issuing Scottish banks to unify their note issue, but it effectively forbade any further issue. Legislation of 1845 imposed on Scottish banks an unprecedented requirement to hold gold as backing for their note issue, which was thereby restricted. By preserving separate note issue in Scotland the act made it difficult for the Scots banks to invade England. Finally by effectively banning the formation of new joint-stock banks the 1844–5 legislation stopped price competition between existing banks. By the end of 1845 there were 17 Scottish note-issuing banks and between 1850 and 1878 the number fell to ten as a result of four amalgamations, one carefully managed collapse disguised as an amalgamation, and two sensational crashes.

The genuine amalgamations were in the 1850s and 1860s and involved the merging of Perth and Dundee banks into larger organisations. The Edinburgh and Glasgow Bank was a major joint-stock bank in serious trouble since 1847 which was taken over by the Clydesdale Bank in 1857 to avoid public admission of the Edinburgh and Glasgow's insolvency. The first of the crashes was that of the Western Bank in 1857. Like the Edinburgh and Glasgow, the Western had been in trouble for some time but failed to learn its lesson. Its paid-up capital of £1,500,000 by 1857 was second only to the Royal Bank's £2,000,000. The Western had the second largest note circulation and the largest number of branches (101) of any bank in Scotland, but in the boom of 1857 it lent unwisely and massively to a limited number of firms. The bankruptcy of three of those firms, plus a general slump originating in America destroyed the Western. As unlimited liability still reigned for unincorporated banks, the main losers, once government action curtailed commercial panic in Glasgow, were the bank's shareholders. They lost nearly £2 million of capital and reserve plus over £1 million of further calls. Twenty-one years later Glasgow in 1878 experienced the even greater shock of the failure of the City of Glasgow Bank. This, like the Western, was a bank run on aggressive lines. It had 133 offices by about 1875, but its deposits were not proportionate to its lending, and it was heavily dependent on the London money market, having sunk a high proportion of its resources in discounts. In a manner by no means atypical of the contemporary Scottish business community, the City of Glasgow was deeply interested in overseas investment, ranging from America to India and New Zealand. Bad judgement in American railways and New Zealand land, combined with the Western's error of over commitment to a few unsound local businesses, placed the City of Glasgow in an impossible position which a board of pious mediocrities tried to conceal by falsification of balance sheets. The final crash came on 1 October 1878, when the rigours of unlimited liability came into play for all shareholders. Eventually calls amounting to £2,750 per £100 share were made with a heartlessness and systematic ruthlessness worthy of a Victorian melodrama, which is what the whole episode was. Two thousand families suffered losses, often on a scale involving bankruptcy.

The remaining seven unlimited banks in Scotland swiftly bought up and reopened most of the City of Glasgow branches. Banking facilities were therefore scarcely reduced by the crisis. The three chartered Scottish banks had always enjoyed limited liability and by 1882 the other seven Scottish banks had availed themselves of legislation granting them limited status. Independent audit and the publication of consolidated if abbreviated balance sheets were voluntarily adopted. Banks ceased to trade in their own stock. The most important overall result of the crisis was probably an entrenched policy of caution in all lending on the part of the Scottish banking system. Aggressive, commercial Glasgow remained a major banking centre but the ascendancy of cool, professional Edinburgh was unshakeable after 1878. In the three decades before 1914 the Scottish banking system displayed rock-like stability. The North of Scotland Bank lost £233,000 in 1888 during a crisis in the herring industry, thereby wiping out its reserve, but not seriously risking failure. The other banks tended to be hyper-reluctant to oblige any agricultural or industrial client without solid guarantors. Apart from a general opening of offices in London in the 1860s and 1870s the Scottish banks were reluctant to brave the wrath of the English banks by supporting the small-scale foray over the border perpetrated by the Clydesdale. All in all, the rate of expansion in Scottish banking fell significantly after 1886 and this fall was accentuated after 1900. The banking system, like the industrial structure of Scotland, was in its own terms mature, presided over by the awesome figures of the general managers of the banks. These eminent men had every reason to be pleased with themselves in the decade before 1914. Profits were healthy and security absolute. Modern critics may argue that more adventurous lending policies would have stimulated innovation and dynamism: they carp at what was, in its own terms, perfection.

The Scottish industrial economy of the late nineteenth and early twentieth centuries had achieved maturity in a comparatively short space of time. In 1885 a Forfarshire manufacturer remarked that:

Thirty years syne we were all sma' bodies here—The Juteocracy of Dundee, the Ironocracy of Lanarkshire and Ayrshire, the Shipocracy of the Clyde, and the Tweedocracy of the Border—all date alike from the Crimean War, as the fine old English gentleman traces his pedigree from the Conquest.

The increase in Scotland's aggregate national wealth is difficult to quantify, because of the absence of separate statistics for what was technically simply the northern part of the United Kingdom. One pointer is the fact that total taxed income in Scotland in 1854–5 was approximately £28 million sterling, and by 1885 the figure was roughly £56 million sterling, so it looks as if Scottish national income may have doubled in this period, and a significant proportion of the increase was being channelled into overseas investment. This was itself a symptom of a mature economy. As the United States and West Germany have demonstrated in the twentieth century, such economies have a natural tendency to export capital looking for higher returns abroad than can be obtained at home. It was a commonplace of late Victorian comment that Scotland invested abroad on a scale per head with no parallel among the other nations of the United Kingdom. The first notable surge of enthusiasm for such investment after 1856 seems to have come in 1873 when Scots seized the advantage of low New York Stock Exchange security prices (due to depression), in order to buy a substantial stake in American railways. Then Edinburgh capitalists lent massive sums to rebuild Chicago after the terrible fire of October 1871 had destroyed some 18,000 buildings there, leaving 90,000 people homeless. Thus opened a new world of American real estate investment and mortgage business. Dundee capitalists were soon lending large sums on the security of real estate in the Pacific North West. Thereafter, despite the inevitable ups and downs of the stock market, Scottish capital continued to flow into the American economy, entering new areas such as mining, especially in California and Colorado, and cattle ranching, especially in Texas where the Scottish-American companies provided not only finance but entrepreneurial drive.

America was, of course, only one area of overseas investment, albeit the most significant one. Aberdeen and Edinburgh investors were extemely interested in the development of Australia and New Zealand. The industries, railways, and commercial agricultures of India, Ceylon, and Burma all attracted Scottish capital, and such links could be self-reinforcing. It was after a spell on the Heelikah estate of the Scottish Assam Tea Company, for example, that William Jackson (1849–1915) returned to Aberdeen and became one of the handful of engineers who devised badly needed machinery for processing plucked tea. Dundee became the home of the investment trust, mainly through the activities of Robert Fleming who set the investment trust boom in motion with the first issue of his Scottish American Investment Trust in July 1873, but Fleming had learned the potential for investment in America in previous employment under Edward Baxter, one of the members of a millionaire linen family. Scottish foreign investment may have risen from £60 million in 1870 to as much as £500 million by 1914, which raises the problem of why a small country with much primary poverty amongst its working masses, and an undoubted shortage of innovative investment, chose to send so much money abroad.

The answer would appear to be that in terms of the market economy on which Scotland's industrial greatness rested, this export of capital was inevitable, and in the eyes of those who managed it, morally and economically right. Their job was to maximise the rate of return on Scottish capital. It was a fact of life that between 1870 and 1914 very attractive terms could be obtained for capital transfers designed to supply the basic investment required by an expanding frontier of settlement in the Americas or Australasia, or by the often ruthless process of directing the land and labour of African or Asian peoples into the commercial agriculture needed by their European masters. That this overseas investment had a circular effect on the development of the Scottish economy is clear. Much investment went into communities or economic complexes dedicated to the production of staple commodities for international trade. That trade's expansion expanded demand for the products of Scotland's mature industrial economy. The wheat of the Canadian or American prairies, for example, had to be taken by rail to eastern ports, and in Canada the locomotive could well be one made in Glasgow while both in Canada and in America the sacks holding the grain were quite likely to have been manufactured in Dundee. The ships which crossed the North Atlantic with the grain were often enough built and engineered on the Clyde. Thus demand for the great staples of the Scottish economy was sustained and enhanced. This meant that these staples still constituted the prime investment areas for Scottish capital at home. It was not reasonable to sink funds into risky new products when old ones offered solid returns. No sane financier was likely to choose to shoulder staggering transition costs to a new industrial structure of a necessarily hypothetical kind. The dynamism of the market can be circular as well as linear.

Scottish agriculture 1840–1914

The dynamism of market forces can also be cruel, as Scottish agriculture learned to its bitter cost in the years after 1870. Yet the years between 1840 and 1870 were on the whole prosperous ones for Scottish agriculture. Two areas of innovation go far to explain the buoyant state of Scottish farming around 1840. One, which is too often neglected by historians, was the rapid spread of efficient and cheap drainage. The agricultural improvement of the eighteenth century had never solved this particular problem. Surface cuts to remove water presupposed convenient slopes and a good natural drainage to connect with, while underground drainage tended to be a complex business involving excavation and the use of great quantities of boulders and brushwood. The result was that rigs remained a very common feature of Scottish agriculture, if only because there was no real alternative. Then in the early nineteenth century tile drainage became available at reasonable cost. In the Carse of Gowrie, for example, it was the tile drains produced by Sir James Richardson in his tile-works at Pitfour which seem to have led the way, but every area of Scotland produced its own pioneers in drainage such as James Smith of Deanston. One reason why the mechanical reaper devised by the Angus clergyman Patrick Bell in 1828 never caught on in Scotland, and has been obliterated in popular memory by the later but vastly more successful American McCormick reaper, was that the still widespread rigs in Scottish fields ruled out its use. In 1846 a Public Money Drainage Act made funds available to farmers specifically for drainage, and Scots farmers made heavy use of this legislation. Combined with an even more systematic use of liming, efficient drainage increased returns on much land.

Mechanisation was the other area of innovation highly favourable to Scottish farming. Direct mechanisation of farm work was uneven in incidence. Mechanical threshing was commonplace by the 1840s, and thereby deprived farm labourers of significant winter income from work with the flail. Reaping, even after drainage improvement, was not mechanised to the same extent, at least for a long time. Farm labour was still cheap, so the main change was simply from the sickle to the scythe. Eventually mechanical reapers came into use, and after 1850 there was a growing tendency on bigger farms to use steam power for threshing and ploughing. Arguably, it was the mechanisation of transport with the coming of the railways which more than any other single innovation

changed the prospects of Scottish farming. Dairying in particular benefited from fast access to urban markets for fresh produce. The south-west
of Scotland developed a thriving dairy industry based on small or
medium sized farms: an industry which stood up well to difficult times
after 1870. In the same way cattle farming in the northern parts of Scotland benefited from long-distance rail haulage. It was a combination of
such haulage and massive land improvement which turned the North-
East into a great cattle-producing area with its own specialist
Aberdeen-Angus breed.

Prices remained healthy throughout the 1850s and 1860s. The repeal
of the Corn Laws from 1846 was, of course, a political gesture. Sir Robert
Peel had carefully calculated that the cost of transporting grain from
eastern parts of Europe to Britain would in normal years more than ade-
quately protect British grain producers. As eastern Europe was the main
source of grain imports, it is not surprising that the price of wheat
remained stable at about 40s. a quarter in the late 1840s rising to 50s by
1852 and to over 70s. in 1854 and 1855. From then onwards it remained
for 20 years at highly satisfactory levels from the point of view of the
farmer. A good deal of the mechanisation and improvement which
occurred on Scottish farms in the mid-Victorian period involved an
increased use of horses, so the price of oats was sustained by this trend,
and by the fact that in Scotland oatmeal was an important constituent in
the diet of the urban poor. That cattle prices and prices for dairy products were well sustained is perhaps best illustrated by the simple statis-
tic that in 1856 the number of cattle in Scotland was officially 967,000.
By 1876 the figure had risen to 1,131,087. It was reckoned that in the mid
1860s the equivalent of 50,000 fat cattle were being sent south annually
from an area about a third larger than the county of Aberdeen. Such
prodigies of specialised development were based on an increasing use of
fertilisers, of which Scottish agriculture consumed very large quantities
indeed from guano to industrial phosphates; on an increased turnip
acreage for winter feed; improved railway and steamer services; and
improved breeds from the beef cattle breeds to milk-producing Ayr-
shires.

Rural society in the Lowlands remained rigidly hierarchical. There
were comparatively few owner-occupiers. For the sake of both prestige
and profit large landowners tended, if anything, to enlarge their holdings
when they could. Nevertheless in favoured areas an able tenant farmer
could make a very good living as well as pay a substantial rent. Fine solid

farmhouses all over Lowland Scotland housed tenant farmers who were essentially agricultural entrepreneurs and who at their best in families like the Hopes of Fenton Barns in East Lothian were also model farmers with an international reputation. Prosperity made the irritant of Scotland's reactionary game laws, which reserved the right to kill game solely to the landlord, tolerable if not acceptable. Tenants only acquired the right to kill rabbits and hares on their own property as late as 1880. Prosperity made the occasional visitation of rinderpest, pleuro-pneumonia, and foot-and-mouth disease a temporary disaster from which the Scottish cattle trade recovered quite quickly. Linked together in prosperity, the laird and tenant farmer held under them a quiescent and cheap labour force. In parts of the Lowlands such as Angus and the Howe O' the Mearns a large part of this force would be single men organised under the bothy system—a species of labour barracks which gave birth to a wealth of song in the shape of the bothy ballads, but which destroyed family life and held men at miserable levels of comfort. Here was a rural proletariat indeed, dedicated to working a commercial agriculture whose prosperity was intimately interwoven with the great conurbations of industrial Scotland.

In 1867, admittedly in a year of poor harvest, the average price of wheat in Britain stood at 64s. 5d. a quarter. Nobody at the time could reasonably have forecast that within twenty years that price would be halved, and that by the 1890s it would be down to 23s. 0d., the lowest price for 200 years. The fundamental reason for this was the flow of grain from Canada and the United States at highly competitive prices on to the British market. The creation of transcontinental railway systems in North America and a dramatic fall in Atlantic shipping costs due to larger, steel-hulled vessels with economical triple expansion engines, abolished the protection which distance had long given to the British farmer. Nor was it simply the grain farmer who suffered, for North America, and indeed Argentina after 1900, shipped great quantities of meat, alive and dead, to Britain. To this must be added meat and dairy products from Australasia which the introduction of refrigeration brought into British markets in the late nineteenth century. The skies rang with the wails of farmers and landlords. Certainly this huge flow of cheap food severely dampened prices and rents. The bonanza years were over, but it does seem that Lowland farming in Scotland weathered this whole crisis much more successfully then, say, the grain producing areas of England.

The reasons for this are not far to seek. Over large areas of the Lowlands mixed farming rather than specialised farming was the norm in Scotland before 1870. Mixed farming was naturally more flexible in its response to changing market conditions. In addition, the specialisations of certain Scottish agricultural regions did not prove injudicious or unadaptable in the 1880s and 1890s. The cereals for which the Scottish climate is best suited, oats and barley, did not experience price falls on the scale suffered by wheat. The dairying industry of the south-west maintained its reputation for efficiency and a scientific approach, pioneering the recording of milk yields, and remained highly competitive in Scottish urban markets. Cattle farming had always been relatively more important in Scotland than in England and cattle prices were not so badly affected as cereal prices by the new flood of imports. In any case, the imported meat and cattle were never very serious competitors for the quality end of the meat trade, so the long Scots tradition of breeding quality cattle paid off in a high degree of resilience in the face of the foreign challenge. In Aberdeenshire the grain acreage remained pretty stable between 1879 and 1914, while the acreage under turnips fell by a mere seven per cent. This was, however, an unusually stable scene. Scotland's total acreage of permanent grass rose during this era from 1,160,000 to 1,490,000 while the grain acreage fell from 1,390,000 to 1,186,000. In percentage terms (15) this was only half the fall which occurred in English grain acreage. Clearly the main response of Scottish agricultural lay in a further swing towards pasture. Rents necessarily fell. Wages fell, then recovered in the 1890s, but remained much lower than industrial wages, and by 1912 Scottish agriculture could be seen to have weathered the storm, though at a price. The market in land was extremely poor in this period, and landlords who had incurred heavy mortgages before the fall in agricultural prices and rents, as many had, were in an extremely difficult position for decades.

In the Highlands another cycle of dramatic economic, social, and political change occurred between 1840 and 1914. To understand its origins it is essential to look at an industry which they shared with the Lowlands, but which was disproportionately important north of the Highland Line—sheep farming. Earlier in the century, when sheep farming was first introduced to the northern Highlands there had been a series of crises in the new industry, ranging from falling prices after the Napoleonic wars to sustained hostility from evicted crofters allied to large-scale sheep stealing. In 1815 raiders are said to have stolen nearly

1,600 sheep from eleven farms in Sutherland. However, between 1838 and 1874 the history of the Highland sheep farms was reasonably prosperous except in the odd extreme winters such as those of 1838 and 1860, when very bad weather caused heavy loss of stock. All the time, however, the grazing habits of the sheep were contributing to their own downfall, for these dainty and destructive feeders destroyed the finer grasses on pastures which they were allowed to overgraze, leaving the way open for coarse grass and bracken to take over. Meanwhile there was a growing tendency for Lowland farms, and especially those on the east coast, to compete with Highland sheep farming by using rotation grasses and turnips to raise sheep intensively on small areas. Colonial wool had been reaching Scottish markets in fair quantities for a long time, but after the mid 1870s both colonial wool and colonial mutton, often superior in quality to and lower in price than Highland products, were freely available on the British market. In the 1860s unwashed Cheviot wool sold at 1s. 0½d. per lb. By the 1890s the price was 6½d. per lb. In the same way a three-year-old Cheviot wether (gelded ram) which in the 1870s sold for 45s. was costing a mere 28s. by 1900. The great age of sheep in the Highland economy was over. The higher, poorer grazings normally stocked with wethers suffered most because the fall in the value of their stock was the highest of all, but all sheep farms were to some extent affected and their rents had to come down.

This coincided with a rising demand for moors for sporting use. The economics of this development hinged on two simple facts. One was that industrial development had created immense personal and family fortunes in many parts of Britain. The other was that in the complex social hierarchy of nineteenth-century Britain the pursuit of aristocratic blood sports was a significant indicator of high social standing. The artist Sir John Millais, for example, at the height of his career enjoyed excellent deer-stalking on Fannich, Loch Luichart, Dunrobin, Braemore, and Loch More between 1867 and 1871, and nothing more emphatically underlined his social and professional acceptability amongst the greatest in the land. From Braemore he went on to Loch More for stalking and salmon-fishing as a guest of the Duke of Westminster. Theoretically stalking deer with a rifle was compatible with sheep-farming. In practice it was not, partly because the gamekeeper wished to raise grouse to broaden the scope of the sport offered by his moor, and found the heather-burning methods of the sheep farmer too indiscriminate. Above all rich men were ready to pay both the grazing and the sporting rent for the sake of a clear shot. The supreme irony thus occurred of a large-scale clearance of shepherds and sheep from extensive areas of the Highlands. In the counties of Argyll, Inverness and Ross, sheep declined in number from 2,187,000 in 1879 to 1,609,000 in 1914. In their place came deer forest; that oddest of all forests where the aim is to avoid any vegetation high enough to obstruct the fire of a rifle or shotgun. Such deer forest increased in acreage from 1,975,209 acres in 1883 to 3,584,966 in 1912. It was on shooting rents that many an ancient house raised or refurbished its stately home in the late nineteenth century. Before we leap to condemn this deliberate creation of vast man-made deserts, it is important to recall that a study of the large estates on the peninsula of Morvern, opposite Mull on the west coast of the Highlands, has concluded that, though latterly run as sporting machines, these properties were not parasites sucking the life out of the region. On the contrary, it has been argued that their proprietors very often ran their estates at a loss by subsidising them from their industrial incomes, and that this process shielded the area from the full blast of agricultural depression while providing much employment and welfare for its people.

What is clear is that the social order and habits of command maintained by a new class of industrialist proprietors and their heirs were no more compatible with the human dignity of the Highland people than the habits of the worst landlords of the old school. It is not surprising that the discontent which had simmered under the surface of Highland society finally boiled over in the early 1880s. Circumstances were favourable. The British government was making a conspicuously bad job of coping with widespread agrarian unrest in Ireland and was easily thrown into blind panic by the thought of another Ireland in the Highlands. Lack of leadership, that chronic curse of Highland society, only inadequately remedied by the Free Kirk after 1843, was less crippling in the 1880s because of the emergence of a second-generation leadership in the shape of sons of Highlanders who had emigrated to Glasgow, often after clearances. The year 1883 saw renewed violence in Skye, the formation of the body eventually known as the Highland Land League, and the appointment by the government of a royal commission under Lord Napier. Royal commissions are usually elaborate devices for wasting time on an issue the government does not really want to tackle, but circumstances were such that a Crofters' Holding Act was a reality by 1886. Absolute security of tenure, compensation for improvements, and controlled rents were the central features of this legislation. The Napier commission had not in fact been very happy about extending absolute security of tenure to uneconomically small holdings, but on this and other points political expediency was the guiding light. A Crofters' Commission was set up in 1887 to administer the act in the crofting counties which were defined as Shetland, Orkney, Caithness, Sutherland, Ross and Cromarty, Inverness and Argyll, with 12 parishes (eight of them in Argyll) excluded.

The argument that one effect of this legislation was to freeze the pattern of crofting, often on unviable units, seems to have a good deal of force. Of course, the crofting landscape was never wholly static. A Congested Districts Board was set up in 1897 with money and power to create and enlarge holdings, and to improve transport by building roads and piers and agriculture by various forms of technical assistance. The Crofters' Commission and the Congested Districts Board were merged into the Scottish Land Court in 1912. Substantial parts of the Highlands in Perthshire, Angus, and Aberdeenshire never came within the remit of these bodies. On the mainland the great estates were not vastly affected by the creation of officially-recognised crofters' rights, if only because crofters had usually already been moved into limited areas near the sea. In the Hebrides the story was different and in the southern part of those islands saw the emergence of a statutory landscape of long rows of crofts with even longer strips of land behind them for arable and grazing. In the Shetland Isles the effect of the crofting legislation was finally to break the vice-like grip of the merchant and laird (often the same man) over the crofter-fisherman. The Truck Acts which attacked conversion of cash payment into payment in kind on very poor terms were already undermining the old ascendancy, and a great boom in the herring fishing in the 1890s and early 1900s gave the newly emancipated community economic confidence at just the right time. In Orkney, as befitted the softer nature of those isles, the change effected by the crofting legislation at first looked less dramatic, though it decisively strengthened the status of the tenant farmer. In the long run the combination of security, low rent, and good soil placed the tenant farmer in a position to buy out his landlord, for the landlord found it increasingly difficult to make any profit from his estate, while the tenant, inheriting a tradition of improved agriculture on reasonable soil, made enough money at least to raise a mortgage to buy his farm. In the last analysis, the provision in the crofting legislation that a crofter could make his tenancy heritable, or assignable to another, destroyed the reality of his landlord's ownership of the

croft, when taken in conjunction with the other provisions of the legislation. In Orkney and Shetland this process was rapidly pushed to its
logical conclusion—outright change of ownership. It was perhaps the
misfortune of the western Highlands that a similar logical progression
was not followed there, but the snag was that crofts in that part of the
world did not have the economic potential supplied by Shetland's fish or
Orkney's rich soil. It is significant that Hoy, the poorest of the Orkney
Isles in terms of soil, was until recently one of the last of those islands
with substantial estates.

The price of success

That the Scottish economy of the period 1840–1914 was, in its own
terms, a success is scarcely questionable. The total population of Scotland in 1841 was recorded as 2,620,184. By 1911 the figure was 4,760,904
and this very substantial increase in numbers had been absorbed by a
society which was confident that it stood in the van of human progress.
The 1901 edition of *Black's Guide To Scotland* referred in its section on
Glasgow to 'the marvellous growth expansion and variety of its industries and commercial pursuits' and such pride was common in all big
Scottish cities. Dundee was 'the principal seat of the linen and jute trades
of the United Kingdom'. Yet Dundee alone gives one reason to pause, for
its predominant textile industry paid its mainly female labour force very
low wages, and employment for men was so scarce that in a Scotland
which like Ireland was contributing a steadily decreasing proportion of
the manpower for the regular British army as the nineteenth century
merged into the twentieth, Dundee was an exception. In August 1914
Dundee was a city which even by British standards sent an exceptional
number of ex-regular reservists to the colours. It was a glowing tribute to
the recruiting effect of heavy unemployment and grinding poverty, the
more so because the Boer War period had seen a higher percentage of
Dundee volunteers rejected on grounds of physical unfitness than was
the case in even the worst districts of industrial Lancashire. Before 1914
the average wage in Dundee textiles was £1 a week, and there were many
earning less. Dundee was, as usual, an extreme case, but the Glasgow
unskilled labour market was overloaded with many thousands of unfortunates faring on average more poorly than a Dundee jute worker, and
even the wages of the more fortunate working classes left only a narrow
margin for a man trying to raise a family.

In such fields as working-class housing there was very little real progress in Scotland between 1871 and 1914. In 1861, 72 per cent of all Scottish families lived in 'houses' of not more than two rooms. In the larger cities these dwellings were usually flats in tenement blocks and Victorian family sizes helped to ensure a large measure of overcrowding with all its attendant evils such as epidemic diseases ranging from dysentry to typhus and tuberculosis. By 1911 47–49 per cent of the population of Scotland lived in one- or two-roomed dwellings at a time when the corresponding English figure was 7.5 per cent. At this date 56 per cent of one-roomed dwellings in Scotland had more than two persons living in them, as had 47 per cent of two-roomed dwellings, and 24 per cent of three-roomed dwellings. These figures were much the same as they had been 50 years before and were not improved by the habit of keeping lodgers which tended to become more prevalent as the size of dwellings increased. In the parliamentary burgh of Glasgow in 1871 nearly a quarter of all families kept lodgers. The housing problem did vary from city to city, but virtually everywhere there were large pockets of very bad housing.

In the last analysis the market economy could not cope with this problem. The Scottish economy could and did mobilise huge capital sums for certain kinds of domestic investment. Railways are an example, though so much of the capital for Scottish railways came from England that it may be better to take dock construction as an example. The Scottish economy was heavily committed to international trade, exporting a great deal of its manufactures and importing huge quantities of raw material and food. The size of ships steadily increased throughout the period 1840 to 1914 as did the complexity and cost of the equipment needed to load and unload them efficiently. The upshot was inevitably that a great many Scottish harbours gave up the struggle to keep abreast with other ports. Those ports which were determined to remain in the first rank had, however, to accept the necessity of massive and sustained expenditure on piers, docks, cranes, repair and shipbuilding facilities and indeed many other matters. Glasgow docks and the river improvement schemes which were essential to them were reckoned to have cost upwards of £11,250,000 by 1900. Leith Dock Commission had to fund a series of very expensive new docks in a harbour which, like that of Glasgow, was entirely artificial. Glasgow and Leith were in a class by themselves but Aberdeen and Dundee shouldered heavy financial burdens in relative terms for the sake of their docks. In 1912 Dundee harbour represented a capital expenditure of some £1,270,000 with an existing debt of £348,000 being funded out of an annual revenue of some £80,000. At this time the average docker's wage was between £1 and £2 a week, when he was in employment.

Building costs were such that it was not possible to create decent housing for such people on the assumption that they could pay an economic rent. Due to unemployment and other misfortunes they could hardly afford the bad accommodation they had. The enforcement of higher standards of construction and sanitation after 1900 very often pushed the cost of tenement housing beyond the point where a decent return could be expected and the result would then be a paralysis in working-class housing which makes it all the more sobering to reflect that the first council house scheme of a modern kind embarked on by a Scottish municipal authority was Logie in Dundee which started in 1919. Glasgow, it is true had a well-publicised City Improvement Trust which started simply as a demolisher of slums and, due to finding itself with too much land on its hands during a period of depression, developed into a builder of model tenements. By 1914 the Trust had spent nearly £600,000 on building new tenements, but it housed a mere 10,000 persons and those mainly prosperous tradesmen and their families. The level of rent excluded the poor from the scheme.

The wealthier classes did pour out money for certain public purposes. The biggest beneficiaries of this largesse were probably the churches, and from Roman Catholic to Wee Free, they all built numerous kirks in town and country. Scottish universities often benefited from local endowment, the exception being usually St Andrews which until 1877 or so looked as if it was mouldering its way towards quiet dissolution. Schools were another strong interest of the Scottish middle class and it tended to create its own system of education within an educational tradition with at least some egalitarian tendencies, either by, as in Edinburgh, turning charitable institutions for the poor into fee-paying institutions for the offspring of the middle classes, or by founding new schools such as Kelvinside Academy in Glasgow. However, the main achievement of the great self-confident Victorian bourgeoisie which dominated Scotland before 1914 was to maintain their own ascendancy within a society which tolerated, nay positively encouraged, enormous inequalities of income, without provoking any serious challenge to their position. Scotland was a Liberal stronghold, and never more strongly so than in 1906.

Like many creations of man's ingenuity, Victorian Scotland died of its own perfection. It was, in its own terms, very prosperous over a long period. Its heavy industries, like its banking system, created a world which seemed to sustain their primacy and guarantee their future indefinitely on a conservative basis. Scottish society was well-integrated at most levels. There was no real clash between town and country: their social and economic systems were mutually reinforcing. Even exceptions to this generalisation did not threaten the fundamental soundness of the system. The Highlands are a case in point. With the failure of the potato crop in 1846 large parts of the north-west Highlands faced a grave subsistence crisis unthinkable elsewhere in Victorian Scotland. Yet the problem was manageable compared to that of contemporary Ireland. The population at risk was probably less than 200,000 and a mixture of landlord generosity from such proprietors as Macleod of Macleod and the Duke of Sutherland, and state aid organised by the aptly-named Sir Edward Pine Coffin saw the crisis through without mass starvation. There was of course heavy subsequent emigration. That it proved necessary eventually to grant crofters special tenurial rights did not destabilise the right of absolute ownership basic to Lowland industry and agriculture. Highland crofters could be and were placed in a special category. They were an exception.

Yet it can be argued that only a radically different pattern of distribution of wealth could have given Scottish society the capacity to generate new consumer-orientated mass-consumption industries in the late nineteenth and early twentieth centuries. It was the absence of broad-based consumer power which goes far to explain the disappointing record of Scotland's tentative but often very early ventures into such fields as electrical engineering and the manufacture of motor cars. During the eighteenth century it does seem that a relatively high income per head of population played a key role in stimulating through domestic demand the early stages of the British industrial revolution. The failure of France to match British development may indeed be closely linked to the failure of French living standards to improve in the eighteenth century (indeed it seems likely that for very many Frenchmen they actually declined). However by the nineteenth century Scotland had developed a very specialised regional branch of the British economy, heavily oriented towards the manufacture and export of capital goods and coarse textiles. The ruling élites in this regional economy were so successful both in business and in the creation and manipulation of political and social controls over the poorly-paid bulk of the population that they preserved the hierarchic order which suited them with remarkable continuity between 1840 and

1914. Ironically, when demand for the heavy industries collapsed, as it did to a greater or lesser extent between 1919 and 1939, this left the old economic and social order cruelly exposed to cold winds of change.

7

Industry and Agriculture in an Age of Crisis 1914–1939

The experience of the Scottish economy between 1914 and 1939 was in many ways a paradoxical one. The First World War did represent a fundamental challenge to the assumptions of the pre-1914 era, yet its immediate impact on the Scottish industrial scene was conservative. It emphasised an existing over-emphasis on the great staple industries of the Victorian period. After 1921 it was quite clear that only large-scale change could spare Scotland the grave repercussions of a post-mature economy in a world suffering from chronic slump and trade restriction. The basic problem was well understood by the 1930s and the state showed unprecedented interest in the field of regional policy. Nevertheless, the results of endless discussion, analysis and prescription were disappointing. The self-reinforcing success of the Victorian age seemed to have been replaced by an age of self-reinforcing failure.

The First World War challenged fundamental assumptions underlying the economy and society which had developed in Lowland Scotland since 1832. Over the period 1832–1914 Scotland as a whole was remarkably, nay strategically loyal to the Whig-Liberal political tradition. Indeed it was the disproportionate support which that tradition enjoyed in Wales and Scotland which enabled it in its turn to enjoy a disproportionate period in power if the period 1832–1914 is taken as a whole. The explanations of this phenomenon are as numerous as might be expected. Presbyterianism in Scotland, for example, was as potent a force as Methodism in Wales in the forging of a Liberal tradition. Nevertheless, it is clear that the fundamental reason for the Liberal ascendancy in Scotland was the health and vigour of the heavy-industry-based Scots economy, for it was on that economy that the prosperity of the Scots middle classes was based, and those middle classes were the bedrock of Scots Liberalism. It would be wrong to regard Scots Liberalism as pacific. Truculent hostility, whether directed at internal opponents or at international rivals, was an undoubted component of the movement. The Scottish middle classes had a substantial interest in the fortunes of the British Empire, especially in India where in the days of the Honourable East India Company Scots had established a tradition of imperial service which survived and flourished when India came directly under the Crown. Short wars in distant places could often find a lot of support in Scotland, though it is worth stressing that there was usually also vocal opposition. The Boer War had seen a sharp division of opinion in Scotland and the leading Scottish 'pro-Boer', Sir Henry Campbell-Bannerman, became the Liberal prime minister in 1906. Scottish Liberalism accepted the idea of Free Trade (absence of discriminatory tariffs) wholeheartedly. It was therefore committed to regional specialisation on a world scale, with all that that implies for increasing interdependence among peoples.

On top of this Scottish Liberalism was also committed to a restricted view of the desirable scope for direct state interference in the working of the economy. Now historians have no difficulty in demonstrating that the idea of an age of 'laissez faire' in the nineteenth century is an illusion. The state always interfered in a whole range of matters. Factory acts were passed to regulate industrial labour, and if they were originally limited in scope, and if the early factory inspectorate in Scotland included men like James Stuart of Dunearn, a former bankrupt who had murdered a man in a duel and whose bias in favour of the employers was quite violent, the fact remains that the scope of factory legislation steadily broadened while enforcement became fairer and stricter. Public health was the subject of increasingly elaborate legislation and administration, especially after the thoroughly frightening visitations of cholera which struck Scotland in the years 1832, 1848–9, 1854–5, and 1866–7. Cholera killed comparatively few people compared with other endemic scourges but it killed them conspicuously, horribly, and in substantial numbers within a short space of time. The last epidemic cleared the way wonderfully for the passage of the Public Health (Scotland) Act of 1867. After 1872 the state enforced a new national system of education, though it was one which had abandoned so many of the virtues of the old Scots parochial schools as to be generally deemed a very mixed blessing. Nevertheless, the 'laissez faire' ideology of many Scots businessmen and politicians before 1914 was neither unrealistic nor devoid of practical usefulness. Such is the pervasive influence of the modern state, and so seductive is the prospect of 'one-way socialism' (state benefits without state control) to the business community, that perhaps only the existence and reiteration of a creed denying the desirability of virtually all state interference with the economy, can ensure the restriction of that interference to modest proportions in the long run.

Obviously, the outbreak in August 1914 of a war between the great powers of contemporary Europe, and Britain's involvement in such a conflict, was in itself a terrible blow to an outlook which at heart assumed that nations were becoming steadily more reasonable, and progressively more aimiably interdependent. Equally destructive of the pre-1914 world was the unexpected way in which the war developed. The languidly ineffective fashion in which the Liberal premier Asquith ran a war of unprecedented size and scope was perhaps in itself a tribute to older values. After all Asquith sat for a rural Scottish seat in Fife and his patrician orations rang out periodically in the unlikely surroundings of the Volunteer Hall, Ladybank. When the utterly unscrupulous Welshman David Lloyd George replaced Asquith in 1916 at the head of a coalition dedicated to total victory in total war, it was clear that no decent limits would be recognised in state intervention in the economy, or indeed in anything else. How ironic then that the immediate effects of the war on the Scottish economy can not unfairly be described as conservative. Only in the longer run were they revolutionary.

War and post-war boom 1914–1921

The nature of the First World War—a bloody struggle fought in the end by armies of millions in trenches in France, where the main business for most of the war consisted of the relentless slaughter of infantry by massed artillery—could scarcely have been better designed to enhance demand for Scotland's traditional products. The introduction of unrestricted submarine warfare later in the war by the Germans increased almost to breaking point the demand for tonnage from Scottish shipyards, which were already the beneficiaries of a Grand Fleet which was itself the culmination of a long race in naval construction with the German Empire.

Day in, day out, however, there was need for vast quantities of textiles, usually of a fairly crude kind. Canvas of all kinds from tenting, to groundsheets, to waggon covers and tarpaulins was in great demand. Shrapnel and the machine gun drove armies into the protective misery of elaborate trench systems, usually lined with sandbags made from jute. By 1915 there was a sandbag shortage. By the end of the war sandbags were being used by the million. Clothing for British armies of unprecedented size placed heavy burdens on Scottish woollen and linen manufacturers. Above all, the metallurgy and heavy engineering of Scotland could be used to meet the most clamant of all military needs—that for guns and shells. Compared with Continental armies, the British Expeditionary Force started the war woefully ill-equipped with ordnance and ammunition. Lloyd George made his mark first during the war as the man who solved the 'shell scandal'. Finally, given the lack of expenditure on roads which had been typical of successive British governments, it was the railways which were bound to bear the brunt of internal transport demands. As the Grand Fleet spent much of its time at Scapa Flow in Orkney, and occasionally used anchorages off the west coast of the Highlands, some Highland railway lines which had been of very marginal viability when built, were busy as never before carrying supplies north for the Royal Navy.

Lloyd George described the war as 'a war of engineers', but it was also a war of chemists. Unheard-of demand for explosives such as TNT kept existing Scottish explosive works busy and called new ones into existence. To some extent war with Germany was bound to stimulate new developments in the British chemical industry, because Britain had become heavily dependent on the German chemical industry in the years before 1914. Lest this be deemed a crime, it may be pointed out that the bottoms of sundry of the Kaiser's battleships in 1914 were protected by the bituminous products of Messrs. Briggs of Dundee. After August 1914 it was essential to replace German dyestuffs, if only to be able to dye millions of uniforms a uniform khaki. Success in producing substitutes for somewhat more unusual German dyestuffs lay behind the development of a business in anthraquinone dyestuffs by James Morton, a Scots businessman of Ayrshire origins, and after the war he and his associates established Scottish Dyes Limited on a large site at Grangemouth. This factory became part of Imperial Chemical Industries eventually, but such technological spin-off from the war effort was relatively rare, as another example shows. Even after the Boer War, when many more British troops died as a result of disease than as a result of Boer bullets, Britain remained wholly dependent upon German chemical manufacturers for supplies of certain bacteriological sugars which were important for military medicine. Late in 1916, when all other sources of raw material for one particular sugar were seen to be unobtainable, it was decided to synthesise the drug from the inulin which could be obtained from dahlia tubers. A combination of sacrificial giving by gardeners and the professor of chemistry, his staff and laboratories in the University of St Andrews produced sufficient quantities of what was needed, at the price of a large-scale massacre of dahlias.

Of necessity, there was a massive extension of government control in the war economy. Raw material buying was one of the areas where this was most striking. By March 1916 the British government was buying the entire Russian flax crop and distributing it to the British linen industry. In October 1917 the appointment of a Flax Control Board by the War Office gave the state's intervention in the industry firm bureaucratic form. From August 1916 the War Office purchased all Indian jute required for military purposes, and found that such half-measures rather than complete control created complex problems which were only finally solved when three different methods of purchasing raw jute had been tried. The British wool clip was entirely under government control from June 1916, but here the normal Scottish pattern of wool marketing was in fact little disturbed by the change. Scottish wool was reasonably uniform, being nearly all blackfaced or Cheviot, so there was no need for elaborate grading as in England, and the general rule was for farmers to consign their wool to large brokers in Glasgow or Edinburgh who then sold the clip to manufacturers and then returned the price to the farmer minus their usual commission. All that happened was that the broker sold to the government at a price fixed by a government valuer according to an official schedule. Nothing else changed. Herein lay an important truth about the vast expansion of state control over industry during the war: it was essentially a process whereby the state used businessmen in new *ad hoc* authorities to organise other businessmen. By the end of the war the government had direct charge of shipping, railways, canal transport, and coalmines. It purchased about 90 per cent of all imports and marketed over 80 per cent of all food consumed, as well as controlling most prices. Yet most Scottish businessmen, quite rightly, did not believe that creeping bolshevism was overtaking them. They were reassured by the spirit and personnel of the new government bureaucracies, and many learned to prefer payment by costs plus an agreed margin to the rigours of market competition.

The war did confirm the ascendancy of the classic pattern of marine engineering, shipbuilding, heavy engineering, steel, coal, and coarse textiles in the Scottish economy. There were new developments. Clydeside, with 250,000 munitions workers, was the most important single munitions centre in Great Britain, but this was necessarily a transient industry. Nearly all the older industries were left weakened in the long run by their wartime development. Streamlining of methods had given the Clydeside shipyards vastly increased capacity by 1919, which meant that they were over-expanded. The collieries were repeatedly disorganised by war pressures. By August 1915 26.8 per cent of Scottish miners had volunteered for military service, and these were usually the youngest and best, production fell despite attempts to replace them by unskilled substitutes. In June 1916 further enlistment of colliers was forbidden and many in the army re-directed to the mines, but there were other difficulties. The state used Scottish railways ruthlessly for two main purposes: provisioning the Grand Fleet at Scapa Flow and feeding steel, ore, and other raw materials into Clydeside. For anything else, rolling stock was hard to come by and coal at one stage was piling up unused around Scottish pitheads. Pre-war production levels vanished for ever. Steel manufacturing was vital to the war effort. Some firms were able to seize this opportunity and grow substantially between 1914 and 1919. Colvilles of Motherwell is the classic example, for it acquired in the course of the war ironworks, steelworks, and collieries, as well as an interest in a shipyard. However, the overall results of the war for the steel industry were really no happier than those for shipbuilding and coal. First, the price of maximum production for a single, desperately eager purchaser, was a fall in quality. A measure of this phenomenon was the use of very sub-standard iron ore mined on the island of Raasay east of Skye by German prisoners of war. Secondly, traditional Scottish overseas markets such as Japan and Australia were being lost during the war to American steel.

While the political establishment closed ranks in a coalition government which was virtually a conspiracy of the two front benches against their back benchers; and the social, religious, and press establishments whipped themselves into an unparalleled frenzy in support of the war; a section of the Scottish working class displayed a commendable degree of realism and detachment. For this the press rewarded them with the characteristically misleading title of Red Clydeside. Syndicalism and pacifism were a good deal more apparent than bolshevism among the leadership of the Clyde Workers' Committee and their followers in the shipyards and engineering shops were quite simply concerned with wages and conditions of work. Among the latter the issue of 'dilution' by the use of semi-skilled labour in areas which normal trade union practice would regard as reserved for skilled workers, was prominent. Lloyd George lavished his oratory on Clydeside in vain. One of the most impudent of his innumerable lies, to the effect that he was as keen a socialist as any man listening to him, received the execration it richly deserved. Consequently he resorted to banning hostile newspapers and jailing Clydeside politicians. In the short run it worked, though politically the spell in jail did most of his victims nothing but good. In the long run, such is the sensitivity of the investor that the Red Clydeside tag probably cost the region dearly in terms of lost opportunities, which loss ironically confirmed its radicalism.

Perhaps the best illustration of the cruel dilemmas inherent in Scotland's war boom is the jute industry centred in Dundee. From 1915 that industry, stimulated by huge government purchases of hessians and sandbags, had enjoyed substantial prosperity, at the price of having to accept substantial increases (in terms of percentages at any rate) in wages. Everyone in the trade knew that the Indian jute mills were simultaneously making huge profits (up to 300 or 400 per cent) whilst conceding very little to their labour force. A Bengal spinner's weekly wage in 1914 averaged 3.45 rupees. In 1919 it was 3.75. For a weaver the figures were 5.65 and 6.75. There was no reason to suppose that the lack of price-competition typical of the war would survive the peace. It was therefore with surprise that the Scottish industry experienced a prosperous 1919, going forward to 1920 with yarn massively foresold and American orders for hessian backing for linoleum high. The crash came after March 1920. Prices and demand plummeted to the depths of the 1921–2 depression. Shipbuilding passed through a very similar experience. Wartime demand was so high that when America entered the war she enlarged her shipbuilding capacity as a contribution to the Allied cause. Japan, Holland, and Scandinavia, deprived of British ships, also expanded their yards. By 1918 world capacity was not far short of what it had been in 1914 but transport difficulties and disorganisation created a shortage of shipping in 1919 much greater than the real shortfall in tonnage. The result was a busy year for British shipyards in 1920. By April

1921 the bottom had fallen out of shipbuilding and shipping rates were tumbling. Few shipping firms displayed the canny instincts of Christian Salvesen of Leith which, having expanded its fleet to meet wartime exigencies, sold four vessels for big capital gains at the top of the market in 1920, and then cautiously began rebuilding its fleet from 1922 when prices were very much lower.

Scottish agriculture responded to the early stages of the war by an increase of 33,000 in its cereal acreage, mainly at the expense of roots, in 1915. Shipping losses in 1915–1916 at the hands of German submarines severely reduced imports of food from abroad and ensured continued high prices for domestic agricultural production. A poor harvest in 1916 brought matters to a head, the situation being exacerbated by unrest amongst an agricultural labour force reduced by recruiting and rightly convinced that higher prices should mean an increase in their own very low wages. By 1917 the government had intervened decisively with guaranteed cereal prices to encourage tillage; general price control of most important foodstuffs; and a minimum agricultural wage. Scottish cereal acreage increased from 1,235,184 in 1916 to 1,494,414 in 1918, an increase of 21 per cent in two years despite shortages of human and animal labour and fertiliser. By 1918 plans were being made to extend the food production campaign into 1919. In the event, the war ended and Scottish agriculture, which had been able to adapt to wartime conditions with notably less trauma than English agriculture, at first found adapting to the outbreak of peace equally untraumatic. Cereal prices remained high, and though a notably good harvest from an artificially expanded potato acreage in 1918 created an unsaleable surplus, it was taken over by the government on terms which ensured little loss to Scottish farmers. Meat prices were at first controlled after the war, so there was no repetition of the great slump after 1815. Then when control was removed meat prices actually went up. More scientific approaches to farming had been sponsored during the war by the Scottish Board of Agriculture, with particular benefit to the seed potato trade. Until late in 1920 all seemed well.

The slump followed fast. By 1921 imports of dairy products to the United Kingdom had doubled; oat imports increased by a third; and more food grains and more meat were reaching Britain. Between 1920 and 1921 wool sank to a quarter of its former value. Between 1920 and 1922 the price of wheat was halved, while oats in 1922 were worth about a third of their 1919 price. Meat prices held up better but the price of sheep fell seriously after the end of 1921. Crudely, farm produce roughly halved in value between 1920 and 1922. For farmers who had borrowed to purchase or stock their farms, this slump in prices could mean bankruptcy, but for the bulk of Scottish farmers the message seemed to be that they must buckle down to coping with roughly the pre-war position, which meant that there must be a return to an emphasis on economical pastoral farming, very often within the context of mixed farming, but with a cutting back of the wartime expansion of arable. Until 1929 that is roughly what happened.

Recovery and depression 1922–1939

Scotland's economic experience between 1922 and 1939 falls into two parts separated by the divide of the Great Crash of 1929 when the collapse of a frenetic boom on the United States stock exchange plunged not just America, but also the whole world economy into sustained depression. Until that year there was a tendency for most sectors of the Scottish economy to show signs of reverting to modest prosperity after climbing out of the post-war depression of the early 1920s. The one blatant exception to this was what was left of the cotton industry of Glasgow and the west of Scotland. It simply could not survive in the face of sustained competition from India, China, and the cotton industry of Lancashire. Only very specialised sectors of the Scots industry, like the thread industry of Paisley, or highly unusual individual mills such as Deaston, Catrine or Stanley survived. The last-named eventually specialised in weaving tapes for the machinery used in rolling filter cigarettes. To all intents and purposes the industry which had been in the van of late eighteenth-century Scottish industrialisation had vanished by 1929.

Other Scottish textile trades had uninspiring but less disastrous experiences in the 1920s. Jute is a case in point. In 1925 John Sime, the very able secretary of the Dundee Jute and Flax Workers' Union toured the Indian jute areas in company with Tom Johnston, a Labour MP and future Secretary of State for Scotland. They produced a report which, after enumerating a series of grim facts such as atrocious housing and low wages in the Indian industry despite high profitability, denied that the products of the Scottish and Indian industries competed with one another to any significant extent. Certainly, it is clear that the products of the Indian and Scottish jute industries tended to lie at opposite ends of the spectrum of jute goods. However, the Sime-Johnston report was undoubtedly politically slanted, for Dundee employers were much given to citing Indian competition as a reason for keeping the wages they themselves paid low. The truth appears to lie somewhere between the two extreme arguments. A good deal of what was produced by the Indian industry did not compete with Scottish products, but there was a substantial area of overlap and competition, which is one reason why Scottish trade unionists were so anxious to unionise Indian labour with a view to raising its wages and hence the cost of what that labour produced. Be that as it may, it is the case that at the better end of the cheaper lines the Scottish industry was able on occasion to take business from India. In 1922 a demand for bags from Cuban sugar producers and from Argentinian and Uruguayan firms outran the capacity of the Calcutta mills so the balance came from Dundee. In 1927 under very similar circumstances the Dundee mills actually managed to supply hessian sacking to Latin America at rates below those quoted by Calcutta. Only after 1929 did the intermittent prosperity of the later 1920s deteriorate massively. All the same, the jute industry was producing, even at its finer ends, a coarse textile, and foreign competition kept it below its pre-1914 level of production in this period.

It was not open to jute to do what Scottish woollen manufacturers did and concentrate on very high quality tweed exports to the United States which by 1928 was absorbing over a third of all Scottish direct tweed exports. This emphasis on quality enabled the Scots industry to employ roughly as many people—about 28,000—in 1924 as it had in 1907, but rendered it very vulnerable to hostile tariffs which hit it very hard after 1930. Paradoxically, the history of the other Scots luxury exported in bulk to the United States—whisky—was almost opposite to that of tweeds in the inter-war period. The production of whisky in legal distilleries, as distinct from illicit stills, had expanded enormously in Scotland after legislation in 1823 established the modern legal framework for the industry. In 1825 5,981,549 gallons of whisky were charged for duty. By 1884 the figure was 20,164,962 gallons. Two main types were produced. One was malt whisky, produced mainly in the Highlands in relatively small quantities. The other was blended whisky which became commonplace after Aeneas Coffey devised the continuous distillation still around 1832. Blended whisky was mainly composed of spirit distilled from imported grain, but it contained a certain amount of malt whisky or more often an admixture of malt whiskies. Very often the big blended whisky establishments were therefore sited in ports like Leith or Glasgow. By 1900 gross overproduction had occurred and rationalisation of the industry set in with the Distillers Company Limited (formed in Edinburgh by amalgamation of six firms) emerging as the dominant organisation in a troubled Scottish industry. For that industry, which leaned heavily on the American market, the 1920s were an age of disaster, or more precisely of Prohibition.

Only in 1933, after 13 halcyon years for the criminals who catered to the national sport of making nonsense of the ban on alcoholic drink, did Americans admit that the Noble Experiment was a ghastly failure. During those 13 years a large section of the Scottish whisky industry had been closed. Of the 112 distilleries working in 1917 77 were no longer working as late as the spring of 1934. However, whisky sales increased by nearly 1,000,000 gallons in 1935 and by October 1936 roughly 100 Scottish distilleries were at work. This was a change indeed from the period in the 1920s when the Distillers Company was not only closing substantial parts of its Scottish distilling capacity but was also buying and closing Irish rivals. Apart from slaking their thirst with its product, most Scots had no real interest in distilling. Neither directly nor indirectly was it a significant employer of labour. Indeed the outsider with the biggest stake in the industry was the Chancellor of the Exchequer who levied increasingly penal rates of taxation on its product.

In the shipbuilding industry and the closely-related steel industry the 1920s were not as depressing as the 1930s but they were far from satisfactory years. Sir James Lithgow, head of the great family shipbuilding firm at Port Glasgow, was the first major figure in Clyde shipbuilding to sense that the industry needed large-scale rationalisation. His own firm was healthy enough in the early 1930s but as early as the later 1920s he had been visiting Montagu Norman, Governor of the Bank of England, with very drastic proposals. With all the assurance of a man who had been chairman of the Shipbuilding Employers Federation in his thirty-eighth year, Lithgow urged extensive rationalisation of the entire British shipbuilding industry. It was not until 1930 that the first practical steps were taken in this direction, mainly because just enough orders came into Scottish yards in the 1920s to keep the existing historically-determined pattern of organisation going. Late in 1923 orders came in which ensured a revival in tonnage launched in 1924 to the tune of several hundred per cent over the previous year. 1925 was predictably depressed with lowered launchings except on the Tay. 1926 was an even poorer year except on the Forth, and there only the Burntisland yard did really well. However the coal strike of 1926 and the resulting steel shortage held up enough work to make 1927 quite busy. Freights were still abysmally low but until a shipping company folds up, it has to renew its fleet and this sort of order at rock-bottom prices kept the Scots yards going until 1929. After that came collapse.

The Scottish steel industry therefore faced a complex of problems in the 1920s without much buoyancy in its main traditional market. Some of its problems were inherently insoluble. It was facing the virtual exhaustion of once-abundant natural resources. Against the 3,000,000 tons of iron ore being mined annually in Scotland in the 1870s must be set the mere 25,000 tons of 1929. Foreign shipment of Scottish pig iron vanished away, and the once mighty Iron Ring on the Glasgow Stock Exchange, an institution which had given the United Kingdom a premier in the shape of its former member Andrew Bonar Law, was abolished. To make matters worse Scotland lacked good coking coal. All it had were semi-coking varieties which increased costs. Capacity had been much over-extended during the wartime munitions drive and it is arguable that the process of rationalisation by closure of surplus capacity which the Scottish steel industry had to embark on after 1919 at times obscured a more fundamental problem—the relative inefficiency of Scottish steel manufacturing methods.

Few Scottish steelworks had blast furnaces sited near them. There were in fact no integrated steelworks in Scotland which meant that a whole series of economies in the use of heat were not available. Hot waste gas from the blast furnaces could not be used later in the process, nor could hot metal be run straight into the steel furnace. In any case, Scottish furnaces were too small, with an average charge of a mere 60 tons. All this enabled more efficiently laid-out English and Welsh plants to undercut Scottish steel plate and angles by as much as £3–4 a ton in the 1920s. What the Scots did do was shift the whole emphasis of their steel industry. It had been an open-hearth industry producing high-grade acid steel from imported Spanish or North African hematite ores. Increasingly, it turned to cheaper phosphoric ores and began to produce basic steel. In 1913 basic steel was only 10 per cent of total output. By 1920 the figure was 38 per cent and by 1930 62 per cent of all open-hearth steel was being made from basic pig iron. By this last year the world slump had pushed the Scottish steel industry towards very drastic reorganisation indeed, and perhaps the expedients of the 1920s were a mixed blessing, for they exacerbated as well as put off the day of reckoning.

The Scottish coal industry therefore faced two sets of problems after 1919. One was to regain overseas markets lost during the war and the other was to find additional domestic or foreign markets to compensate for the decline in the demand for coal from Scottish iron and steel producers. Between 1919 and 1924 two sets of circumstances masked the underlying realities and gave an unduly favourable impression of how the industry was coping. The first of these was the survival of government control after 1919. Effectively this ensured that uneconomic Scottish coalfields were subsidised by more profitable English and Welsh ones. The size of the Scottish deficit was extraordinary. In 1920 it was of the order of £5,250,000, and in the last months before decontrol in 1921 it was averaging about £1 million a month. Many Scottish mines were too small and too backward in their methods, nor were there enough big new pits being sunk to match the large modern English pits being sunk in the eastward extensions of the Yorkshire and Nottinghamshire coalfields. The second circumstance which flattered to deceive was the paralysis of much overseas competition due to temporary political factors. Many European coalfields required several years to recover their pre-war capacity and the process was seriously interrupted by such episodes as the French invasion of the Ruhr in 1923. Prices were further sustained by the American coal strike of 1922, and indeed by the bitter British coal strike of March 1921 which ushered in decontrol. Naturally the mines situated on the eastern side of Scotland benefited very much more than those on the west from a situation where, as in 1919, export prices were very much higher than domestic ones. Fife exported nearly a third of the coal it produced in that year whereas Ayrshire pits exported a mere 4 per cent of their output. Progressive firms like the Fife Coal Company tended to expand their holdings between 1919 and 1923 and to press on with schemes for modernisation. Then in 1924 came the expected slump in exports. For the United Kingdom as a whole this amounted to some 22 per cent, but for Scottish ports the falling-off was nearer 29 per cent, and the fall in income from exports was roughly double the fall in quantity.

The troubles of the British coal industry spawned government enquiries throughout the inter-war period. The Sankey Commission of 1919 was deeply divided between owners' and miners' representatives and in any case the government ignored its recommendations. However, after the 1921 strike the state was sufficiently worried about unemployment in the mines to offer a temporary government subsidy of £23 million in 1925–6 to enable owners to cut prices while keeping up wages. Eventually the owners insisted on cutting wages, increasing hours from 7 to 8, and making regional and not national wage agreements. The result was the terrible seven-months miners' strike of 1926, which included in its course the General Strike when a reluctant trade union leadership found itself involved in a potentially revolutionary confrontation with the government. As soon as it decently could the British Trades Union Congress backed down, leaving the miners to be ground down to a defeat which left an aftermath of suffering expressed succinctly in an increase of 1s. 7d. in the pound in the cost of poor relief in Scotland in 1926.

The 1926 strike was the turning point in the inter-war history of the Scottish coal industry. By 1927 the prices for Scottish coal exports were down to the levels of 1914, and this after a substantial measure of inflation. The Samuel Commission on the British industry was set up in 1925, so after the strike an effort was made to implement its major recommendation: that amalgamation be encouraged. In practice such amalgamations as occurred owed more to private than to government initiative but by 1927–8 there was an ambitious Scottish cartel scheme whereby inefficient mines were to be closed and their owners compensated out of a levy on all domestic sales of coal. It was not a wholly effective scheme, but it did foreshadow the compulsory cartel system embedded in the Coal Mines Act of 1930. Nowhere in Scotland was there an increase in the mining labour force between 1913 and 1931. In some of the older mining areas with a tradition of heavy involvement with iron and steel manufacture, such as Lanarkshire, there had already been falls in the labour force of up to 50 per cent. Only in the east in Fife and the Lothians was there any significant new investment and development in this period.

For most of Scottish industry 1930 was the year which marked the coming of deep depression, collapsing prices, and mass unemployment on a scale much greater than even the unemployment seen in 1922–3. The implications of such levels of unemployment were alarming. Dundee is a good example of this, for unemployment levels in its predominant jute trade reached over 70 per cent in 1931 and 1932. There were over 37,000 unemployed jute workers in Dundee in July 1932; in 1937 there were still nearly 28,000. Between 1929 and 1939 there was a substantial fall in the level of employment in the jute industry from 35,000 to 26,000. The work force was still predominantly female, so the bulk of the jobs lost—perhaps as many as 8,000—were female jobs, while male employment dropped by only a little over a thousand. There was no expansion of other manufacturing industries in the city at this time to compensate for this catastrophic decline in employment in jute. Employment in shipbuilding went up by a few hundreds, but other engineering industries actually declined between 1931 and 1939, and gains of about 1,000 jobs each in printing and publishing and the food and drink industries had actually been lost again by 1946. It was not that no effort was made to attract new industry to the city: quite the reverse. There was a Development Committee of the City of Dundee which represented the civic government, business, and trades union interests of the city, and which produced a substantial book expounding the attractions of Dundee to 'Industrialists at Home and Abroad'. Bound in jute, and with the perhaps rather unfortunate title-cum-invitation to 'Do It At Dundee', it was outstandingly unsuccessful in what it set out to do.

However, the experience of Dundee was only an extreme case of what was going on all over industrial Scotland. Heavy industry was very hard hit and with it the whole of the west of Scotland where unemployment in the 1930s averaged 25 per cent of the work force. In Clydeside shipbuilding there were dramatic swings of fortune amongst long-established firms. Harland and Wolff, a firm whose most famous establishment was the Queen's Island yard in Belfast, had long been established on the Clyde and had long displayed expansionist ambitions there. In the 1890s, for example, Harland and Wolff had tried to invade Dumbarton but had eventually been compelled by circumstances to abandon their bid to take over three shipyards there. Just after 1918 Harland and Wolff were under the vigorous chairmanship of Lord Pirrie, who was also chairman of Lamport and Holt Limited (a firm of shipowners trading to South America), and vice-chairman of the Royal Mail Group. There was talk of Harland and Wolff opening a yard on the Tay and a local authority there thought it expedient to buy all the land adjacent to the only unused deep berthage on the river in order to be in a position to offer Harland and Wolff a very expensive (for the incoming firm) welcome. Nothing came of the rumour, but acting through the Royal Mail Group Lord Pirrie purchased many berths on the Clyde, including Napier's site at Govan; London and Glasgow Engineering and Iron Shipbuilding Company Limited, also of Govan; A. and J. Inglis of Pointhouse; D. and W. Henderson of Meadowside; Caird and Company of Greenock; and Archibald McMillan and Son Limited, of Dumbarton.

When Pirrie died in 1924 he was succeeded at the head of his empire by Lord Kylsant, who collected shipping lines with the zest that Pirrie collected shipyards, despite the fact that the key Royal Mail Group's own finances were extremely shaky, even when it was helped by government money available under the Trade Facilities Act. Kylsant bought control of the White Star Line in 1926, and in 1928 the Commonwealth Line and the Shaw Savill and Albion Line. Failure to repay government loans in 1929 led to a protracted exposure of the feet of clay on which the Royal Mail colossus stood, culminating in the arrest and conviction of Kylsant in 1931 for issuing a false prospectus.

By 1930 Sir James Lithgow had become head of the National Shipbuilders' Security Limited, formed with government encouragement and with the support of virtually the entire British shipbuilding industry, not to mention the Bank of England. It could raise funds by a one per cent levy on the sales of participating firms and the money was used to buy up and close down obsolete and or redundant shipyards. The success of this operation was limited by the fact that the basic problem was an absence of orders for ships. All the rationalisation in the world could not supply the surviving yards with enough orders to make them prosperous. In 1931 work was suspended on a new Cunarder at John Brown's and the unfinished hull of what was to be the *Queen Mary* brooded over a stricken Clyde. Occasional flashes of luck would keep a given Scottish yard busy. Thus in 1932, a bleak year in the industry, the Burntisland Shipbuilding Company had ten launches and vastly boosted the statistics for the Forth. On the Clyde it was a great event when the government in 1933 gave help towards finishing the *Queen Mary*. She was launched in 1934 and even in 1935 her fitting-out kept Brown's humming with activity. The only firm that had some measure of continuous activity was Lithgows—mainly because of a close relationship with the big shipping firm of J. and C. Harrison. Sir James Lithgow and his brother Henry, in close co-operation with Montagu Norman, actually carried out the first big rescue operation in Clyde Shipbuilding when they took over two collapsing giants Beardmore's and Fairfield's. They also bought a large stake in Colville's, the steel firm, in 1934. The Lithgows' motives for doing all this in the early 1930s appear to have been largely altruistic. They believed they had a duty to maintain industry and employment in the west of Scotland. Rearmament in the late 1930s provided just enough work to keep the Clyde yards going. War broke out just in time in 1939, for after the launching of another huge Cunarder in 1938, the *Queen Elizabeth*, the position as regards civilian orders was every bit as bleak as in 1930. On the whole, Scottish shipbuilding had been reasonably competitive up to 1936, but after that year foreign competition plus a worsening depression bit very deep. Fortunately the Admiralty was in no position to imitate Aberdeen trawler owners of the late 1930s in having ships built for it in Germany.

In a slightly less extreme form the problems which beset Clyde shipyards could be found in most of Scotland's staple industries in the 1930s. The woollen industry was more successful than most, but even it was plagued by mounting foreign tariffs. From a labour force of 28,000 in 1924, employment fell to 24,000 in 1930, due mainly to a loss of European markets. There was a rally in the late 1930s due to a more buoyant domestic market but with a downturn in the trade cycle in 1937, the prospects were deteriorating just before the war. Woollen carpets, a particularly successful section of the industry, showed this same cycle very clearly. Carpet firms suffered badly from American and Canadian tariffs in the early 1930s and from economic distress in the important Australian market. They recovered with the help of relative domestic prosperity between 1933 and 1937 and then faced short-time again at the end of the decade.

This was, relatively speaking, a success story. The steel firm of Stewarts and Lloyds actually abandoned its Mossend works in the Monklands near Glasgow and transported a great deal of its labour force with it to Corby in Northamptonshire, where it built a big new integrated steelworks over extensive beds of slightly phosphoric ores. There was really no alternative. The firm needed basic steel for the tubes which were its main product (basic steel is particularly suitable for welding). By the early 1930s basic steel was just not being made in Scotland while depreciation and protection made it too expensive to import it by 1932. From that year Stewart and Lloyds built the last basic Bessemer steelworks in Britain at Corby and the converters it laid down were superseded only in 1964–5. What was left of the Scottish steel industry, deprived of the old demand from the Clyde shipyards to a very large extent, naturally huddled together in the cold. In 1934 three major firms were left in the Scottish industry. These were Colvilles, with plants at Motherwell, Cambuslang and Glengarnock; the Lanarkshire Steel Company with works at Motherwell; and the Steel Company of Scotland with works at Blochairn and Newton. Between 1934 and 1936 government pressure produced further amalgamation, with the ubiquitous

Sir James Lithgow, a director of Colvilles, playing an important role in the process. By 1936 it was complete. Colvilles controlled the other two big firms.

The logical corollary of such concentration was investment and development. After 1936 there were indeed some signs of this. Colvilles controlled all Scottish steel production except that of the Scottish Iron and Steel Company Limited of Coatbridge. At the end of 1936 Colvilles strengthened its vertical integration by buying the extensive coalfields of Archibald Russell Limited. With an authorised capital of £6,000,000, most of which had been issued, and net profits of £739,000 for 1936, Colvilles were in a strong position to invest. This they did from 1937, mainly in Clydebridge and Clyde where new blast furnaces, coke ovens, a new plate mill and other equipment were installed. It all fell short of a fully integrated modern plant. Partly this was because of an underlying dilemma. Integration implied that furnaces should be near the steelworks, but the latter, for historical reasons rooted in their need to be near coal and ore, were inland. Yet furnaces using imported ore or scrap (of which Scotland used a lot) needed to be near deep berthage to be operated economically. From before 1930 the idea of a totally new location on the lower Clyde was discussed, but the degree of discontinuity implied in this was so massive as to make any positive decision impossible before 1939.

Scotland's failure between 1921 and 1939 was primarily a failure to attract or develop new industry. In the period 1930–9, with a major world depression and consequent collapse of world trade, it is difficult to imagine a more vulnerable regional economy than the heavy capital goods, export-oriented type which Scotland had inherited. Contemporaries were perfectly well aware of this by the late 1930s and a myriad of well-meaning public bodies, from the Ayrshire Development Council to the Scottish Development Council itself, laboured to repair this weakness. C. A. Oakley, a very shrewd and well-informed contemporary observer, was quite clear in 1937 that Scotland's heavy and textile industries would never again employ such a high proportion of the working population as they had in the past. He concluded that 'Her greatest need is therefore for new industries'. The problem is to explain why they did not develop on anything like an adequate scale.

One favourite theory has been that the Scottish economy since as early as 1800 had been losing the capacity to harness scientific advance to industrial purposes. The result, it is argued, was cumulative technological backwardness as the old links between academic science and industry atrophied under the often protracted reigns of Victorian captains of industry who persisted in their rule-of-thumb approach long after it was clear that industrialisation on the Continent involved a new and vital relationship between the research lab and the workshop. In the first place, outside the field of the chemical industry where a crucial, but very limited, component of scientific knowledge was contributed by medical graduates, this view probably exaggerates the academic contribution to early Scottish industrialisation. Joseph Black's lectures on latent heat were indeed attended by James Watt, but they had no direct bearing on his inventions. Secondly, it probably underestimates the extent to which Scottish universities in the late nineteenth and early twentieth centuries received endowments ultimately deriving from industrial fortunes and often devoted to scientific ends. It would be difficult to find an academic physicist more heavily involved in contemporary engineering developments, from the theory of the steam engine, to electrical engineering and telegraph cable laying, to aluminium smelting, than William Thomson Lord Kelvin, professor and then Chancellor of the University of Glasgow between 1846 and 1907. Indeed it has been argued that the ultimate limitation on Kelvin's superb mathematical talent was that he believed in the finality of engineering concepts to the point where he could not see their inadequacy for certain purposes.

Besides, there is the connection, so often neglected by historians, between the flow of innovations and market opportunity. H. J. Habbakkuk has demonstrated not only that Britain steadily lost her comparative lead in technology to the United States in the nineteenth century, but also that to a large extent this was due to poorer growth prospects in the British economy. Where market conditions were favourable to expansion, British businessmen could be just as dynamic and innovative as American. In the field of machine tools, for example, it does seem that Scottish engineering firms held their own very well until the inter-war period. Before 1914 precision machine tool manufacture in the west of Scotland tended to be carried on in general engineering businesses, because of the limited scope for specialisation, but this did not impair the quality of the product. Shipbuilding machine tools were very successfully manufactured in Scotland, and those Scottish firms who produced them showed admirable readiness to adopt developments pioneered in the United States where a different wage structure and a different climate were bound to produce different patterns of development.

The inter-war period with a depressed shipbuildings industry, a flourishing second-hand market for machine tools, sharp German and American competition, and sustained financial crises, was a singularly adverse environment for massive development. Nevertheless, firms like Craig and Donald, James Bennie, Loudon Brothers, G. and A. Harvey, and James Allan Senior and Son, all of whom amalgamated in 1937 to form the Scottish Machine Tool Corporation, were by any standards competitive. Their record in the English market alone proves this. What no degree of technological awareness could alter was the bleak economic setting in which they had to operate.

The fact appears to be that just as the economic success of Victorian Scotland was self-reinforcing, so the economic failure of inter-war Scotland was the product of a series of mutually reinforcing interlocked factors. High on the list of these factors was the extreme localisation in Scotland of concentrated heavy engineering complexes and coarse textile manufacture. Originally these concentrations gave rise to substantial external economies due to the build up of skills and the juxtaposition of complimentary firms. They were, however, always very vulnerable to the fierce swings in the trade cycle characteristic of the capital goods industries, and with sustained depression their position was desperate. They had never paid particularly high wages and between 1922 and 1939 unemployment in Scotland remained persistently higher than the United Kingdom average. In 1924 the UK percentage was 10.3 and the Scottish one 12.4. In 1932 the figures were 22.1 and 27.7 respectively and in 1939 10.8 and 15.9. The contrast with England was even sharper for the UK figures included not only the Scottish ones but also those for Ulster and South Wales, both areas with abnormally high unemployment. The upshot was that purchasing power in inter-war Scotland was generally so low compared with, say, the south of England, that Scotland held little attraction for businessmen interested in the new mass produced consumer goods. Electrical power increasingly freed industry from the need to be located on or near coalfields, so the draw of large prosperous metropolitan markets like London became enormous. It is significant that an observer writing of the Scotland of the late 1930s reckoned that Edinburgh had the best industrial prospects of any Scottish city. Edinburgh has always had the largest and most prosperous middle-class population in Scotland.

One absolutely inevitable consequence of sustained depression, given Scottish employers' enthusiasm for cutting wages under such circumstances, was labour trouble. Scotland acquired between 1919 and 1939 a reputation which it had not previously possessed for extreme labour militancy with strong left-wing political overtones. As reputations go, it was hardly deserved. In view of what was happening to Scotland's staple industries, it would have been a miracle if there had not been major strikes, and the 'bolshevism' of the 'Clydeside Brigade' of Labour MPs was largely non-existent. Their clearest mind, John Wheatley, was an orthodox Catholic, and their most flamboyant personality, James Maxton, was an aimiable but distinctly woolly-minded sentimental socialist. However, it was not difficult to acquire a revolutionary reputation between the wars. To take a Scottish example: the Distillers Company Limited was all the keener to run down its Irish interests because it saw in Eamonn de Valera, the future premier and president of Eire, a symptom of universal revolution. That this was a trifle hard on a wing-collared Catholic professor whose views on most economic and social questions might be described as strongly reactionary rather than just conservative, was neither here nor there. From this point of view, the Scottish working class settled for a typically British compromise in the inter-war period. It raised enough hell to frighten off investors, but not nearly enough hell seriously to shake the existing social order. It is true that the large scale amalgamations in shipbuilding, steel, machine tools, and textiles could lead to the pensioning off of old entrepreneurial families. This did not invariably happen. Of the two big textile conglomerates which emerged in Dundee one, Low and Bonar, which was centred on the old linen firm of Baxter Brothers, did eliminate families like the Baxters. The other, Jute Industries, originally a much looser structure centred on what had been the world's biggest jute firm, Cox Brothers Lochee, did not dispense with the services of the old families. Its board in 1936 included old names like Cox, Sandeman, and Walker. Whether new or old, the managerial class in no way lost its grip on the industrial and social hierarchies between 1919 and 1939.

The single most revealing area of economic activity in Scotland, for a student of the social order, was housebuilding. High interest rates and material shortages restricted building in the 1920s, and it fluctuated a great deal in the 1930s, but there was no parallel in Scotland to the very substantial housing boom which played a central role in the significant growth achieved in the English economy in the 1930s. In 1938 22.6 per cent of Scottish working-class housing was officially classed as overcrowded. The English figure was 3.8. Two Housing Acts, the Chamberlain Act of 1923, and the Wheatley Act of 1924 offered meaningful incentives for the construction of private and public housing until their provisions were cancelled in 1929 and 1933 respectively. After that the emphasis was on slum clearance. In fact in Scotland in the 1930s more homes were demolished than were built, and even in the period 1934–6, when interest rates were very low, private housebuilding in Scotland was not buoyant.

Scottish farmers endured a desperately difficult decade between 1921 and 1931, but were on the whole more fortunate in the rest of the 1930s. Their troubles were compounded when, in the face of a torrent of cheap agricultural imports, the government by the Corn Production (Repeal) Act, 1921, abandoned its financial underpinning of wheat and oat prices and jettisoned its commitment to certain standards of husbandry and a minimum agricultural wage. An acreage payment, of which Scotland's share was £4.4 million, survived but a run of bad summers and late harvests in 1922, 1923, and 1924, left the industry at a low ebb. Even in the 1920s, however, compensation appeared in the shape of legislation in 1923, 1926, and 1929 which left agricultural land and buidings free of rates which were only levied on the farmhouse proper. In addition to de-rating the farmer who had bought his farm benefited from the Agricultural Credits (Scotland) Acts of 1925 and 1929, while a very important precedent was set in 1925 with the Beet Sugar (Subsidy) Act. The arguments for establishing a beet sugar industry were primarily strategic. In Scotland suitable conditions for the crop really only existed in the east-central area, so it was logical that Fife should be the centre of the Scottish industry and that the essential processing factory be built outside Cupar, the county town. To secure adequate acreage for the factory to process, a subsidy proved essential. It could be defended on strategic grounds, on grounds of creating work in rural areas, and on the ground that it saved foreign exchange. After a lengthy if marginal existence the factory was closed in the early 1970s in an irreversible gesture which, with the percipience typical of modern government, was completed just before a substantial rise in world sugar prices.

Prices steadied until 1930, when another massive slump occurred. Prices for certain kinds of sheep fell by as much as 40 per cent. Grain prices slumped heavily. In Edinburgh in December 1933 the highest price for wheat was just 20s. 6d. a quarter and for oats 15s. 9d. Provincial prices were even poorer. Potatoes fell to ruinous levels, especially for remoter areas with high transport costs. Cereal, milk, livestock, and wool prices tumbled, and with them the value of land. Inevitably there was a substantial fall in both the oats and the barley acreage, while temporary grass increased by 160,000 acres and permanent by over 260,000 acres. What saved Scottish farmers from even more drastic change was the abandonment of the sacred principles of Free Trade by the so-called National Government after the election of 1931.

One of the first results of this development was a Wheat Act passed in 1932 which established a guaranteed price for millable grain sold. Wheat was relatively unimportant in Scotland and it was not until 1937 that price guarantees were offered for oats and barley, the most important Scottish cereals. As they were often retained on the farm as animal fodder, this could only done on an acreage basis. Meat prices had fallen so low that restrictions on foreign imports into Britain had to be introduced in 1932. By 1934 temporary beef subsidies were operative and by 1937 the Livestock Industry Act had made them permanent at levels of 5s. 0d. per hundredweight for ordinary home-bred cattle, and 7s. 6d. per hundredweight for quality beasts. When to all this is added the fact that producer boards were formed for the marketing of Scottish milk, potatoes, and bacon pigs, and that these bodies, with the support of two-thirds of the producers in their regions could coerce the remaining producers by depriving them of the right to sell to anyone but the board, it is clear that a high degree of state intervention in agriculture had been accepted. Admittedly most of it was the one-way socialism of benefits without control, and this was underlined by the 1937 legislation which allowed a subsidy of 50 per cent cost for lime and 25 per cent for slag applied to the land. However, there was a measure of control, and not just in the shape of marketing boards. Under the Agricultural Wages (Regulations) Scotland Act 1937 minimum wages, overtime payment, and holidays for Scottish farm labourers were all regulated by a statutory board. Within this framework it must be said that Scottish agriculture made a steady recovery from the depths of 1931 and even made striking progress in technical matters like the adoption of tractors (though not combine harvesters), and the establishment of a high-quality seed potato export, especially to England.

The key to this very much greater willingness of government to accept direct responsibility for the agricultural sector of the Scottish economy was undoubtedly the fact that the National Government enjoyed at first an overwhelming and then a very handsome majority and could ignore once emotion-laden shibboleths such as 'the free breakfast table'. That said, the freedom with which government used its ability to manoeuvre is perhaps best explained by the still very close links between the countryside and the political, social, and economic élites of the United Kingdom. Thomas Shaw, a Scots advocate who was later a Lord of Appeal of the House of Lords, took his territorial title from the estate of Craigmyle in Aberdeenshire. A passionate salmon fisher, he became friendly towards the end of his life with Neville Chamberlain, who when premier in the late 1930s fished his way from one Highland estate to another by way of recreation. Lord Craigmyle's last illness struck him at Glenapp Castle, home of the widow of Lord Inchcape, an Arbroath man who became a great shipping magnate. Great civil engineers like Alexander Gibb and Weetman Pearson, the first Viscount Cowdray, bought estates in the north of Scotland in the inter-war period, partly for prestige, since assimilation to the landed gentry was still the supreme social accolade, and partly to secure secluded retreats. The Wills tobacco dynasty, for example, could retire to estates and a castle in Glen Lyon. The young Lord Dunglass, later the Earl of Home, later Sir Alec Douglas-Home, and later still Lord Home of the Hirsel, was not only a major Border landowner but also an up-and-coming young man in Chamberlain's pre-war government and in the long run a future premier. It was certainly the ability to manoeuvre within this sort of élite which saved the young Forestry Commission from extinction in the fierce government economies of the 1920s. Set up by legislation of 1919, the Commission was entrusted with the task of buying land and planting it on a sufficient scale to establish a strategic timber reserve for wartime, and to help the balance of payments in peacetime. Its first Chairman, the sixteenth Lord Lovat, resigned in 1927 to take a government post, but only after using his immense charm and ability to save the Commission from the 'Geddes Axe' of economy in 1922 and the equally grave threat of Winston Churchill as Chancellor of the Exchequer in 1925. The third Chairman, another Scottish landowner Sir John Stirling Maxwell, managed to fend off an early threat from an economy-minded National Government. It was all very much the world of John Buchan's novel *John Macnab*.

Though often Tory in formal party allegiance, the political, social and industrial leadership of inter-war Scotland was essentially the old Liberal ascendancy rallying under fresh banners. John Buchan, though a declared Conservative, was clear that his creed embodied all that was best in Victorian Liberalism. What was discernible was a shift in balance. Before 1914 and even more before 1900 the Scots with easiest access to the magic circles at the top of the political and social ladder were those already born into the aristocracy like Lord Rosebery and A.J. Balfour. Bonar Law was the harbinger of a whole host of middle-class Scots who ascended Olympus between 1919 and 1939. When Lord Meston of Agra and Dunottar was given his title in 1919 on the occasion of his retirement from the Indian Civil Service, he was the first alumnus of the University of Aberdeen to achieve a peerage since Sir George Gordon of Haddo was created the first Earl of Aberdeen in 1682. That fact suggests that pulling out plums from the honours pudding had not been particularly easy even for successful Scots meritocrats. After 1919, however, the situation was different. John Buchan was advanced to a peerage and the Governor Generalship of Canada for literary and political services. The period also saw the irresistible rise of John Anderson, that most awesome of Edinburgh science graduates, through the civil service ranks to the status of the supreme man of business to the British Establishment, a status eventually confirmed with the title of Viscount Waverley.

Whether this kind of leadership was altogether desirable for a stricken industrial community may be doubted. Despite crippling depression, this élite was at heart well pleased with itself, and it was perhaps too successful by half in maintaining social and political continuity. Discontinuity was the only hope for change in Scotland, but even the long swing of the political pendulum towards Labour in the Scottish constituencies was strikingly reversed in the election of 1931. Walter Elliot, a Glasgow Tory who was for four years Minister for Agriculture in the National Government after 1932, alleged that the whole business of a Labour premier deserting his party to hand effective power to a huge Tory majority, carefully wrapped up as a National Government, could only be explained by assuming that God was a violent partisan of the then Conservative leader Stanley Baldwin. Though this is an example of the tactlessness which helped to keep Elliot out of high office after the Second World War, it did have a grain of truth in it. Seldom can so uninspiring a group of politicians as Ramsay MacDonald and his Liberal and Conservative allies have received such a crushing electoral endorsement as the British people gave the National Government in 1931. That government did provide a framework of protection within which Scottish agriculture could at least partially be stabilised. In the industrial field the most depressed areas of Scotland were designated Distressed Areas, and soon re-designated Special Areas in accordance with the politicians' genius for slapping new labels on old luggage. By the end of 1938 the Commissioner for the Special Areas had spent £4.9 million in Scotland, but the brutal fact was that the basic problems of the Scottish economy had barely been touched. The odd industrial estate had been established with light industries which usually wanted female labour when unemployment was most severe amongst men. The fact that only rearmament prevented another plunge into depression in 1938–9 showed that the declining heavy industries were still far too important in Scotland.

Surprisingly little progress had been made in tackling the complex of problems first exposed to widespread discussion by the 1921 slump. Compared with the economy of south-east England, the economy of Lowland Scotland was still depressingly undynamic. That it was not the only British regional economy in this position was cold comfort.

8

The Shaping of the Modern Scots Economy 1939–1960

Between 1939 and 1960 Scotland changed from an acknowledged exceptionally depressed area in a far from buoyant inter-war Britain into part of what was naïvely described as 'the affluent society' of the 1960s. Standards of living, overall, reached imprecedented heights. Significant economic, political and social changes occurred. Yet closer examination reveals a surprising degree of continuity. Few fundamental industrial problems were solved. Deprivation was relative but then deprivation is usually a relative question. The problems of the Scottish economy retained the ultimate stamp of credibility in the eyes of Westminster politicians—they affected the way Scotsmen used their votes.

The outbreak of the Second World War in September 1939 was bound to have profound effects on the Scottish economy and, on balance, those effects were likely to be deleterious, at least in the long run. In the short term, of course, the war was likely to solve the unemployment problem in Scotland by removing a great many men, and later women, into the armed forces and by enormously increasing demand for coal, steel, iron and all the products of Scotland's heavy industry. Even before the outbreak of war rearmament had been keeping something like 20 per cent of the capacity of the active Clyde shipyards busy. Indeed, in the course of the war there was actually a swing back towards the traditional heavy industries which in 1939 employed roughly 16 per cent of the employed population but which by 1945 had increased that figure to 25 per cent. In the immediate pre-war period factory closures were only marginally lower than the figures for new factories opening in Scotland. It so happened that the Second World War was much more fruitful of technological advance and innovation than the First World War. The major scientific discoveries of the period 1939–45 included magnetron valves, radar, jet engines and many other aerospace developments, nuclear power, electronic computing and control systems, antibiotics, DDT and other insecticides, and a host of others too numerous to name. It was therefore a major tragedy that very little production in these fields came to Scotland. Only 32 government factories were built in Scotland during the entire course of the war, so diversification in the older industrial areas was minimal. Dispersal of industry in the United Kingdom was never carried very far. After the Battle of Britain in 1940, the British were in no danger of losing air superiority. They did suffer from bombing, especially night bombing, until the German invasion of Russia in June 1941 led to a major diversion of German air strength to the eastern front. However there was never anything like the sustained fury of the Allied air attack on Germany in 1944–5, which meant that the British government never felt obliged to make a major effort to disperse industrial production. On the contrary, it increasingly felt that the optimal course was to reinforce existing big concentrations of industrial activity, thereby minimising the cost of assembling an adequate labour force. It is true that apart from a heavy aerial attack on Clydeside in March 1941, Scotland did not experience anything like the scale of destruction which afflicted certain English cities, but this was a very marginal factor which post-war circumstances did not allow to be of any real significance.

Curiously enough, the period of wartime dominated by the Coalition government formed by Winston Churchill in 1940 saw a burst of constructive and positive activity in the economic field emanating from that most unlikely of all sources—the Secretaryship of State for Scotland. This latter post had been recreated in the late nineteenth century mainly as the result of a campaign led by Lord Rosebery, who wanted it to be a powerful position with himself as the first incumbent. His political elders and betters were careful to exclude him from the job, which was in many ways a mere shadow of what Rosebery had envisaged. To make assurance doubly sure, the Secretaries of State for Scotland were hand-picked for mediocrity and dullness, and any of them showing a flicker of originality or charisma was almost instantly removed even if he had to be kicked upstairs, like Lord Pentland just before the First World War, to do so. It was Churchill's determination to secure the services of Tom Johnston, Labour MP for West Stirlingshire and a civil defence regional commissioner, as Secretary of State for Scotland, which explains the new dynamism. Johnston was able, to some extent, to insist on his own terms before he accepted the post, and he showed immense shrewdness in what he asked for. He wanted and secured a Scottish Advisory Council of ex-Secretaries (usually referred to as the council of state), which he used to launch some of his more enterprising schemes, for if they were approved by this body, of all bodies, it was possible to argue that they must be bipartisan and non-controversial. Seldom has the British Establishment been handled with so deft a touch. It is a measure of just how immemorable the membership of the council of state was that it is extremely difficult to find a photograph of this august body.

Johnston was certainly the greatest Secretary of State for Scotland to date. In 1942 he established the Scottish Council on Industry to improve communication between government and industry. With some difficulty he managed to create a separate Scottish Tourist Board. Nor was he backward in the field of social welfare. Scotland was the first part of the United Kingdom to operate rent tribunals to control the level of wartime rents, and by an ingenious use of civil defence hospitals (originally designed to take mass casualties from air attack), to examine and treat war workers, he virtually created a national health service for Clydeside. Nor could Johnston be accused of a mandarinic pursuit of centralised power. He foresaw the grave implications for effective local democracy in the whole concept of central planning and in the *Memories* he published in 1952 he summed up his own creed as 'federal action, yes, . . . but the big centralised stick, no'. Furthermore he was as hostile to a big bureaucratic stick in Edinburgh as in London. It was in fact an unholy alliance between Edinburgh bureaucrats and Westminster politicians which effectively abolished traditional Scottish local government in the early 1970s.

Yet it is fair to say that this shrewd, dynamic and urbane character never came near the central issues affecting Scotland's industrial future. His triumphs tended to be in areas peripheral to the industrial economy proper. This is true even of what was arguably his greatest achievement—the establishment by legislation of 1943 of the North of Scotland Hydro-Electric Board. Johnston was picking up a development of long standing in the Highlands, but one which had rather lost impetus since 1929. The first major hydro-electric station in Britain opened at Foyers in Inverness-shire in 1896. It powered an aluminium works downriver from the Falls of Foyers. The second British hydro-electric site was Kinlochleven in 1909. Then there was a pause before development resumed with Falls of Clyde (1926), Rannoch (1930), Tummel (1933), and Galloway (1935–6). Opposition could be bitter to such schemes, partly because of the visceral fear displayed by businessmen for such exercises in state capitalism and partly because of the objections of the landed interest to the inevitable interference with their absolute property rights which such schemes and their catchment areas involved. A public enquiry by the respected and deeply patriotic Lord Cooper of Culross, the greatest Scots lawyer of his day, was therefore a necessary prelude to successful legislation on hydro-electric development. Vested interests were assured of more than generous financial compensation. This was already a well-established procedure. The Galloway scheme, for example, had seen a quarter of a million pounds spent on compensation, much of it for damage to fisheries.

Johnston showed characteristic wisdom in resigning his post at the end of the war. He would not have been allowed so free a hand under the Labour government of Clement Attlee which assumed power after a decisive Labour victory in the general election of 1945. This turned out to be a centralising regime *par excellence*. The fact is that Johnston was the beneficiary of very unusual circumstances. War created an unparalleled sense of national solidarity within the United Kingdom, so it was quite safe to have an able man as Secretary of State for Scotland and to give him a relatively free hand. He was unlikely to establish any kind of autonomous power base, as Johnston's post-war retreat into administrative posts in the gift of government showed. Churchill had sat for a Scottish seat in his time. His career as MP for Dundee ended with an on-the-whole well-merited rejection at the polls in 1922 by a community tired of being neglected except at election time. During the Second World War Churchill wanted a quiet and cooperative Scotland, which Johnston helped secure for him.

The National Government had operated a party truce whereby the major parties simply did not oppose one another in by-elections. The party in possession was thereby guaranteed a virtual free run for its candidate and the electorate deprived of any serious influence on the government. Intriguingly, when the Greek scholar Douglas Young stood as a Scottish Nationalist candidate for Kirkcaldy burghs on a strong anti-military and industrial conscription platform in 1943, he ran the Coalition candidate quite close. Young had 42 per cent of votes cast to the Coalition man's 52 per cent. However, the general election of 1945 saw the Labour Party win 37 Scottish seats, with three seats going to its (moribund) near relation the Independent Labour Party, compared with 32 for the Unionists (Conservatives) and two for independents. The future of the Scottish economy was therefore to some extent in the hands of a Labour movement which had inspired a large measure of support for itself within Scottish society.

The Labour government had no belief in what has come to be called devolution, and it was a fact of life that the Scottish economy had for generations before 1945 been an integral part of the British economy. Furthermore, as time passed a strong equalising trend within that economy became apparent. Rates of taxation were naturally identical, but prices, terms of employment, and wage rates tended to become remarkably homogenous throughout the United Kingdom. The Second World War strongly stimulated the development of a close relationship between the Trades Union Congress, as representative of its affiliated unions (by 1950 there were 186 of them with nearly 8 million members), and the state. On most advisory bodies of consequence a tripartite membership became standard, with the state, the central employers' body, and the TUC being the usual bodies represented. By 1945 national agreements regulated terms and conditions of employment in virtually all well-organised industries and services. In some industries such as building and railways they covered almost all eventualities. In the latter case it is easy to see why agreements covering all British lines were natural. The Scottish railway companies had lost their separate identity at the time of the 1923 grouping of all major British railway lines by virtue of the Railways Act of 1921. In place of five wholly Scottish concerns, only two main-line companies were left in Scotland between January 1923 and January 1948—the London Midland and Scottish and the London and North Eastern—and both of these were, as their names suggest, Anglo-Scottish. In other industries the strength of the trade union involved was enough to secure general British agreements. The degree of national regulation could be less than absolute. In coalmining only minimum wages were settled, while in engineering general wage changes were prescribed but not district rates. District wage differentials therefore survived, but decreased steadily in number and significance. For the Scottish economy, the crucial point was that in an established industry it was no longer possible to think in terms of attracting work to a region by means of significantly lower wages which could lower the costs of the product.

As it happened, the Labour government assumed office in 1945 just after the last of a series of classic reports on location of industry and town planning was published. These reports—the Barlow, Scott, and Uthwatt Reports—had spotlighted three fundamental problems. One was the socially disruptive effect of sustained depopulation in rural areas. Another was the complex of problems created by the continuous growth of a limited number of large conurbations, and the third was the decline in the export and internal markets for a number of big traditional industries, among them such Scottish industries as coal, shipbuilding, iron and steel, linen and jute. In the latter case these industries, it was recognised, were regionally concentrated, and the expanding industries which might provide work to compensate for the contraction in employment in the older ones were originally localised elsewhere. War work between 1939 and 1945 had tended to absorb this stubborn regional structural unemployment but it could and did reappear, so this particular problem was the main concern of post-war location policy.

In practice the short-term trend in Scotland after 1945 was to emphasise precisely the older staple industries. Such promising war developments as the manufacture of vehicles and aircraft were rapidly wound up. Only with difficulty was the Rolls-Royce engine works retained at Hillington in Glasgow. Though Britain sacrificed fewer lives on the battlefield in the Second World War than in the First World War, the extent of worldwide destruction between 1939 and 1945 was quite unprecedented. The industrial economies of two of Britain's most formidable rivals, Japan and Germany, were virtually paralysed for a number of years after 1945, and there was huge demand especially for the replacement of capital goods. Shipbuilding was an interesting case in point. There was strong demand for ships in the early post-war period. The output of new ships from Scottish yards in 1948 was valued at £45 million, of which £12 million was for export. In addition ship components were made and sold, and there was some repair work, though not as much as would be normal in English yards. The Clyde produced the bulk of Scottish output, but if Rosyth naval dockyard be excluded, about a seventh of the Scottish industry's output came from centres like Aberdeen, Dundee, Leith, Burntisland and Ardrossan. Whereas in the year 1932 76 per cent of the labour force was unemloyed, unemployment in Scottish shipyards between 1945 and 1951 never went above 7 per cent, and the record would have been even better had not shortages of steel obstructed production. In the period 1949–51 Scottish yards launched no less than 15 per cent of new world tonnage, and the Clyde alone was producing a third of all new British tonnage in these years. Not much wonder that shipbuilding, with its ancillary trades included, had an output superior to mining and was much the biggest Scottish manufacturing industry in 1951.

On the other hand, at that date it could be said that Scotland made no aircraft, passenger cars or tinplate. Of the 23 motor vehicle factories opened in Scotland from time to time only one—Albion Motors—survived, and it was a manufacturer of commercial vehicles. In general it could be said that though the metal trades employed about a sixth of the Scottish working population and half of those in manufacturing, there was still in 1951 a strong emphasis on the heavier end of the trades—ships, locomotives, heavy iron and steel products and so on. Technologically, the Scottish iron and steel industry was still not in the forefront of modern development. It made, for example, very heavy use of cold metal (scrap) and employed a lower charge of hot metal than any other regional British steel industry. Not only was there still no properly integrated steel works in Scotland, but it was also the case that the Scottish industry specialised in the heavy end of the market. The greatest part of Scottish output lay in plates and heavy rolled products where Scottish firms produced 30.4 and 16.1 per cent respectively of all British production in 1949–51. Scotland also produced a good deal of wrought iron, steel tubes, and alloy steel. Against this must be set her very low share of total British production of light rolled products, wire and sheet steel. It was estimated that in 1950 when Scottish steelmakers produced a little under 500,000 tons of finished, total consumption of steel in Scotland was about 289,000 tons, or 60 per cent of the domestic production. Scotland was therefore a heavy net exporter of steel, especially heavy steel products, but a net importer of light steel products such as strip steel, tinplate, wire, tyres, wheels and axles.

The nationalisation of iron and steel came comparatively late in the programme of the Labour government. An Iron and Steel Act, which provided for the maintenance of roughly the existing structure of the industry under state ownership, was passed in 1949, but opposition in the House of Lords was able to postpone vesting day until February 1951. Late in 1951 the Conservatives defeated Labour at an election, so the experiment in nationalisation was brief in iron and steel, for the new government repealed its predecessor's legislation. With another traditional Scottish industry, coal, nationalisation was early and permanent. Legislation was passed in 1946 and on 1 January 1947 the Scottish Division of the National Coal Board assumed responsibility for 275 Scottish mines previously owned and managed by 120 separate firms. The Divisional Board opted to leave 79 small mines working dispersed pockets of coal under their existing management, operating under special licence. The other 196 mines came under the direct management of the Board on Vesting Day. They were not a particularly inspiring heritage, having a history of depression and ruthless short-term exploitation during the war period. The Board estimated that half the collieries it was managing were in such a state of physical and economic decline that they would have to be closed within the next 20 years. Before the First World War, Scotland's share of British coal production had actually been rising. From a peak output of 42.5 million tons in 1913, Scottish coal production fell to an average of not much more than 30 million tons between the wars. After 1945 production was running at just over 20 million tons per annum, and given the circumstances it is not surprising that between 1948 and 1952 it rose to an average of only 23–24 million tons.

Domestic demand for fuel was high, nor was it always possible to satisfy it. Despite much complacent talk by Clement Attlee and Herbert Morrison, there is good reason to doubt whether the Labour government at first had, or could see the need for, an organisation capable of long-term economic planning. This weakness became very apparent in the winter of 1947—admittedly the coldest winter since 1881–2—when an acute fuel crisis led to sudden massive cuts in electric power supply to industry and a rise in British unemployment figures to over 2,000,000. Emanuel Shinwell, an old Clydesider who sat for a Dundee seat, was the Minister of Fuel and Power who emerged with a deservedly tarnished reputation from this fiasco, for it was known that his ministry had ignored repeated expressions of concern, especially from Sir Stafford Cripps, the Chancellor of the Exchequer, in preceding months. It is hardly surprising that unemployment among Scots miners never exceeded 1 per cent between 1947 and 1951, though one must remember what a revolution this represented in an industry which in 1932 had had no less than 34.7 per cent of its labour force out of work. The total labour force in the Scottish coal industry, including its clerical staff, in 1950 was 91,300.

Changes in importance between the main Scottish mining areas were inevitable after 1945. In particular the Lanarkshire field was suffering from over-extensive exploitation in times past and unfavourable mining conditions. Over 70 per cent of its coal came from seams less than three feet thick, as compared with 13 per cent in Fife and 26 per cent on average in Britain as a whole. Indeed it was reckoned that in the Central West area of the Lanarkshire coalfield in 1951 pits were operating at a loss of over 6s. per ton of saleable coal. More disturbing was the fact that output per head in Scottish mines, which in 1935 had been high in relation to England and Wales, was being overtaken by other British mining areas and by 1950 had in fact been clearly outstripped by them. Scottish coal became progressively more expensive than English or Welsh coal. It was fully a third costlier than coal from the East Midlands of England, the cheapest of all British coal in the early 1950s. Until 1950 the market was so favourable that the Scottish Division made a profit, but in 1951 and 1952 this turned into a loss.

What was needed was a massive development programme and it is wholly to the credit of the National Coal Board that it allowed its Scottish Division to plan some fifteen large new collieries to exploit at one and the same time economies of scale and the deep coals of Fife, the Lothians, Ayrshire and the upper parts of the Firth of Forth. In 1947 the average depth of mining in Scotland was a mere 900 feet. Private enterprise had achieved its remarkable levels of efficiency in the mid 1930s by exploiting the last workable decades of this level of mining. Whether it would ever have made the transition to deeper levels may be doubted, for new pits had to be sunk at depths of 2,000–3,000 feet, or more. Technically these levels were a feasible proposition because of significant improvements in technique of which preliminary boring provides a good example. In the early 1900s a bore sunk at Balfour Mains in Fife took five years to reach 4,534 feet. By the later 1950s a bore sunk at Brucefield near Clackmannan could reach a depth of 4,406 feet in under 13 months. What was daunting was the scale of capital investment required, and it must be said that, operating on this level, when the Scottish Division was wrong it tended to be crashingly and expensively wrong. The new show colliery, with associated mining housing, at Rothes in Fife is the supreme example. Sunk at punishing expense on the advice of outside experts, and in the teeth of local mining opinion, it proved utterly unworkable almost at once. In the long run this investment programme probably saved the Scottish industry. In the short run it was easier to notice the fiascos, falling output, poor productivity, and rising absolute and relative costs.

There was no significant recovery in the textile field between 1945 and 1951. Cotton, woollens, linen and jute had long ceased to be an expanding part of the Scottish economy. At best they could hold their own. Jute provides an illustration of this. After dreadful inter-war depression, the industry received a mild boost from pre-war civil defence preparations and then the usual stimulus of war demand superimposed on a substantial export drive in the early stages of the war. Jute was regarded as a strategic raw material and placed under a Jute Control Office which, after Dunkirk and the fall of France had to restrict imports to save shipping space. Less essential usages of raw jute had to be progressively curtailed and at one point it looked as if supplies of the raw material might be cut off altogether. The only major supply source was Bengal and in 1942 the shipping route through the Bay of Bengal was cut by Japanese activity. As it happened, this proved temporary, but the jute industry finished the war working on restricted capacity and supplies. Its labour force, which had been recorded as 27,478 in July 1939, was recorded as 15,234 in July 1946, and as 15,566 in July 1950. The vexed problem of supplies of raw jute did not resolve itself at all quickly after the war. British India became independent in 1947, not as a unit but as two dominions—India and Pakistan. East Bengal, where most of the jute available on world markets came from, was transmuted into East Pakistan and the appalling civil disorder and political tension which accompanied Partition ensured that jute remained in relatively short supply. As late as 1952 it was reckoned that with its shortage of labour and other problems the Scottish jute industry was producing only 75 per cent of its pre-war output.

In the long run, this was a blessing to the city of Dundee, for it marked a measure of discontinuity with the old total ascendancy of the jute trade. The gap left by the decline of jute was to some extent filled by new light engineering industries. There had been a spectacular expansion in metalworking and light engineering in Dundee during the war. Much of this was purely temporary in nature involving the making of ball and roller bearings, jerricans, carbide tools, torpedoes and torpedo nets. However, the fund of skill built up in these lines proved invaluable to existing firms in such fields as electrical engineering, which wished to expand after 1945, and to incoming firms like the American-owned Timex corporation which established a large factory for the manufacture of clocks just on the edge of the old Duncan family estate of Camperdown in the north-western part of Dundee. The Kingsway industrial estate rapidly built up with firms making cash registers, dry batteries, watches, toys and sound equipment. Significantly, a good many of these firms were American-owned, and attracted to the area by what was by their standards cheap female labour. The fact that these factories were relatively remote from their markets did not matter greatly because their products had very high values compared with their weights.

Elsewhere in Scotland light engineering works and similar new developments were being opened in the period 1945–51. Most consumer industries were represented in Scotland, but with a bias towards the older ones such as food and drink, and a relatively small representation in newer fields such as chemicals and building materials. In quantitative terms Scotland was still far too heavily dependent on old heavy industries which fared as well as they did mainly because of the existence of a seller's market after the war. It is perhaps worth emphasising that the most radical changes brought about by the Labour government between 1945 and 1950 were primarily social. The establishment of a National Health Service put an end to the reliance on voluntary funds and fees which had hitherto been the common lot of Scottish hospitals. Universal free medical care was a startling and levelling innovation. Social security was vastly improved, and in education, though selectivity remained unchallenged, access to secondary and higher education was effectively opened to all who showed adequate talent. All in all, a beneficial social revolution was carried through, even if its ultimate product tended to be a meritocrat whose self-esteem made the pride of ancient aristocracies seem a mild phenomenon by comparison. What the Labour government did not have was any systematic, let alone dynamic, industrial policy. Its major acts of nationalisation were nearly all rescue operations on industries with a long history of trouble under private enterprise. Many had been so ruthlessly used during the war that it would have been difficult to set them on their feet under private ownership immediately after 1945. The railways are an example of this. The Scottish railways had been abolished as a distinct system by legislation of 1921. Thereafter the grouped British railway system had a very difficult time due to depression and rising competition from road transport which the railways could hardly cope with due partly to the elaborate statutory restrictions and regulations which bound them. When the government assumed control of all main-line railways and several local ones at the end of 1939, it had to negotiate a financial settlement with the companies. What emerged was far from generous. The railways kept all their net revenue in 1940, but in 1941 only 67 per cent of it; in 1942 the figure was under 48; in 1943, 41; and in 1944, 48. Nationalisation was the only alternative to a traumatic run-down of a demoralised and under-capitalised industry.

Only at the very end of its period of power did the Labour government cast its eye on vigorous and profitable industries, with a view to their nationalisation, but by then the government was tired and palpably losing the will to rule.

It is therefore not too unfair to describe the policy of the Labour government as essentially a mixture of liberal social reform, state welfare, and enlightened capitalism if one assumes that an enlightened capitalist is prepared to accept state control of certain industries, especially when the alternative is collapse. One snag about this approach is that it can easily make nonsense of market economies without providing any real alternative. Housing in Scotland was an early and ominous example of the phenomenon. At one level Scottish housing was a success story between 1945 and 1951. A population which had hardly changed in size since 1931 had 230,000 more houses and nearly a million more rooms by 1951. It was a big step forward, even if in 1951 there were still nearly as many people in Scotland living two to a room as there were in England and Wales with a population nine times larger. Between the wars the number of houses built in Scotland at 337,000 was less, but not much less per head of population than the number built in England and Wales. What was significantly different was the percentage of these houses built in Scotland which were built for a local authority. At 67 per cent this was very much higher than the figure of 25 per cent for England and Wales. After 1945, due to shortages of materials and the operation of an elaborate licensing system, building by private enterprise was very restricted and council house estates became a more and more prominent feature of Scottish towns and cities. However, even allowing for a central government grant towards building them and a statutory local subsidy, it was reckoned that in March 1952 the average Scottish council house tenant would have to pay 3½ times his current gross rent before he was paying the real cost of his accommodation.

The reasons for these extremely uneconomic rents were of varied origin. One was the heritage of the Rent Restriction Acts. Another derived from genuine concern at the inability of the poorest-paid to pay an economic rent. On the other hand the income of the average Scottish working-class household was estimated to be 2½–3 times as great in 1953 as in 1938. Yet Glasgow alone had an annual deficit on its housing account of £1.1 million in 1952–3. Sheer political cynicism must take its place in the list of explanations. These low-rented municipal dwellings created and secured voters, often for nominally socialist politicians who were active capitalists, usually in lines not unconnected with the construction industry.

This was the less reputable side of a regime which between 1945 and 1950 sustained much the most serious, hard-working, and effective government which twentieth-century Britain has produced to date. Its only rival in terms of legislative achievement was perhaps the pre-1914 Liberal government, but that government had by 1914 brought the United Kingdom to the verge of civil war. Attlee's government confirmed and strengthened the unity of the realm. Yet there was a vein of potentially dangerous cynicism in the Labour regime, at the top as well as the bottom. It had reneged decisively on Labour's long-standing commitment to devolution in Scotland and Wales. It reinforced the arrogance of a Westminster élite in control of a highly centralised political system, and by enormously expanding the role and power of the state machine it enhanced the self-regard of the mandarins of the higher bureaucracy. Too often the public was subjected to exercises like the 1947 white paper on industry and employment in Scotland, which pretended that the government had a transforming strategy for Scottish industrial development, when it had no such thing, or to such pieces of puff as the gutless and powerless Highland Advisory Panel, set up to give the impression that something was happening.

Yet on balance the Labour government's record is less remarkable for genuine innovation than for a high degree of continuity with the policies of the wartime coalition government. A final illustration of this point can easily be found in the case of agriculture. After a fumbling and confused start, the government had during wartime extended a system of guarantees, subsidies and controls throughout the farming industry. In Scotland the main results of this were a substantial increase in tillage. In 1942 the tillage acreage at 2,098,000 was a mere 2,000 short of the 1918 figure. This level was maintained in 1943 and 1944 and only began to fall in 1945. To keep labour on the land it was essential to increase its wages, so a minimum agricultural wages policy was embarked upon which effectively doubled farm wages between 1939 and 1945. Guaranteed prices and acreage payments would have been rendered essential by this increase in wage costs alone, but there were many other justifications for a policy of direct subsidy. Government was anxious to contain the retail price of certain commodities without discouraging their production. An early introduction of rationing helped to control the situation, but in the case of potatoes though consumption rose by two-thirds per head, acreage rose by 70 per cent and rationing proved unnecessary during the war. To compensate partially for loss of pasture land, special subsidies were offered for reseeding old and marginal pastures and for hill cattle and hill sheep.

After the war absolute shortages and import problems ensured that much of the wartime system would be upheld. Thus the Agriculture Acts of 1947 and 1948 ensured the continuation of guaranteed farm prices and gave tenant farmers greater security of tenure. The total of direct subsidies varied from year to year but Scotland usually secured about an eighth of the United Kingdom total. In 1950 Scots farmers received about £3 million out of a total of £20 million, mostly through grassland ploughing grants, and hill sheep and cattle and calf-rearing subsidies. Obviously the Highlands, with a very large proportion of marginal hill land, benefited massively from such arrangements. The Agricultural Marketing Act of 1949 confirmed the role of the marketing boards set up in the 1930s, cleared the way for the creation of Milk Marketing Boards and greatly increased government influence over these bodies. In forestry the story was similar. As ever, war had seen a ruthless sacrifice of timber reserves and as early as 1943, when a white paper on post-war forestry policy was presented, government was preparing plans to repair these ravages. A Forestry Act, 1945 was passed by the coalition government and accepted as the basis of the Labour government's policy. On purely Scottish matters the Forestry Commission was made responsible to the Secretary of State for Scotland (on British issues the Commission was jointly responsible to him and the Minister of Agriculture). That R. L. Robinson (from 1946 Lord Robinson), the Chairman of the Commission from 1932 to 1952, found it easier to extract money from a Labour government than from any conceivable alternative, is not to be doubted, but the target of 5 million acres of state and private forest in productive condition within 50 years of the end of hostilities was emphatically bi-partisan.

In a sense, therefore, the general election of October 1951 which returned the Conservatives to power was never likely to mark a very startling break with major post-war policies. The impetus to further nationalisation was checked. Steel and road haulage were partially de-nationalised, but that was all. There was a progressive dismantling of rationing, restrictions and controls, but again many of these measures had always been avowedly temporary and would have eventually disappeared, albeit more slowly, under a Labour regime. In the Scottish constituencies Labour and Conservative emerged from the election with the same number of seats. Yet the timing of the election did in fact make it a crucial one. The Labour governments between 1945 and 1951 had been operating under desperately difficult circumstances. Apart from the transition from war to peace, there was the need, successfuly met, for a huge increase in the volume of exports simply to maintain British capacity to import. Terms of trade for the UK had worsened notably since the days of cheap food and raw material imports before 1938, and within this general balance of payments problem there were specific difficulties like the chronic dollar shortage. By 1951 the Korean War boom had lifted America out of a temporary depression; there was an unmistakable upswing in world trade; and there was a very considerable improvement in the balance of payments, due to a fall in the cost of raw materials, which greatly benefited Britain by giving her a more favourable set of terms of trade. Whoever was in office in 1952 was, barring accidents, set for a fairly long run in power. Dynamic leadership was not really needed. In any case the premier, Winston Churchill was a very old man who suffered a series of strokes shortly after assuming office again. Though his colleagues, and party carefully obscured the facts, his doctor has given a picture of a premier who was senile, severely handicapped mentally and physically, and semi-comatose towards the end of his last period in office. His successor, Anthony Eden, had a short and catastrophic premiership culminating in the débâcle of Suez, after which major national disaster there was, incredibly, no systematic enquiry into the abysmal performance of the military and political leadership. Hugh Gaitskell, the Labour leader, reserved his fighting talk mainly for his own party, and Harold Macmillan, Eden's pseudo-Scottish successor, was able, much to his own surprise, to survive in office for years rather than months.

If the Scottish economy was not changing fast enough under Labour, it was even less likely to change under these governments, which basically ran the *status quo* while benefiting from a healthier world economy. In theory 'traditional monetary weapons' were used as the main source of economic control after 1951, but the fact that in 1957 the government set up the Radcliffe Committee to investigate the nature of the monetary system and how far it could be controlled does not inspire great confidence in the precision with which these weapons were wielded. In fact in Scotland the prosperity which buoyed the government's fortunes in England was less apparent. The annual average percentage of the workforce in Scotland which was unemployed between 1953 and 1959 was 3.1, compared with a UK figure of 1.6. Scottish unemployment by 1960 was about a third higher than it had been in 1948. Its incidence, of course, varied across the face of the country. Edinburgh and the Lothians had relatively low unemployment rates, while the Highlands had twice as high an unemployment rate as Scotland as a whole. In absolute terms Glasgow and the three adjacent counties of Lanarkshire, Renfrewshire, and Dumbartonshire contained half of all unemployed persons in Scotland. Nor did these figures tell the whole story. Between 1951 and 1960 there was a net outflow of labour from Scotland which was twice the size of the outflow from any other British region. The population of Scotland had fallen relative to that of England and Wales over a long period, largely due to emigration. In 1801 at 1.6 million Scotland's population was almost a fifth of that of England and Wales (8.9 million). By 1951 the figures were 5 million and 44 million, so Scotland had fallen to a ninth of the population of the larger unit. Scottish population was virtually static between 1914 and 1951 and increased very little to 1960 because over three-quarters of the natural increase in population was emigrating, mainly to jobs in England.

Diversification of its industrial base was undoubtedly what Scotland needed, and there was much discussion of this, but comparatively little progress. The total employment provided at 31 March 1961 by incoming firms which had opened in Scotland since the war was 45,000 or 6.1 per cent of total employees in the manufacturing sector of the Scottish economy. It was by 1960 clear that Scotland had already lost out on the main British developments in fields such as aircraft and vehicle production, as it had in electrical engineering, both in its capital goods production aspect, and in its communications equipment and consumer goods aspect. Nor were the omens very favourable, given current trends, in the new wave of science-based, research-developed industries. The very sensitive relationship which such industries had with their markets and their tendency to lean heavily on military and Post Office orders made the south-east corner of England their natural habitat. It was easy enough for politicians in the 1960s to suggest, with the wave of a confident pipe-stem, that science-based industry could be located in depressed areas at the whim of government. The reality was different.

In the field of town-planning, it was possible for government, central and local, to exercise a much more effective influence on development. Here the outstanding problem in the 1950s was Glasgow. Its halcyon era between 1875 and 1914 had made it the greatest of British provincial cities. It was the second city of the British Empire and one of the six largest cities in Europe. From its long agony in the inter-war period and understandable concern during the Second World War about its post-war future there emerged a report, originally sponsored by Tom Johnston and written by a committee under the leadership of the architect Sir Patrick Abercrombie. This report, published in 1946 as the Clyde Valley Plan, urged that in the interests of both city and region there should be systematic dispersion of industry and population. The Scottish Office, under a Secretary of State for Scotland who reflected faithfully the views of Westminster, accepted this recommendation and in 1947 designated the new town of East Kilbride under the New Towns Act of 1946, as a first step towards dispersal. Glasgow Corporation was understandably unenthusiastic about East Kilbride, which was not technically part of an overall plan for Glasgow, and which was a rival for resources and jobs. Meantime Glasgow, using its own unsatisfactory planning procedures and its inadequate resources, had tried to cope with its clamant housing problems by creating a series of peripheral working-class dormitory suburbs such as Drumchapel, Easterhouse, Castlemilk, Pollock and Priesthill. Devoid of social amenity (not even a pub before 1969) and ugly to boot, there were an aesthetic and social disaster. A second new town, Cumbernauld, was designated in 1956, this time specifically in order to receive overspill population from Glasgow. The Housing and Town Development Act (Scotland) 1957 marked a swing in Treasury opinion against new towns, which like so much else, had turned out to be vastly more expensive than politicians had originally expected, and towards housing overspill in existing but expanded centres. Meantime Glasgow, squeezed by the enforcement of a green belt policy around its existing built-up areas, finally succumbed to a general overspill policy. By 1960 the city was sponsoring population movement out of Glasgow into developing areas where it was hoped that the state would use regional incentives to promote industry.

The euphoria which modern planning allied to modern public-relations techniques can so easily create was inappropriate in Scotland around 1960, for in real terms the Scottish economy was beginning to fall sharply behind the UK economy which itself was faltering, by international standards. The Scottish percentage share of the United Kingdom gross domestic product fell from 9.3 per cent in 1951 to 8.7 per cent in 1960. This can be converted into a rough guide to relative standards of living by taking gross domestic product per head, in which case the Scottish figure fell from 92 per cent of the UK figure in 1951 to 88 per cent in 1960. At a time when unemployment in Scotland was well above the average for the United Kingdom as a whole it was depressing that investment patterns in Scotland showed more emphasis on capital deepening than on capital widening; or put it another way, more emphasis on producing the same output with less labour than on producing a wider range of products with more labour. Even by European standards Scotland was not a poor country and by world standards it was a rich one. Nevertheless, the Macmillan regime, despite the premier's frequent public references to his canny Scots grandfather, was in many ways an irritating one for a majority of Scots and that irritation assumed recognisable political form.

In the general election called in 1955 by Anthony Eden shortly after he became premier, the Conservatives had won 36 out of 71 Scottish seats. Thereafter came the Suez crisis of 1956 and the rise of Harold Macmillan. Stylish and able, Macmillan was never overburdened with economic principles. He inherited and continued a tradition of appeasing the labour movement. This dated from the early days of Churchill's second government when the old man, turned appeaser at the last, sent Walter Monckton to the Ministry of Labour to work a policy of buying off serious trouble. Macmillan's own peculiar contribution to politics was the discovery that in the short run government-induced inflation, if nicely timed, could make the economy more vigorous and the winning of elections easier. An admiring colleague, Reginal Bevins phrased it thus: 'if you raise demand, supply will meet it'. Such a formulation implicitly recognises that Macmillan was lucky enough, at the start, to be playing with an economy with a deal of slack in it. The general election of 1959 saw the Conservatives float through to a victory unthinkable when Macmillan succeeded in 1956. In Scotland Macmillan's slogan 'You've never had it so good' was less successful than in the south of England. In the context of the Scottish regional economy, it was of dubious accuracy. Labour captured 38 Scottish seats to the Unionists' (i.e. Conservatives) 32. Scotland was moving against the current towards a key position in British politics. Labour's electoral hopes in a close-fought election were likely to depend on a disproportionate number of Labour MPs from Scotland. The underlying reasons for this political swing, which was to be decisive when it persisted in 1964, were economic. It is all summed up by the example of an exuberant work on *The New Architecture of Europe* published in 1961 which selected the buildings of the Rothes Colliery, alone in Scotland, as worthy of illustration on the ground that 'Sinewy directness characterises all components, particularly the masterful dominating winding towers'. To most Fifers the main point was that the wretched mine was worse than useless for winning coal. Macmillan had style not to say dash but he did not, in Scotland, deliver the goods. Arguably he hardly did that in England either, but, when he claimed the credit for prosperity there in the late 1950s, there was at least plenty of it around.

9

The Scottish Economy and the
Transit of Britain 1960–1976

From 1960 to 1976 Scotland passed through years when politicians promised more than ever before in the field of economic growth, and delivered very little. By the end of 1976 virtually every known gimmick in the way of internal and external manipulation of the British economy had been tried, and had failed. Not surprisingly, nationalism reared its head in a Scotland relatively disadvantaged in times of depression and financial stringency, and faced with a Westminster leadership quite remarkable for its lack of justified or unjustified popular appeal. By 1969 the British government was becoming worried about the situation and produced a hypothetical Scottish budget for 1967–68 demonstrating to its own satisfaction that Scotland had a deficit of £300–400 million due to the very large imbalance between revenue raised and state expenditure (of which regional policy expenditure was a relatively small part). This particular exercise had, in an Irish context, wasted much parliamentary time in the nineteenth century and may safely be dismissed as equally futile in the twentieth century. It presupposes that a hypothetical Scots government would shoulder all the burdens deemed necessary by a British government, and accept the British Treasury's view of what its revenues should be. Both assumptions are wildly improbable. In any case, the United Kingdom was still very much a unitary state, and the serious issue was the behaviour of Scottish voters at the polls, which in turn seemed to be much affected by their economic experience. Paradoxically, it was the efforts of politicians to manipulate the economy for political ends which seemed to be at the root of the crisis.

By 1960 it was clear that something like a 'political cycle' was emerg-

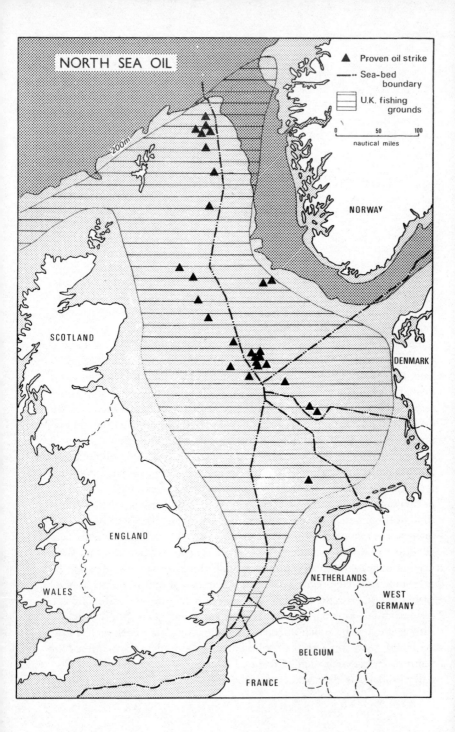

NORTH SEA OIL

▲ Proven oil strike

·-·-· Sea-bed boundary

U.K. fishing grounds

0   50   100
nautical miles

NORWAY

200m

SCOTLAND

DENMARK

ENGLAND

WALES

NETHERLANDS

WEST GERMANY

BELGIUM

FRANCE

ing in the British economy. The obverse of this particular coin was the so-called 'stop-go' policies adopted by government to manage the complex of problems created by inflation and deflation. Until about 1955 it was possible to believe that the British government could successfully and simultaneously pursue the twin objectives of high domestic investment and growth, and a fully convertible pound sterling. A major crisis in that year, not notably well handed by the then Chancellor R. A. Butler, had exposed the truth that in order to protect a vulnerable pound sterling against speculation, it might be necessary to sacrifice domestic growth. As government began to manipulate the economy so as to generate a boom just before an election, a dreary and repetitive pattern began to emerge whereby a reckless budget was followed by electoral victory which was followed by 'overheating' in the economy which in turn necessitated restrictive measures which would be put into reverse next time the regime came under political pressure. This pattern was particularly damaging for regions like Scotland with an acute need for sustained investment in new enterprises.

This last point became a sore one in the winter of 1962–3 when unemployment in specific regions was very high. Interestingly, the economics editor of the *Observer* inclined to deprecate this emphasis. In a book published in 1964 he argued that unemployment in regions like Scotland was not notably worse in December 1962 than it had been in December 1958 (the Scottish figures in thousands of workers were 100.6 in 1962 as against 95.5 in 1958). According to this line of thought it was the movement of demand in the economy as a whole which was the trouble. Obviously there was truth in this remark, but there was also a hint of London-centred lack of interest in the underlying structural problems of Scottish industry. Be that as it may, it is undoubtedly the case that by the early 1960s both the Conservative government and big business were showing signs of conversion to the concept of planning. The reasons for this were legion. Post-war planning had been associated with direct controls but in the early 1960s it was fashionable in official circles to point to the French national plan and greatly to exaggerate its voluntary nature. Really big businesses found it difficult to take major investment decisions without some idea of how the government hoped to manage the economy in the medium term and the government itself was becoming increasingly neurotic about Britain's comparatively slow growth rate, which was ironic because in historical terms Britain was growing faster than ever before. Only in the halcyon days of the third quarter of the nineteenth century had rates of growth of gross national product per head even approached those achieved by the UK in the 1950s. The comparison was of course being made with other countries and especially western European ones.

For Scotland the main consequence of the new vogue for planning was the emergence of a new emphasis on regional policy. Of course regional policy dated back to 1934 when the distressed areas were designated. Upgraded linguistically to special areas, these were renamed and further promoted to development areas by the 1945 Distribution of Industry Act. The 1960 Local Employment Act tried to make the system at once wider and more flexible by replacing these big statutory units by smaller 'development districts' defined in the first instance by the possession of an unemployment figure of 4.5 per cent or more. By the late 'sixties political pressures had produced a reversion to more sweeping geographical areas and the whole of Scotland was classified as a development area, apart from the Edinburgh–Leith conurbation. Such was the indignation in the excluded area that the government had resort to its infinite resources in nomenclature and on 6 June 1968 the citizens of Edinburgh and Leith were encouraged by a visit from Sir Joseph Hunt, chairman of the Hunt Committee on the Problems of Intermediate Areas. Truly all areas had become development areas, but some more so than others.

Planning presupposes plans, so in 1963 the government produced a white paper on Central Scotland. This has been described as 'somewhat tentative and incomplete', but it did at least show an interesting shift of emphasis, for instead of concentrating on the problems of resuscitating the older depressed areas, it was full of briskly optimistic language about sponsoring growth areas for new industries. The government did not envisage state-ownership of these industries. Rather it relied on a combination of indicative planning, such as the white paper itself; the 'persuasion' which existing planning powers enabled government to apply to private industry bent on expansion; and the provision of an adequate infrastructure of transport, housing and other facilities. Undoubtedly the language of the *Central Scotland Plan 1963* reflected a changing emphasis in contemporary economics. Immediately after the war the government implemented policies derived ultimately from the work of J. M. Keynes, and successfully stabilised employment at very high levels indeed. Keynes did not really provide an answer to the inflation which these policies were likely to breed, but by the 1960s a generation of post-Keynsian economists were obsessed with the theory of growth. The very name of the Scottish Development Department formed in 1962 underlined this growth-oriented approach. Nor was the Central Scotland plan of 1963 meant to stand alone. Very soon economics professors and staff from five Scottish universities were involved in a series of sub-regional plans deriving from it, and in other specific research projects.

The crucial question was how far all this furiously-publicised planning activity was likely to produce results. From the point of view of Westminster it would clearly be gratifying in the short run if the public relations bonus built into these exercises proved sufficient to generate a swing to the Conservatives in the next general election. That this did not happen is at least partially due to the fact that the economic scene in Scotland in the early 1960s was one of light and shade, and there was increasing public awareness that the overall balance was unsatisfactory. In 1953 Lord Bilsland, the President of the Scottish Council for Development and Industry, had introduced a survey of Scottish industry written by C. A. Oakley, Controller for Scotland of the Board of Trade, with a suitably unctuous reference to 'a new Elizabethan era, which Scotland hails with confidence'. By the end of the decade neo-Elizabethanism had been consigned to the limbo it merited and the Scottish Council for Development and Industry sponsored a *Report on the Scottish Economy* (commonly known as the Toothill Report) published in 1961. Though criticised at the time as pompous and complacent, and the language of the report was both, it did in fact spell out in some detail the way in which the loss of jobs in basic industries was not being compensated for by adequate new development.

Indeed, the pace of decline in many Scottish industries visibly accelerated after 1960. The railways were an extreme and unusual example. The nationalised rail system inherited not only a run-down industry, but also one which had been over-expanded in uneconomic directions. Only the crudity of railway accounting, which hardly improved after 1945, obscured this truth. However, with rising competition for passengers and goods from private cars and road hauliers in the 1950s the railways faced a financial crisis which made it essential to identify loss-making services. Dr Richard Beeching of Imperial Chemical Industries was brought in to provide the sense of detachment which would make the preordained radical proposals more palatable. His 1963 report was very drastic indeed, proposing rail closures which, if carried out in full, would greatly have emphasised the physical isolation of the north and south-west of Scotland where, at least in 1963, the road systems were admitted to be inadequate and well below modern standards. Michael Noble, Secretary of State for Scotland from 1962 to 1964 sat in the crossfire between the nationalised railways and the inevitable Scottish pressure groups formed to fight the Beeching proposals. The result was a partial suspension of the closure programme. Arguably the whole 'New Look' in nationalised industries sponsored by the Conservative government from 1960 was bedevilled by a half-baked approach to accounting problems. This was true of the railways but perhaps the most blatant example was the Forestry Commission, much the biggest landowner in Scotland, which was pursued by the Treasury to name an acceptable percentage profit on operations and to maintain it. Predictably, too high a figure was agreed and the resulting inability to sustain it created unnecessary embarrassment. The government never allowed the Commission to operate on genuinely commercial lines (such as selling half-acre bungalow plots round all its most scenic forests or auctioning shootings), so there was no realism in the new 'commercial viability' criteria when they were applied to businesses which the government regularly compelled to behave in uncommercial ways.

The coal industry in Scotland was, of course, a prime target for the new business spirit among the Treasury knights. Ordered to eliminate uneconomic pits, the Scottish Division of the National Coal Board in 1962 predicted the closure of 27 pits by 1965. By that year, however, competition from oil plus competition from more favourably-situated British pits (now actively encouraged by an 'economic price' selling policy) had created massive losses in the Scottish Division which in due course scheduled 23 of Scotland's remaining 71 pits for closure, with a suspended sentence hovering over another 13. Increased coal prices accelerated the drift towards oil-firing on the part of such formerly massive customers as the steel giant Colville's. It was all very depressing, but the miners' agitation for a stay of execution was regarded by all reasonable and moderate men as yet another example of irresponsible extremism refusing to face the facts.

Virtually all the big staple Scottish industries were in the toils by the early 1960s, from shipbuilding to textiles. In shipbuilding the crisis was at first concealed. It was rooted in a steady fall in demand for the products of British shipyards. What was most disturbing about this was the fact that the world's seaborne trade was steadily rising. It increased from 460 million tons in 1939 to over 2,000 million tons in 1969, and such an increase required a big expansion in shipping. World merchant shipping tonnage actually increased by over 100 per cent (from 8.7 million to 18.7 million tons) between 1959 and 1969. In the period 1950–4 the United Kingdom produced 31 per cent of the world's new tonnage. Within a decade the figure had fallen to 13 per cent and in the same time Scotland's share of U.K. launchings fell slightly from 38 per cent to 34. Foreign competition, especially from Japan but also from West Germany and Sweden, was the main explanation. By the early 1960s many Clyde yards were operating on the narrowest of margins, occasionally taking unremunerative work in order to keep ticking over.

The jute industry also faced mounting overseas competition. Most Indian manufacturing capacity was in that part of Bengal which went to the Indian Union. East Pakistan was a jute-growing area with little industrial development, so it set out to catch up with the once dominant Calcutta mill complex, building by 1962 14 jute mills capable of processing a quarter of its jute crop. The Jute Control Office established in Britain during the war could in fact shield the Scottish industry because it was the sole legal importer of raw jute and jute goods, and it resold the latter to quota-holders at Dundee prices. When trading in raw jute was returned to private hands in 1954, protection was continued under a system known as Jute Control whereby Indian manufactured goods were resold in the British market with a mark-up, at first of 40 per cent, and after 1957 of 30 per cent. The Scottish industry concentrated more and more on the more expensive end of the market. In the 1950s it derived advantage from the boom in broad-loom backing for tufted carpets, as much in the United States as in Britain. Wages increased by 100 per cent between 1948 and 1958 (in India the figure was 46 per cent). By the mid-1960s, however, a series of problems were raising their heads. Raw material and transport costs were rising and the development of polypropylene, a side product of the petro-chemical industry, had at last created a synthetic rival capable of challenging jute at low price levels.

There were concrete achievements to set beside the disturbing trends. The Forth Road Bridge was completed in 1964 and the Tay Road Bridge in 1966. Both were made possible by government loans which were to be liquidated by revenue from tolls, though the Forth Road Bridge had the cost of its approach roads added into the capital burden, which then became somewhat excessive. The container revolution in the shipping of goods by sea was catered for by the creation of terminals equipped with the specialised handling facilities required to load and unload a limited number of very large pre-packed boxes. Of necessity, only a few big ports could afford such investment. By the end of 1968 container terminals were operative at Greenock, Leith and Grangemouth. The growth of the last-named port after 1945 was spectacular and hinged almost entirely on its petro-chemical connections. Although the combination of new road bridges and containerisation strengthened the position of a big port like Leith, it helped kill stone dead declining smaller harbours like Alloa and Bo'ness. Less ambiguous in its results was the siting of a new steel strip-mill at Ravenscraig in Lanarkshire in 1958. This was in fact a purely political decision arrived at after protracted argument within the government culminating in a compromise whereby a larger project was literally split down the middle and half given to both Scotland and Wales. Arguably the location of a British Motor Corporation plant near Bathgate in 1961 (specialising in heavy trucks and agricultural tractors), and the opening of a Rootes' plant at Linwood in 1963 (initially specialising in the Hillman Imp car), were equally political decisions forced on reluctant firms by a government determined to mop up surplus labour in the west of Scotland. Both plants nearly collapsed in their early years due to a combination of low productivity, high overheads, and transport costs.

Hardly surprising was the poor showing of the Unionists (i.e. Conservatives) in Scottish constituencies in the general election of 1964. The Lowlands expressed annoyance by returning 43 Labour MP's. Peripheral Highland areas returned 3 Liberal MP's (later strengthened by a Liberal victory in a Border constituency), and the Tories were reduced to 24; a fact which lost them the election for Harold Wilson assumed power with a majority at Westminster of four. Here was an unmistakable protest against 'stop-go' economic management and regional policies more remarkable for promise than fulfilment. It does seem that British politicians, both Labour and Conservative had been deeply impressed by the so-called 'Kennedy Revolution' in American politics. When John F. Kennedy was elected the 35th President of the United States late in 1960 the revolution which carried this conservative Democrat into office was one of technique rather than substance. It involved an emphasis on style, a whipping-up of a mystique, and above all a massive and expensive use of all the media to project a favourable image. From the Scottish point of view, the main repercussion had been an exponential expansion in the amount of hot air regularly emitted by British governments on Scottish economic problems.

Lacking a decisive majority until March 1966, the new government at first trod warily in matters Scottish. It had inherited a difficult economic position. When ill-health finally prised Macmillan away from power in 1963, he left two very dangerous interlocked legacies. One was an increasing emphasis on the premier's personal ascendancy in politics. Colleagues were 'little local difficulties' or scapegoats to be sacked in droves when it came to the crunch. The other was an inflationary-cum-expansionist bias in finance well sustained by Reginald Maudling, Chancellor in Sir Alec Douglas-Home's brief government. In office Labour churned out plans and schemes for revitalising the Scottish economy. In 1965 the Highlands and Islands Development Board was established by statute, partly to coordinate the jungle of overlapping administrative authorities in the Highlands. Its financial resources were limited and the Scottish Office made it clear that it regarded the Board as a body devoted to relatively small issues such as minor industrial developments, forestry, land-use, fishing, tourism and agriculture. In its first five years the Board claimed to have created 5,000 new jobs and to have assisted over 200 fishing boats. In the six years to November 1971 it spent £9.25 million, but it must be emphasised that this was a modest sum compared with the recurring expenditure of single large government departments in the Highlands. The Board helped to ensure that the Highlands, with only 5 per cent of Scottish population, were securing 10 per cent of government expenditure in Scotland by the late 1960s. All the same, the Board's contribution to this situation was much smaller than its resounding title suggested.

The wilder enthusiasms of the Board's first chairman, Sir Robert Grieve, such as a proposed Moray Firth metropolitan growth area of half a million people, were studiously ignored by Westminster, though he does seem to have been one of the voices, if only one, which persuaded the government to site a fast breeder nuclear reactor at Dounreay near Wick in Caithness, and to place a big new aluminium smelter development at Invergordon on the Moray Firth. The wider vision of the High-land Board was, however, quite mild compared with the sweep of the government's *Plan for Expansion* for the Scottish economy announced with resounding fanfares in January 1966. This document made a very sensible analysis of what was wrong with the Scottish economy, arguing that old and declining industries must be slimmed, reorganised and modernised; that there must be a shift of resources into, and a retraining of manpower for, new growth industries such as cars and electronics; and that a particular effort must be made to assist specific declining regional economies such as those of the North East and the Borders (the Highlands were presumably already in hand). Government action was clearly essential to achieve these ends. It was therefore proposed that the whole of Scotland, except the Edinburgh–Leith area, would be treated as a development area in which investment grants of up to 40 per cent could be offered to new industrial enterprises. Over the period 1965–70 it was forecast that public investment in Scotland would amount to over £2,000 million. Daringly, the government set itself to reverse the disturbingly high rate of emigration by creating sufficient job opportunities in Scotland to retain the natural population increase. It was magnificent, but was it war? Even at the time doubts were expressed as to whether the Labour government had either the will or the means to work such a transformation. Besides, the plan came out before the election of March 1966 which gave Harold Wilson's Labour government a clear UK majority of 97, and effectively freed the government from having to pay too much attention to public opinion.

In Scotland there was less of a swing to Labour than in the UK generally. Scottish seats were distributed: Labour 46, Conservative 20, and Liberal 5. Scotland was, however, no longer politically strategic and politics were dominated by the government's protracted and quite misguided attempt to defend what turned out to be an unrealistic value for the pound. If devaluation was politically impossible in 1964, it was certainly not so in 1966, and the reasons for its rejection seem to have been a complex brew of British government stubbornness, and massive American pressure against devaluation. One result of the Second World War had been a heavy dependence by successive British governments on the United States. The Macmillan era had reinforced that dependence and the Labour leadership was as susceptible as the Conservatives to American representations backed as they were by the loans which made a long delaying action against the inevitable possible. For Scotland the main consequence of the course of action chosen by Harold Wilson and his Chancellor, James Callaghan, was a massive dose of deflation in 1966, with the usual concomitants of soaring unemployment and a mass emigration, which at 50,000 was one of the highest annual totals ever seen. 'Stop-go' had indeed been changed—cynics said for 'permanent stop'. The face value of Wilson's other electoral pledges plummeted.

Coolly observed, they had never been very convincing. As early as 1965 a major Clyde shipyard—Fairfield's Govan Yard—had to be rescued from liquidation by a government–private enterprise consortium. Contraction in orders for the Royal Navy had driven Fairfield's into merchant shipping work at extremely competitive prices leaving little margin for error, and by October 1965 the firm was bankrupt. The government stepped in in December to rescue its modernised yard, though not its associated marine engineering firm of Fairfield-Rowan. An attempt was made under the consortium to integrate state and private enterprise, and management and labour, in an unprecedented fashion. Fairfield's triggered off a radically new attack on the problems of British shipbuilding which was expressed most influentially in the so-called Geddes Report of 1966 on the UK shipbuilding industry. This document called for the reorganisation of the industry into larger units capable of effecting economies of scale and, thus, of competitiveness in the expanding world market for ships. On the Clyde two large combines were formed in the period 1967–8. The strong Scott-Lithgow group which united the yards on the lower reaches of the river was formed in 1967. By 1969 £7 million had been spent re-equipping these yards to the point where they could and did accept orders ranging from quite small ships to 250,000 ton tankers.

The other consortium, Upper Clyde Shipbuilders (UCS), was born of a difficult labour (union problems delayed its creation until 1968). Nor was the child a healthy one. Of the five firms incorporated in its structure, only one was profitable. The other four had a combined loss of £2.4 million before entering Upper Clyde Shipbuilders. This ill-assorted group included Fairfield's, through which firm the government had a 17.5 per cent holding in the consortium. Understandably, private investors were most reluctant to invest in the new venture, which meant that the government, through the Shipbuilding Industry Board, had to provide the vital capital. By 1970 the government's stake in the firm was 49.4 per cent. In that year Yarrow's, the only profitable firm in the grouping bought themselves out into independence. They were well out, for UCS started with a back-log of losses on pre-existing contracts to the tune of £12 million, to which it promptly added losses of £9.8 million on its own contracts, many of which were taken at far too narrow margins. Knowing that the financial situation was desperate and that the management would have to admit this if there was a long strike, the unions chose to play an aggressive game which, incredibly, made UCS a pacesetter in wage levels. The management was equally irresponsible. It was slow to modernise or rationalise, and knowing that the public purse underpinned it, it chose not to know the extent of loss. Unbelievably, when liquidation came in 1971 the latest audited accounts were dated August 1968.

What was unique about UCS was not its bankruptcy. In 1969 the Burntisland Shipbuilding Company on the Forth went bankrupt as the result of one mis-costed job, leaving Robb Caledon of Dundee and Leith the only significant shipbuilder on the east coast south of Aberdeen. What was unique was the clarity with which UCS illustrated the harrowing consequences of state finance without effective control. Lunacy would not be too strong a term for the record of labour and management. Furthermore the impact of the devaluation finally forced upon the country in November 1967 helped to sustain this atmosphere of crisis ameliorated by state hand-outs. A new Chancellor, Roy Jenkins, devoted himself to making devaluation work at the cost of severe deflation, which increased unemployment, depressed already poor investment levels, and ironically stimulated wage demands by strategically-placed union groups. It was classic 'stagflation'. When in April 1970 the official *Scottish Economic Development Quarterly Report* preened itself on 'reversing trends in emigration', the basic explanation was that unemployment in England was now so high that Scots preferred to go on the dole at home. There it must be said that the government was spending money on a larger scale than ever before to mitigate the full effects of the crisis. Regional policy was costing upwards of £300 million a year by 1970, much of it going on subsidies, advance factories, infra-structure development and other techniques designed to attract industry which could be discouraged from expanding in south-east England by a refusal of industrial development certificates. On balance, the increase of unemployment in Scotland was modified, if not stopped.

The Scottish National Party won a striking by-election victory at Hamilton in 1967. Given the record of successive governments, the only surprising feature of this development was that it came so late and was not sustained in the general election of 1970 when the party won only the Western Isles. Scotland returned 44 Labour MPs, 23 Conservatives, 3 Liberals, and a Nationalist. Overall in the UK Mr Edward Heath, a leader the Conservative party was preparing to ditch because of his lack of popular appeal, had a clear majority, to the surprise of most observers. Theoretically, this should have marked a very drastic change in state attitudes towards the regions. From 1967 the Labour government was paying a Regional Employment Premium which literally paid firms for keeping workers on their books in the Development Areas. The late

1960s saw the rise of a conservative school of economic thought which may be described as 'monetarist' in that it blamed inflation primarily on state willingness to increase the money supply. It also criticised the propping up of industrial 'lame ducks' and had doubts about the efficacy of regional subsidies which it saw as a burden on growth areas which was not producing self-sustaining economic vigour in the subsidised regions. When in mid-1971 UCS appealed to the new government for an additional £6 million of working capital, it met with a refusal which precipitated liquidation. In that same year a white paper on financial policy for ports indicated that government grants for harbour development would in future be much more closely tied to proof of commercial viability. It was announced in October 1970 that the Regional Employment Premium, by now costing £100 million a year, would be phased out from 1974, and the Industrial Reorganisation Corporation established by the Labour government to help finance rationalisation in industry would be wound up. Here was the 'Quiet Revolution' which promised to curb the expansion of state activity and spending in order to enhance traditional market mechanisms.

That the 'Quiet Revolution' was largely jettisoned by the end of 1972 may be ascribed to the juxtaposition of two events against a difficult financial background. In a bid to control rising inflation the government started subsidising price restraint in the nationalised industries. Fanned by decimalisation of the coinage, inflation became so acute that the government tried to impose a legal wage freeze, which led directly to the miners' strike of spring 1972, in which the government was both beaten and humiliated. In a sense, the new regime had already reneged on most of its declared basic principles. After a great deal of trouble including a work-in at UCS, the government had announced in February 1972 that instead of slimming down Upper Clyde shipbuilding to two yards, as its advisers had urged, it intended to sink another £35 million in a company to be called Govan Shipbuilders which would embrace three of the four UCS yards. More public money was later used to help a private American firm take over the fourth, the Clydebank Yard. The miners' strike was rapidly followed by a budget in which the Chancellor completed several political somersaults, not least in the field of regional policy. A year after investment grants and the Industrial Reorganisation Corporation had been abolished the Chancellor, Anthony Barber announced that he intended to 're-establish the regional differentials'. Indeed he claimed to be giving development areas a more clear-cut preference than they had enjoyed under any previous system. He certainly extended grants to plant and machinery, as well as allowing free depreciation.

It seems that the U-turn completed by these measures was partially rendered necessary because the miners' strike coincided with the passage of legislation for Britain's accession to the Common Market. This had total priority in Heath's mind, which is perhaps why men like Mick McGahey, a miners' leader from Fife, could stare him down. Labour was opposing the terms of entry. Almost certainly a Labour government would have negotiated and accepted similar terms, but lest too much be made of this argument, it must be said that the Labour leadership would thereby have violated the views of its own supporters even more than those of the public at large. Effectively, passage of the legislation was secured by collusion with an organised rota of Labour MPs, who of course did not wish to vote against their own Whips too often. A fight to the death with the miners could have destroyed this co-operation by exacerbating party warfare.

The Common Market had in fact always been primarily a political choice, right from Macmillan's first bid for entry in 1961–3, when General de Gaulle, to the fury of the Americans as much as the British, vetoed British entry. Yet at the level of the man-in-the-street it was sold to British opinion largely on the basis of the growth rate of continental western European economies; an argument impressive but irrelevant since it proceeded from causes that had nothing to do with the Common Market. As early as December 1961 the then President of Dundee Chamber of Commerce was full of 'opportunities almost unlimited' at the prospect of entry. He had to wait. Late in 1966 a Labour government very much on the defensive and looking for a political *coup* to restore its prestige reopened negotiations, but in 1967 General de Gaulle again used his veto, as might have been expected, since the Labour government was if anything more deferential to the General's *bête noire*, America, than the Tories. Official or semi-official publications like *Oceanspan* published by the Scottish Council for Development and Industry in 1970 forecast a 'European' future for central Scotland, where raw materials imported at deep anchorages in the Clyde would be processed before being exported from Forth ports. To some extent *Oceanspan* followed the pattern of the related 1968 *Grangemouth–Falkirk Plan* by extrapolating existing tendencies, but in 1970 the extrapolation was on a misleading scale, as the events of subsequent years showed. Scotland always had been a European land, and Common Market entry was not followed by economic boom.

What Westminster seemed to lack was any sense of its own limitations. Some of the regional planning exercises it sponsored seemed to be based on wishful thinking. Thus the sub-regional plan for Tayside, *Tayside: Potential for Development*, which appeared in 1970 was entirely based on the assumption of an increase of 300,000 in what was in fact a declining regional population. It is easy enough to see why the politicians were obsessed with the idea of growth. Rapid growth makes it infinitely easier for a government to be re-elected, and it tends to blur all difficult political decisions in the euphoria of expansion. However, it is still important for a politician to be able to distinguish between incantation and effective policy. The failure of Common Market entry early in 1973 to produce by osmosis an acceleration of British growth rates to levels comparable with France and Germany was underlined by the fact that continued Market membership was 'sold' to the public in the 1975 referendum more by the argument that the economy was now, two and a half years after entry, in such bad shape that any attempt to withdraw would lead to instant collapse, than by anything else. By then the Conservative government had fallen under dramatic circumstances. It had long been the intention of the Conservatives, after the Common Market decision was past, to win a decisive majority on a trade union issue. Failure to do so in the face of the 1974 miners' strike marked the end of an era, indeed possibly the end of a political system.

The Labour government, which succeeded to office without a majority early in 1974 and then secured a narrow majority later that year in a second general election, did not represent so much a sharp break with its predecessor, as a more pessimistic view of the price which had to be paid to achieve essentially bi-partisan objectives. When Harold Wilson chose to resign in 1976, the move was widely interpreted, rightly or wrongly, as a sign that the problems gathering round the regime—soaring unemployment, recession, huge and worsening trade deficits, and accelerating inflation—were in the foreseeable future insoluble. It was therefore deeply ironic that the only discernible long-term policy held by his successor James Callaghan and his Chancellor Denis Healey hinged on an industry inextricably bound up with Scotland—North Sea oil. The discovery of a huge natural gas field off the northern Dutch coast in 1959 lured world oil companies into North Sea oil prospecting, using the technique of drilling from maritime platforms first perfected in offshore

Caribbean oilfields. After international agreement on the division of the continental shelf, part of which is the North Sea, serious drilling started in the mid-1960s. Early in 1970 the situation was still uncertain, but by the end of that year it was clear that major oilfields which were commercially viable had been discovered. The oil was very expensive, by Middle Eastern standards, but by 1973 it was clear that neither cheap Arab oil, nor cheap British coalminers could be taken for granted any more. North Sea oil was a feasible, nay a lucrative proposition, and most of it in the British sector lay off the coasts of mainland Scotland, or Orkney or Shetland. There being no damned nonsense about merit in politics, the prospect of oil revenues seemed to offer British politicians a quite fortuitous escape-route from their problems.

What North Sea oil offered Scotland was more difficult to say. It was bound to create jobs since Scottish harbours were the main bases for the operation and Scotland was the predestined landfall for the vital pipelines. Just how many jobs had been created by late 1974 is difficult to say, for in addition to direct employment in building and servicing facilities for drilling and pumping, there was a good deal of indirect stimulus like induced construction. One informed estimate gave a total of roughly 30,000 jobs in oil-related employment. Towns like Aberdeen and Fraserburgh, with large concentrations of such work representing massive spending by oil companies, had touched unheard-of levels of prosperity, and property prices by 1975. Dundee harbour was doing very well out of servicing facilities for the oil rigs, while at Montrose the old fishing village of Ferryden on the south side of the South Esk had been blitzed and reconstructed to provide onshore oil facilities. However, in a wider context these figures do not greatly impress. Employment in primary and manufacturing industry in Scotland fell by 79,000 between 1967 and 1971 and even in agriculture, mining and fishing alone the fall was 27,000—not far short of 1974 oil-related employment. Even if the figure for the latter were to rise to 50,000–60,000 by 1980, it would still not be the equivalent of the 1967–71 job loss, and half the new employment facilities are likely to be in construction work, which cannot possibly last indefinitely. Areas with a high stake in platform construction like the Cromarty and Moray Firths were likely to fade early, while the North-East and Shetland had the best medium-term prospects. However, it was clear by 1975 that the oil boom would be finite. Unlike the Norwegians, who were pursuing a careful and shrewd policy of controlled exploitation in their North Sea oilfields, the British government was from the first desperate for quick exploitation, initially to cover the staggering costs of development, much of which was financed by foreign companies and much of which was carried through with imported equipment and materials. Latterly oil-revenues had become a lifeline and governments were palpably hanging on until they came on stream in sufficient quantity to save the day. By the later 1990s the oil revenues were likely to be falling steeply.

So large were these oilfields that it was confidently expected that from about 1980 all the UK's needs could be met (though for technical reasons some continuing importation of oil was likely) and a surplus would be left over for export. Financially, the UK government was likely to benefit massively with a tax revenue from oil of over £3,000 million in 1980 rising to an annual £4,000 million until decline set in after about 1995. Naturally, even a Conservative government showed no desire to share this windfall with its Common Market partners, and no government of any kind was likely to contemplate serious sharing of the money with, say, Shetland or mainland Scotland. The UK being a very unitary state, the sort of split of mineral royalties which occurs in most federal states between provincial and central governments was unthinkable. Or was it?

In abstract it was very desirable that at least a significant proportion of this once-for-all cash transfusion be devoted to investment designed to restructure the economies of the Northern Isles and mainland Scotland. Regional policy had helped to keep down levels of unemployment which would otherwise have become distressing, but no government, Labour or Conservative, had possessed the programme, the will, or the means to tackle the underlying structural problems of the Scottish economy. Indeed a good deal of regional policy was probably misconceived from an early stage. The pulp mill at Corpach outside Fort William established by a combination of government and Wiggins Teape money in 1962 (after all the other private sponsors had withdrawn) was typical of the heavily-capitalised projects employing many outside specialists (in this case often Glaswegians) which governments set up in the Highlands. By the time of Anthony Barber's 1972 regional incentives, it could be argued that Barber was making it in general profitable to set up capital-intensive industry in labour surplus areas. Meanwhile the loss of employment in existing industry was accelerating. In the Clyde shipbuilding faced yet another visceral crisis in 1977, despite a drop in its labour force to 23,000 from the 98,000 of 1945. World orders dropped from 35 million tons in 1975 to roughly 13 million tons in succeeding years due to world recession. In Dundee jute firms were transferring to synthetic fibres which required a third less manpower for production and were slashing jobs heavily as they re-equipped and concentrated. Even in Shetland, where the expansion of the local fishing fleet in the 1960s had been an outstanding example of local initiative, the future did not look reassuring because the Common Market Commission was pressing for a fisheries policy calculated to damage the local fleet's chances of further expansion.

Scotland became an industrial nation within a politically stable Britain operating a market economy. By 1914 that market economy had ceased to be dynamic in Scotland. Many different options were tried within the market framework. Municipal socialism had a long history in Scotland, being pioneered on the grand scale by Glasgow Corporation before 1914. It expanded relentlessly after 1919 until local government was much the biggest single employer of labour in Scotland. Private philanthrophy had long sustained individual estates in the Highlands, and in 1918–19 it had its last glorious fling when the English industrialist Lord Leverhulme bought Lewis and Harris with a view to drastically modernising them. His schemes broke on the rock of not unjustified local dislike of his high-handed methods. Neither of these opinions proved capable of reversing the pattern of stagnation. The mixed economy after 1945 produced a higher standard of living, but was increasingly used by a grossly over-centralised political system as a means of manipulating the electorate. 'Fine tuning' to produce the 'window in space' where the consequences of inflation had not yet caught up with its author, the government, proved an irresistible temptation to premiers disposing of infinitely more personal power than say Louis XIV, because at that moment of high apparent prosperity, a renewed mandate was assured. These tactics killed the market economy, but nobody, and least of all the Labour leadership, wanted to try really socialist economics.

In all this Scotland's identity should have vanished with her distinct regional economy. Her vaunted banking system with its own note issues was by the 1970s a mere facade concealing English control. In the same way, all her major publishers had been taken over by English or American money. Her electronics industry, employing 30,000 in 1970, was a series of assembly-lines whose research and development side was furth of Scotland. Nationalisation or Westminster subsidies pervaded basic industry. Farming incomes, despite a transfer from subsidy to import levies and guaranteed prices, were still controlled by London's man-ipulation of the Common Market agricultural unit of account—the 'green pound'. Yet by 1977 there were enough Scottish Nationalist MPs to ensure that a Labour government was moving a Devolution Bill in the House of Commons. The idea had originally been rendered current coin by the Conservatives before the 1970 election, which they expected to lose, and by 1977 it had been talked about to the point where some politi-cians seemed actually to believe in it. They were few. The rest divided between those who thought it an unfortunate necessity with 11 Scottish Nationalists already around Westminster and those who thought it a potential disaster. The proposed Scottish Assembly was, of course, intended to have no effective financial power and be largely cosmetic. Real power was to remain at Westminster, parts being progressively transferred to the even remoter regime in Brussels and Strasbourg. However, some politicians tend to underestimate the opposition. Given a political lever, it seemed unlikely that the Scots would not use it, and very probable that they would use it to assert a degree of control over their economic destiny. With investment plans in petro-chemical facilities at Grangemouth alone running at £1800 million in early 1977 it was quite naive to think that economics, and in particular the economics of North Sea Oil, would not remain central in Scottish politics.

Bibliography : General

The chapter bibliographies are selective lists. They comprise significant secondary work and primary sources easily available in print. A bias towards the readable excludes most modern statistical material as such, though it is subsumed in the secondary studies cited. To acknowledge the debt I owe to certain unpublished dissertations, I have cited them under appropriate chapter bibliographies.

For general political and cultural background, two works in the Edinburgh History of Scotland are vital. These are G. Donaldson, *Scotland : James V to James VII* (Edinburgh, rev. ed., 1971) and W. Ferguson *Scotland : 1689 to the Present* (Edinburgh and London, 1968). Both are excellent and have ample bibliographies. There is also a good bibliography in S.G.E. Lythe and J. Butt, *An Economic History of Scotland 1100–1939* (Glasgow and London, 1975), a book which covers a huge sweep of time, and is therefore very selective towards the end, but which contains some technically very impressive work in its central portion. R. H. Campbell's *Scotland Since 1707* (Oxford, 1965) is a standard economic history, especially strong on the eighteenth century. Another bibliography of high quality can be found in T. C. Smout's, *A History of the Scottish People 1560–1830* (London, 1969, and also in Fontana paperback). This very distinguished social history is the first of two promised volumes. First-class regional studies are rare, with the welcome exception of A. Slaven, *The Development of the West of Scotland 1750–1960* (London, 1975). *Scottish Themes* edited by J. Butt and J. T. Ward (Scottish Academic Press, 1976) is that rare phenomenon, a non-disastrous academic *festschrift*, and it contains much relevant material. Thematic books are mentioned in chapter bibliographies, but J. A. Symon's *Scottish Farming* (Edinburgh and London, 1959) has a broad enough sweep to justify special mention. It also has a very useful bibliography.

Too much Scottish economic history has been based almost exclusively on those two remarkable multi-volume printed sources the *Old Statistical Account* of the late eighteenth century and the *New Statistical Account* of the 1840s. Both are very useful but primary manuscript material, for Scottish economic history since 1660 is voluminous and only partly explored. The Scottish Record Office in Edinburgh holds great quantities of official and private manuscript record, usually admirably calendered. Business records have in recent years attracted a good deal of attention and are best approached, like all manuscript material not in public archives, through the National Register of Archives (Scotland), which is part of the Scottish Record Office, though possessed of its own identity. It liaises with all regional surveys and with bodies like the Business Archives Council of Scotland. In recent decades official and semi-official plans and statistics have poured from government presses on a scale reminiscent of nineteenth-century Ireland, where if the Union could have been saved by enquiries and statistics it would have been saved many times over.

A good deal of primary material for certain kinds of Scottish economic and social history is available in the shape of edited volumes issued by scholarly publication societies, or by the Scottish Record Office. A selection of such individual edited volumes as are relevant to the themes of this book will be found in the chapter bibliographies. General collections of documents illustrating Scottish economic development over a period of time are rare, and must be used with care because of the huge element of selectivity which is inevitable in their construction, but R. H. Campbell and J. B. A. Dow jointly edited a *Source Book of Scottish Economic and Social History* (Oxford, 1968). It confines itself to the period after the Union of 1707, coming up to the twentieth century. For the earlier period there is some interesting material in Section II of *A Source Book of Scottish History, Volume Three, 1567–1707*, edited by W. C. Dickinson and G. Donaldson (London and Edinburgh, 2nd edn., 1961). However, at this level of selectivity, document collections can only be an introduction, albeit a stimulating one, to the wider literature.

1 The Physical Setting (pages 11–16)

G. Y. Craig (ed), *The Geology of Scotland* (Edinburgh and London, 1965)

The Scottish chapters in J. Mitchell (ed), *Great Britain: Geographical Essays* (Cambridge, 1962)

A. O'Dell and K. Walton, *The Highlands and Islands of Scotland* (London and Edinburgh, 1962)

F. Thompson, *The Highlands and Islands* (London, 1974)

H. W. Meikle (ed), *Scotland* (London and Edinburgh, 1947)

P. Bailey, *Orkney* (Newton Abbot, 1971)

J. R. Nicholson, *Shetland* (Newton Abbot, 1972)

2   The Scottish Economy c.1660–90 (pages 17–43)

Articles

G. Donaldson, 'Sources of Scottish Agrarian History before the Eighteenth Century', *Agricultural History Review*, VIII, 1960, pp. 82–90

T. C. Smout and A. Fenton, 'Scottish Agriculture before the Improvers—an Exploration', ibid, XIII, 1965, pp.73–93

A. I. Bowman, 'Culross Colliery : A Sixteenth-Century Mine', *Industrial Archaeology*, Vol. 7, No. 4, pp. 353–72

Books

G. Donaldson, *Shetland Life under Earl Patrick* (Edinburgh and London, 1958)

W. W. Findlay, *Oats : Their Cultivation and Use from Ancient Times to the Present Day*, Aberdeen University Studies Number 137 (Edinburgh and London, 1956)

A. McKerral, *Kintyre in The Seventeenth Century* (Edinburgh and London, 1948)

Printed Primary Sources

D. G. Barron (ed), *The Court Book of The Barony of Urie in Kincardenshire 1604–1747* (Edinburgh, Scottish History Society, 1st Series Vol. 12, 1892)

C. B. Gunn, *Records of the Baron Court of Stitchill 1655–1807* (Edinburgh, Scottish History Society, 1st Series Vol. 50, 1905)

The Black Book of Taymouth (Edinburgh, The Bannatyne Club, 1895)

Sir A. Mitchell (ed), *Geographical Collections relating to Scotland made by Walter MacFarlane* (Edinburgh, Scottish History Society, 1st Series Vols. 51–53, 1906–8)

Theses

John A. di Folco, 'Aspects of Seventeenth Century Social Life in Central and North Fife', St Andrews University, unpublished B.Phil. thesis 1975

G. S. Pryde, 'Scots Burgh Finances prior to 1707', St Andrews University, unpublished Ph.D. thesis 1926

3   **Crisis, Union and Reaction 1690–1727**
(pages 44–66)

Articles

A. Fenton, 'Skene of Hallyard's Manuscript of Husbandrie', *Agricultural History Review*, XI, 1963, pp. 65–81

A. L. Murray, 'The Scottish Treasury 1667–1708', *Scottish Historical Review*, XLV, 1966, pp. 89–104

T. C. Smout, 'The Glasgow Merchant Community in the Seventeenth Century', *ibid*, XLVII, 1968, pp. 53–71

A. M. Carstairs, 'Some Economic Aspects of the Union of Parliaments', *Scottish Journal of Political Economy*, Vol. 2, 1955, pp. 64–72

Books

G. P. Insh, *The Company of Scotland Trading to Africa and the Indies* (London and New York, 1932)

J. Prebble, *The Darien Disaster* (London, 1968)

G. S. Pryde, *The Treaty of Union of Scotland and England 1707* (London and Edinburgh, 1950)

T. I. Rae (ed), *The Union of 1707 : its Impact on Scotland* (Glasgow and London, 1974)

T. C. Smout, *Scottish Trade on the Eve of Union* (Edinburgh and London, 1963)

G. P. Insh, *The Scottish Jacobite Movement* (London and Edinburgh, 1952)

Printed Primary Sources

G. P. Insh (ed), *Papers relating to the Ships and Voyages of the Company of Scotland Trading to Africa and the Indies 1696–1707* (Edinburgh, Scottish History Society, 3rd Series Vol. 6, 1924)

D. Defoe, *A Tour through the Whole Island of Great Britain*, Vol. 2 (Everyman edn.)

4 The Beginnings of Radical Industrial and Agricultural Change 1727–1780 (pages 67–100)

Articles

A. J. Durie, 'The Markets for Scottish Linen, 1730–1775', *Scottish Historical Review*, LII, 1973, pp. 30–49

R. A. Dodgshon, 'Farming in Roxburghshire and Berwickshire on the eve of Improvement', *ibid*, LIV, 1975, pp. 140–54

C. Gulvin, 'The Union and the Scottish Woollen Industry, 1707–1760', *ibid*, L, 1971, pp. 121–37

H. Hamilton, 'Scotland's Balance of Payments Problem in 1762', *Economic History Review*, 2nd Series, V, 1953, pp. 344–57

A. J. Durie, 'Linen-spinning in the North of Scotland, 1746–1773', *Northern Scotland*, Vol. 2, 1974–5, pp. 13–36

Books

T. M. Devine, *The Tobacco Lords* (Edinburgh, 1975)

A. J. Warden, *The Linen Trade* (2nd edn, London, 1867) There is a reprint (1967) of the less historically valuable 1st edn of this book.

A. G. Thomson, *The Paper Industry in Scotland 1590–1861* (Edinburgh, 1974)

J. E. Handley, *Scottish Farming in the Eighteenth Century* (London, 1953)

B. Duckham, *A History of the Scottish Coal Industry Vol. 1 : 1700–1815* (Newton Abbot, 1970)

S. G. Checkland, *Scottish Banking. A History, 1695–1973* (Glasgow and London, 1975)

A. J. Youngson, *After the Forty-five* (Edinburgh, 1973)

Published Primary Sources

W. Mackay (ed), *The Letter-Book of Bailie John Steuart of Inverness 1715–1752* (Edinburgh, Scottish History Society, 2nd Series Vol. 9, 1915)

J. Colville (ed), *Letters of John Cockburn of Ormistoun to his Gardener 1727–1744* (Edinburgh, Scottish History Society, 1st Series Vol. 45, 1904)

H. Hamilton (ed), *Selections from the Monymusk Papers (1713–1755)* (Edinburgh, Scottish History Society, 3rd Series Vol. 39, 1945)

R. H. Campbell (ed), *States of the Annual Progress of the Linen Manufacture 1727–1754* (Edinburgh, H.M.S.O., 1964)

V. Wills (ed), *Reports on the Annexed Estates 1755–1769* (Edinburgh, H.M.S.O., 1973)

R. J. Adam (ed), *Home's Survey of Assynt* (Edinburgh, Scottish History Society, 3rd Series Vol. 52, 1960)

Thesis

Annette M. Smith, 'The forfeited estate papers, 1745—a study of the work of the commissioners for the forfeited annexed estates', St Andrews University, unpublished Ph.D. thesis 1975

5 The Triumph of Commercialisation and Industry 1780–1840 (pages 101–155)

Articles

R. Campbell, 'The Industrial Revolution : a Revision Article', *Scottish Historical Review*, XLVI, 1967, pp. 37–55

T. C. Smout, 'Scottish Landowners and Economic Growth 1650–1850', *Scottish Journal of Political Economy*, XI, 1964, pp. 218–34

H. Hamilton, 'The Failure of the Ayr Bank, 1772', *Economic History Review*, 2nd Series, VIII, 1955–6, pp. 405–17

M. L. Robertson, 'Scottish Commerce and the American War of Independence', *Economic History Review*, 2nd Series, IX, 1956–7, pp. 123–31

E. Richards, 'The Prospect of Economic Growth in Sutherland at the Time of the Clearances, 1809–1813', *Scottish Historical* Review, XLIX, 1970, pp. 154–71

Books

H. Hamilton, *The Industrial Revolution in Scotland* (1st edn 1932, reprinted London, 1966)

H. Hamilton, *An Economic History of Scotland in the Eighteenth Century* (Oxford, 1963)

A. and N. L. Clow, *The Chemical Revolution* (London, 1952)

R. H. Campbell, *Carron Company* (Edinburgh, 1961)

J. Butt (ed), *Robert Owen* (Newton Abbot, 1971)

P. Cadell, *The Iron Mills at Crammond* (Edinburgh, 1973)

E. Richards, *The Leviathan of Wealth* (London and Toronto, 1973)

A. R. B. Haldane, *The Drove Roads of Scotland* (London and Edinburgh, 1952)

A. R. B. Haldane, *New Ways through the Glens* (London and Edinburgh, 1962)

J. Lindsay, *The Canals of Scotland* (Newton Abbot, 1968)

J. Thomas, *A Regional History of the Railways of Great Britain Volume VI Scotland : The Lowlands And The Borders* (Newton Abbot, 1971)

M. Gray, *The Highland Economy 1750–1850* (London and Edinburgh, 1958)

L. J. Saunders, *Scottish Democracy 1815–1840* (London and Edinburgh, 1950)

J. E. Handley, *The Navvy in Scotland* (Cork, 1970)

N. T. Phillipson and R. Mitchison (eds), *Scotland in the Age of Improvement* (Edinburgh, 1970)

Printed Primary Sources

R. Owen, *A New View of Society and Report to the County of Lanark*, ed V. A. C. Gatrell (Penguin, 1969)

E. R. Cregeen (ed), *Argyll Estate Instructions* (Edinburgh, Scottish History Society, 4th Series Vol. 1, 1964)

R. J. Adam (ed), *Papers on Sutherland Estate Management 1802–1816* (Edinburgh, *ibid*, Vol. 9, 1972)

Theses

D. G. Lockhart, 'The Evolution of the Planned Villages of North-East Scotland *c.*1700–1900', Dundee University, unpublished Ph.D. thesis 1974

A. N. L. Hood, 'Agricultural Change in the Carse of Gowrie 1750–1875', University of Dundee, unpublished Ph.D. thesis 1974

6 **The Building of a Mature Industrial Economy**
1840–1914 (pages 156–205)

Articles

A. Tyrrell, 'Political Economy, Whiggism and the Education of Working-class Adults in Scotland 1817–1840', *Scottish Historical Review*, XLVIII, 1969, pp. 151–65

U. R. Q. Henriques, 'An Early Factory Inspector : James Stuart of Dunearn', *ibid*, L, 1971, pp. 18–46

E. Richards, 'Problems on the Cromartie Estate, 1851–1853', *ibid*, LII, 1973, pp.149–164

E. Richards, 'How tame were the Highlanders during the Clearances?', *Scottish Studies*, Vol. 17, pt. 1, pp. 35–50

Books

T. Ferguson, *The Dawn of Scottish Social Welfare* (London and Edinburgh, 1948)

T. Ferguson, *Scottish Social Welfare 1864–1914* (London and Edinburgh, 1958)

C. Gulvin, *The Tweedmakers* (Newton Abbot, 1973)

M. C. Reed (ed), *Railways in the Victorian Economy* (Newton Abbot, 1969)

B. Lenman, C. Lythe and E. Gauldie, *Dundee and its Textile Industry* (Dundee, Abertay Historical Society Publication, No. 14, 1969)

P. Payne (ed), *Studies in Scottish Business History* (London, 1967)

D. Bremner, *The Industries of Scotland* (originally published 1869, new edn Newton Abbot, 1969)

A. Muir, *The Fife Coal Company Limited* (Leven, n.d.)

A. Muir, *The Story of Shotts* (Edinburgh, n.d.)

A. Muir, *Nairn's of Kirkcaldy 1847–1956* (Cambridge, 1956)

P. Gaskell, *Movern Transformed* (Cambridge, 1968)

B. Lenman, *From Esk to Tweed : Harbours, Ships and Men of the East Coast of Scotland* (London and Glasgow, 1975)

S. G. Checkland, *The Mines of Tharsis* (London, 1967)

J. Hunter, *The Making of the Crofting Community* (Edinburgh, 1976)

Printed Primary Sources

E. Gauldie (ed), *The Dundee Textile Industry 1790–1885* (Edinburgh, Scottish History Society, 4th Series Vol. 6, 1969)

I. MacDougall (ed), *The Minutes of Edinburgh Trades Council 1859–1873* (*ibid*, Vol. 5, 1968)

H. and L. Mun (ed), *William Melrose in China 1845–1855* (*ibid*, Vol. 10, 1973)

7 Industry and Agriculture in an Age of Crisis 1914–1939 (pages 206–231)

H. J. Hanham, *Scottish Nationalism* (London, 1969)

E. M. H. Lloyd, *Experiments in State Control* (Oxford, 1924)

D. T. Jones, J. F. Duncan, H. M. Conacher, W. R. Scott, *Rural Scotland During The War* (Oxford, 1926)

W. R. Scott and J. Cunnison, *Industries of the Clyde Valley during the War* (Oxford, 1924)

S. Pollard, *The Development of The British Economy 1914–1950* (London, 1962)

C. A. Oakley, *Scottish Industry Today* (The Scottish Council, 1937)

C. Coote, *A Companion of Honour : The Story of Walter Elliot* (London, 1965)

T. Woodehouse and P. Kilgour, *The Jute Industry* (London, 1921)

D. R. Wallace, *The Romance of Jute : A Short History of The Calcutta Jute Mill Industry 1855–1927* (2nd edn, London, 1928)

J. Graham Kerr (ed), *Glasgow* (British Association, 1928)

A Century of Agricultural Statistics : Great Britain 1866–1966 (H.M.S.O., 1968)

8 The Shaping of the Modern Scots Economy
(pages 232–250)

A. K. Cairncross (ed), *The Scottish Economy* (Cambridge, 1954)

G. McCrone, *Scotland's Economic Progress 1951–1960* (London, 1965)

C. A. Oakley (ed), *Scottish Industry* (The Scottish Council, 1953)

A. Schonfield, *British Economic Policy since the War* (rev. edn, Penguin, 1959)

G. D. N. Worswick and P. H. Ady (eds), *The British Economy 1945–1950* (Oxford, 1952)

T. Johnston, *Memories* (London, 1952)

S. G. Checkland, *The Upas Tree : Glasgow 1875–1975* (University of Glasgow Press, 1975)

A Short History of the Scottish Coal-Mining Industry (The National Coal Board, Scottish Division, 1958)

R. Bell, *History of the British Railways during the War 1939–1945* (London, 1946)

Scotland's Older Houses (Scottish Housing Advisory Committee, H.M.S.O., 1967)

W. Vamplew, *Salvesen of Leith* (Edinburgh and London, 1975)

9   The Scottish Economy and the Transit of Britain 1960–1976 (pages 251–269)

Scottish Council (Development and Industry), *Inquiry into the Scottish Economy 1960–1961* (Edinburgh, n.d.)—The Toothill Report

T. L. Johnston, N. K. Buxton, D. Mair, *Structure and Growth of the Scottish Economy* (London and Glasgow, 1971)

J. G. Kellas, *Modern Scotland : The Nation since 1870* (London, 1968)

J. G. Kellas, *The Scottish Political System* (Cambridge, 1973)

S. Brittan, *The Treasury under the Tories 1951–1964* (Penguin, 1964)

P. Donaldson, *Guide to the British Economy* (rev. edn, Penguin, 1973)

W. Beckerman (ed), *The Labour Government's Economic Record : 1964–1970* (London, 1972)

J. Bruce-Gardyne, *Whatever happened to the Quiet Revolution?* (London, 1974)

C. Callow, *Power from the Sea* (London, 1973)

D. I. MacKay and G. A. Mackay, *The Political Economy of North Sea Oil* (London, 1975)

A. MacGregor Hutcheson and A. Hogg (eds), *Scotland and Oil* (Edinburgh and New York, 1975)

M. Lovegrove, *Our Island's Oil* (London, 1975)

North Sea Oil and the Environment : A Report to the Oil Development Council for Scotland (Edinburgh, H.M.S.O., 1974)

C. A. Goodlad, *Shetland Fishing Saga* (Lerwick, 1975)

M. Gaskin, *The Scottish Banks : A Modern Survey* (London, 1965)

Index

281